GW00685345

Bali

BALI

CULTURAL TOURISM AND TOURISTIC CULTURE

by

Michel Picard

English translation by Diana Darling

ARCHIPELAGO PRESS

Produced with the assistance of the French Ministry of Culture

*Published by Archipelago Press
an imprint of Editions Didier Millet,
593 Havelock Road,
#02-01/02 Isetan Office Building,
Singapore 169641
Republic of Singapore*

*English translation first published by
Editions Didier Millet Pte Ltd 1996*

[First published in French as Bali: Tourisme Culturel et culture touristique, Editions L'Harmattan, Paris 1992, ISBN 2-87868-018-9; revised and updated for this English edition]

*English translation: Diana Darling
English editor: Tim Jaycock
Art Director: Tan Tat Ghee
Designer: Norreha Sayuti
Maps by: Lee Woon Hong, Editions Didier Millet, after Hélène Borel, Edimages-Graphique*

Printed in Singapore
ISBN: 981-3018-94-1

CONTENTS

Preface

> Percayalah pada saya, Bali takkan berubah. Bali akan tetap Bali. Dulu, 100 tahun lalu, sekarang, maupun ratusan tahun yang akan datang. Bali tak pernah menggadaikan dirinya untuk pariwisata. Orang Bali sudah bertekad bahwa pariwisatalah yang harus tunduk kepada Bali. Pariwisata untuk Bali, bukan Bali untuk pariwisata.
>
> *Believe me, Bali will not change. Bali will always be Bali. In the past, a hundred years ago, today, and even a hundred years from now. Bali has never sold itself to tourism. The Balinese people are determined that it is tourism that must submit to Bali. Tourism is for Bali, not Bali for tourism.*
> (Declaration of the Governor of Bali, Ida Bagus Oka, excerpt from *Bali: Apa Kata Mereka*, Denpasar, 1991, p.11)

Tourism is first and foremost an extension of the monetary economy, the marketing of the landscapes and cultural expressions of the people of the world, the conversion of regions and societies into tourist products. But beyond the commoditization of the world, another process is at work that affects the identity and the new stakes and meanings of culture.

This book was born out of a dissatisfaction with the way in which questions are commonly formulated when international tourism penetrates a society. The study of the cultural implications of introducing tourism into a society is hampered by a normative approach: observers too often ask whether the indigenous culture is degraded or preserved, harmed or reinforced by tourism. In other words, the debate is blocked by the question of whether the impact of tourism on the culture is positive or negative. The real issue, though, is to understand and elucidate the actual cultural implications of the touristification of societies.

I have undertaken this work of critical elucidation within the framework of the Unité de Recherche en Sociologie du Tourisme International (URESTI) at the Centre National de la Recherche Scientifique (CNRS) in Paris. As with all intellectual endeavor, it could not have been accomplished without the help and encouragement of many people, too numerous to name all of them here. Nonetheless, I cannot allow to pass unmentioned the sharp stimulation I found in the epistemological exigence of my colleagues at URESTI, Marie-Françoise Lanfant, Claude-Marie Bazin and Jacques de Weerdt. Nor could I forget the kind and loyal support of Jean-François Guermonprez, or the enlightened advice and unselfish assistence of Catherine Basset, Fritz deBoer, Edward Bruner, Bruce Carpenter, Christian Clause, Georges Condominas, John De Coney, Jean Couteau, Deborah Dunn, Cristina Formaggia, Hildred Geertz, John Hall, Mahisa Retna Handayati, David Harrison, Kunang Helmi,

Rio Helmi, Hedi Hinzler, Michael Hitchcock, Jafar Jafari, Romi Joyce, Marc Jurt, Denys Lombard, Jean Michaud, Marie-Claude and Didier Millet, Yuko Naumann, Eric Oey, François Raillon, Peter Sane, Henk Schulte Nordholt, Jean-Didier Urbain, Adrian Vickers, Carol Warren, Made Wijaya, and Robert Wood, to cite but a few. Georges Cazes merits special mention here for having published the French version of this book in the collection "Tourismes et Sociétés" of which he is the editor at Editions L'Harmattan, Paris. Finally, I would like to express my warmest thanks to Diana Darling for the graciousness with which she carried out the daunting task of conveying my French thoughts in elegant English.

The conclusions of this study are based on observations made in Bali between 1974 and 1994, and in particular on fieldwork effected between 1980 and 1982. This research was carried out under the auspices of the Indonesian Institute of Sciences (*Lembaga Ilmu Pengetahuan Indonesia*, LIPI) and benefited from the guidance of Professor I Gusti Ngurah Bagus, Director of the Department of Anthropology at Udayana University in Denpasar. I thank him for his kind encouragement, as I do also all the other Balinese who endured my disconcerting questions, and most particularly Anak Agung Gede Raka Arimbawa, Jero Arsa, I Made Bandem, Anak Agung Made Djelantik, I Made Djimat, I Ketut Madra, Ida Bagus Adnyana Manuaba, I Gede Putu Riyasse, I Made Sija, I Putu Suasta, as well as the much missed I Gusti Ketut Kaler, I Nyoman Oka, I Ketut Rinda, I Gusti Ketut Sangka and I Gusti Made Sumung.

PART ONE
The Touristification of Bali

Bali is a tiny island in the Indonesian archipelago, situated eight degrees below the equator between Java and Lombok. On the map of the Republic of Indonesia — a vast territory stretching five thousand kilometers from Sumatra to New Guinea and covering two million square kilometers of land and five million square kilometers of sea — Bali is barely visible. The island is only 140 kilometers from west to east and 80 from north to south; and yet, although it occupies less than 0.3% of the surface of Indonesia, it is one of the nation's 27 provinces. But Bali's renown is disproportionate to its size, and the name of Bali is incontestably better known in the world than that of Indonesia.

Bali's renown is the result of its fame as a "tourist paradise", a reputation built on the vestiges of an orientalist vision of the island as a "living museum" of Indo-Javanese civilization, an enclave of Hinduism at the heart of the largest Muslim country on earth. Indonesia lies across the confluence of the Indian Ocean, the China Sea and the Pacific Ocean — and this has allowed the archipelago's substratum of Austronesian cultures to be fertilized with cultural and commercial currents from the civilizations of India, China, Islam and Europe. But Bali ignored the Islamization that swept through the rest of the archipelago, and appears to have conserved its Hinduist local culture to a remarkable degree. Also, colonization came later to Bali and was less brutal, saving Balinese society to some extent from the traumatizing upheaval experienced elsewhere. Finally, the Balinese seem to have shown a particular genius in the course of their history for assimilating outside influences in a selective way, adopting only those that suit them, and integrating them harmoniously into their own cultural fabric. The result today appears as an original combination of objects and images, customs and beliefs that, despite their diverse provenance, have become acknowledged as "typically Balinese".

As custodians of the Hindu heritage forsaken by their Javanese neighbors, the Balinese are sharply aware of their identity and seem anxious to prove themselves worthy of their distinction within the Indonesian nation. Balinese identity is inscribed foremost in its religion, whose omnipresent ceremonies maintain a pattern of relationships which on the one hand are genealogical, with their deified ancestors, and on the other are territorial, with their places of origin and residence. These relationships are maintained through a close network of temples (*pura*) — walled enclosures of holy ground, rather than buildings, where human beings may make contact with their gods. Bali has been called "the island of a thousand temples"; in fact, there are tens of thousands of temples — temples of house courtyards and local clans; temples of villages and kingdoms; temples of mountains, lakes, forests, and springs — all constituting in a tangible way the historical memory of the Balinese. This memory is kept vibrant through the periodic celebration of temple festivals (*odalan*), when the deities are invited to descend and receive homage at their respective shrines. It is during these ceremonies that the Balinese unleash their artistic talents in an extravagant profusion of processions and offerings, music, dance, and theater, for which they have become famous in the West (1).

Balinese society is remarkable for the complexity of its organizational forms, at once diverse and fluctuating. This complexity is largely a legacy of its history, which saw successive waves of Indo-Javanese influences that affected the island's different regions in various ways, resulting in a heterogeneous social terrain. The "village" (*desa*) is not so much a socio-political group nor, strictly speaking, a territorial unit, although of course it occupies territorial space. It is, rather, a religious congregation, composed of a group of people collectively responsible for the three temples associated with the *desa*, and comprising an entity designated by the term *Kayangan Tiga*: the "Navel Temple" (*pura puseh*) where the village's guardian deities and founding ancestors are venerated; the "Village Temple" (*pura desa*) where the village council meets, and which is associated with fertility rites; and the "Temple of the Interior" (*pura dalem*) where the disruptive influences of the not-yet-purified dead are placated and the deity of death is honored. Village membership is in this way defined by vertical relationships to a temple network rather than by horizontal relationships among the members of a community. The village meets periodically in council under the guidance of an "elder" (*klian*) who is the custodian of the *adat*. Generally glossed as "custom", *adat* is essentially a religious concept, in the sense that it refers to a social order founded by the ancestors according to an unchangeable cosmic order.

If there is a community to speak of, it is that which is defined by the *banjar*, a residential entity whose responsibilities are at once legal, fiscal, and ritual. They are mainly concerned with social control and public order on the one hand, and on the other, with communal co-operation in public works and ceremonial undertakings, the most important of which is the burial and eventual cremation of the dead. Like the *desa*, the *banjar*, too, meets regularly in council, in a public pavilion called the *bale banjar*. These meetings are attended by all male heads of families, all of whom have an equal voice. The council is guided by a commonly elected "elder", who may be dismissed by the *banjar* members, and its decisions are carried unanimously (2).

Bali owes its uniqueness not only to its history but also to its geography. As the westernmost of the Lesser Sunda Islands, Bali is part of a volcanic chain that connects continental Southeast Asia with Australia. An east-west arc of volcanoes divides the island, culminating in the "Great Mountain" (Gunung Agung) in the east, whose

---

(1) On the Balinese temple system and ceremonies, see Belo (1953) and Goris (1960a, 1960b).

(2) The reader who is not satisfied with such a superficial treatment of Bali's social organization may refer to the following works: Geertz (1959), Geertz & Geertz (1975), Guermonprez (1990), and Warren (1993).

height is over three thousand meters. The island was literally created by volcanoes, and the rivers flowing from the crater lakes have carved deep gorges throughout the land, sculpting some of the most spectacular landscapes in the archipelago. To the north, the steep slopes leave only a narrow coastal strip along the Java Sea. To the south, broad fertile plains descend gently toward the Indian Ocean. While the north was always accessible by sea and open to outside influences, the heart of Balinese culture lies in the south where most of the population lives. It is also on the southern coast that one finds the main white sand beaches; the rest of the coast is girded by black sand or rough rocks.

Curiously enough for an island society, the Balinese orient themselves not toward the sea but toward the mountains. One may be tempted to attribute this peculiarity to the inhospitable character of the coastal waters of the Indian Ocean which, with its lurking coral reefs and treacherous currents, makes navigation difficult and has protected the population from foreign incursions. Perhaps more significantly, the social space of the Balinese is configured in a hierarchical cosmos based on the complementary opposition of "the world on high" (*kaja*) — the direction of the mountains, particularly the sacred mountain Gunung Agung, considered to be the source of fertility and life, the seat of the gods and deified ancestors — and "the world below" (*kelod*), the direction of the sea, considered to be a lair of demons, associated with sickness and death. This cosmic orientation is based on the flow of water: pure water descends from the mountains to the sea where it discharges the impurities that it has accumulated along the way.

The fertility of the soil and the technical and organizational skills of the Balinese allowed them to develop, very early in their history, a highly productive irrigated rice culture. Most of the rice fields occupy the coastal plains of the south and rise toward the mountains in terraces contoured to fit the slightest curve of the terrain. The irrigation works and distribution of water among the rice fields are carried out by cooperatives called *subak*, who are responsible for the regulation of the rice cycle. Object of both cultivation and cult, rice is at once the nutritional base of the Balinese and the matrix of their culture.

For over a thousand years, the Balinese rice culture was productive enough to nourish the population. But the Balinese are becoming too numerous. At the turn of the 20th century, Bali's population was less than one million; today it approaches three million (which makes the Balinese the seventh largest ethnic group in Indonesia, accounting for 1.5% of the archipelago's 195 million inhabitants). Bali's surface is only 5,600 square kilometers, and a large portion of that is uninhabitable. The demographic density — nearly 500 people per square kilometer — is more than doubled in the southern part of the island. Anxious to limit urbanization, the government considered two solutions to solve the problem of Bali's over-population: transmigration to under-populated regions of the archipelago; and birth control. Although the Balinese showed little enthusiasm for leaving their ancestral land, the family planning program was successful beyond all expectations.

Under the pressure of a growing population in recent decades, landed property was broken up and the rice fields became too scanty to support the farmers. Unable to put new lands under cultivation, the government strove to intensify rice production by requiring farmers to plant new strains of high-yield rice with shorter growing cycles. This increased the harvests to such an extent that Bali was soon able to export rice to other islands — but this success exacted a price from the Balinese in an increasing dependence on imported technology and inter-island trade. This in turn accelerated the monetarization of subsistence farming and weakened traditional social relationships. In the quest for cash income, farmers are forced to seek other means of support, and now they form a reserve force of cheap labor.

Thus it appears that the Balinese had little choice in what followed. In the absence of mineral deposits, infrastructures and land suitable for large plantations, industrialization is not viable — and even if it were, it would be at the cost of an irreversible upheaval in the rural foundations of Balinese society. Hence the island's only resources would appear to be the richness of its cultural productions and the beauty of its landscape. Under these conditions, tourism is generally presented as the only solution capable of raising the living standards of the Balinese without forcing them to renounce their traditional way of life.

The truth is that this "touristic vocation" of Bali — a notion that today seems to impose itself almost irrefutably, shared as it is by the Balinese as well as by their visitors — is the outcome of a singular history and a complicated series of policy decisions. These decisions were made outside Bali. Tourism is thus a situation that has been imposed upon the Balinese and which they are constrained to accept. We shall see under what circumstances Bali became a tourist paradise by examining the development of tourism in Bali in the context of the island's integration into, first, the colonial empire of the Netherlands East Indies, and then the Republic of Indonesia.

Chapter One

A Living Museum

The island of Bali is celebrated throughout the world for the beauty of its landscape and above all for the richness of its religious and artistic traditions. It is tempting to attribute this enviable reputation to the charm of the Balinese and their island — but the paradisical image that Bali bears today is not merely a promotional cliché. This image has a history: it is the result of series of conceptual constructions elaborated in the West and eventually embraced by the Balinese.

Although tourism in Bali can hardly be said to begin with the arrival of the first European sailors at the end of the 16th century, it is clear that the touristification of the island took place in the context of a more general intervention by foreigners. Indeed, modern Balinese history is essentially a story of conquests — of the displacement of its decision-making centers beyond its shores and the resulting erosion of the authority of its indigenous leaders. Moreover, as the colonial powers penetrated the society, Western discourse on Bali proliferated to such an extent that it drowned the voice of the Balinese. The result is that Balinese discourse itself is now framed in foreign concepts, and the effect is often bewildering, even to the Balinese themselves.

The touristification of Bali implies more than building hotels and marketing a tourist destination: it is a double dynamic — the seizure of Balinese society by an outside power, and the appropriation of its voice by a foreign discourse. It is within this shift of power relationships and in the boundaries of meaning that one must consider the touristification of the island. I will first describe Bali's incorporation into the Netherlands East Indies empire and its opening to tourism. I will then show how the orientalist vision of Bali as a living museum of Indo-Javanese civilization conditioned the shaping of its tourist image.

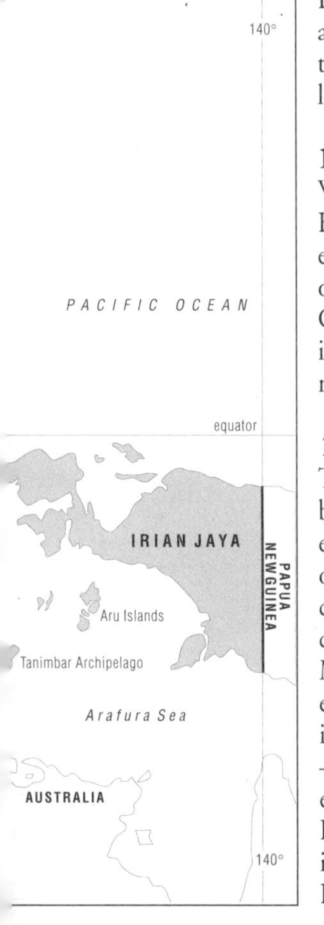

1. Dutch colonization

Well before the arrival of Europeans in the archipelago, Balinese society had already been profoundly marked by foreign influences — those brought about by the civilizations of India and Java, as well as the more diffuse influence of China. The Balinese incorporated traits from all of these, integrating them into an Austronesian cultural base in a manner remarkable for its original syncretism.

The Indo-Javanese myth of origin

The history of the Hinduization of Bali is not well known, but archeological remains and inscriptions indicate the existence of a Hindu-ized Balinese dynasty around the end of the first millennium (Bernet Kempers 1977). Dynastic chronicles recount that in the 14th century, Bali was conquered by the armies of the Hindu-Javanese kingdom Majapahit, who established a court at Gelgel in the southeast of the island. Allegedly, after the fall of Majapahit early in the 16th century, its princes and priests, artists and literati — fleeing the inexorable advance of Islam in Java — emigrated *en masse* to Bali, bringing with them the Hindu heritage of Majapahit to the court of Gelgel, and inaugurating an era of splendor that would later be seen as Bali's golden age.

The importance of the conquest of Bali by Majapahit, besides its tangible consequences, lies above all in the mythic interpretation later given to it by the Balinese, and in particular, in the fact that it is here that the local aristocracy (*triwangsa*) founds its legitimacy by claiming descent from Javanese lords who established themselves in Bali after the conquest (1).

Toward the end of the 17th century, dynastic conflicts led to the court of Gelgel being moved to Klungkung. This signaled a decline in the prestige of the central power and led to the contesting of its authority. The following centuries were marked by the dispersion of power and the establishment of more or less autonomous kingdoms (*negara*), whose sovereigns (*raja*) — while acknowledging the formal primacy of the raja of Klungkung — constantly sought through wars and matrimonial alliances to shift the relations of power to their own advantage.

The fall of the kingdom of Gelgel and the proliferation of noble houses (*puri*) that followed provoked intense competition among the lords. This competition was expressed particularly in a multitude of ceremonial and artistic works, by which each lord sought to establish recognition of his status among his peers and to assure the protective blessings of his ancestors. Over the centuries this profusion of cultural performances has become a major characteristic of Bali. Indeed, the Balinese political system at the eve of Dutch colonization has been called a "theatre state" (Geertz 1980).

The Island of Plunderers

If Sir Francis Drake had called briefly in 1580, Bali's first documented contact with the West dates from 1597, when the first Dutch fleet to attempt the voyage to the Orient debarked in the island in search of food and drinking water. According to the ship's log, the Europeans were greatly impressed by the prosperity of the Balinese and even more so by their hospitality, which differed favorably from their reception in Java. News of this discovery caused a sensation, no doubt because of its descriptions of the court of Gelgel's barbarous luxury and Hindu customs — a sharp contrast with the more austere Islamic sultanates of Java. In spite of this generally favorable first impression, however, the image of Bali that was soon to impose itself on the West was one of savagery: formidable warriors, quick to abandon themselves to the frenzy of

(1) For the Balinese, the reference to Majapahit serves as a means of drawing distinctions, in the sense that the division of Balinese society into four hierarchical classes *(wangsa)*, inaccurately called "castes" in the literature because of a misleading lexical analogy with India, is justified by way of Majapahit being considered as an "origin point" *(kawitan)*. According to this myth of origin, the descendants of different groups of Javanese conquerors — respectively titled *Brahmana*, *Satria*, and *Wesia* — collectively comprise the nobility *(triwangsa)*, as opposed to the common people *(jaba)* who form a residual category today regrouping some 90% of the island's population. More than a sociological reality, this is an ideal model according to which the *Brahmana* compose the priestly "caste", the *Satria* are the kings and princes, and the *Wesia* the lords and the functionaries of the kingdom. On the question of hierarchy in Bali, one may refer to Geertz & Geertz (1975) and Guermonprez (1987).

amok, the Balinese were seen as inveterate plunderers of shipwrecks, and their princes as slave-trading despots, cruel and debauched, whose widows were forced to fling themselves onto the cremation pyres of their lords (Boon 1977; Vickers 1989, 1994).

During the next two centuries, Europe heard little more of Bali, mainly because it had neither spices nor lands that were favorable for plantation farming. In fact, the island's main commercial activity with the Dutch was the slave trade, stimulated by the labor requirements of the United East India Company (VOC), created in 1602 and installed in Batavia on the northwest coast of Java. Throughout the 17th and 18th centuries, the VOC progressively consolidated Dutch influence in Java and, driven by its commercial interests, extended its control over ever vaster regions of the archipelago until the Dutch government finally took it over in 1800 (Ricklefs 1981). After the Napoleonic Wars, the Dutch became anxious about English rivalry in the region, and with Bali lying so close to Java, this little island took on a new strategic importance. The Dutch managed to establish diplomatic relations with the rajas, which led to treaties the Balinese either misunderstood or ignored, thereby clearing the field for a military intervention. The pretext provided by the Balinese custom of *tawan karang*, or the right to salvage any wreck stranded off the coast of Bali, triggered off a "punitive" action in 1846 after a Dutch ship was looted.

It took no less than seven expeditions for the Dutch armies to subjugate the entire island. The kingdoms of Buleleng and Jembrana, in the north and west, were compelled to acknowledge this foreign sovereignty from the 1850s onward. One after the other, the rajas of Karangasem, Gianyar and Bangli chose to submit themselves and thus conserve a relative degree of autonomy. The remaining independent kingdoms of Badung, Tabanan and Klungkung were subdued by military force between 1906 and 1908 (2).

The circumstances of the final conquest of Bali merit recounting. The pretext of the right to shipwreck recurred when a Chinese schooner foundered off the shores of Sanur in the southern kingdom of Badung. The owner claimed damages, addressing his plaint to the Dutch authorities established in Singaraja on the north coast. They in turn claimed damages from the raja of Badung, whom they considered responsible for the plunder. The raja declared the claim unfounded and rejected it. This refusal finally led to the landing of troops on Sanur beach in 1906. The soldiers rapidly ploughed their way to the *puri* of Denpasar where a strange spectacle awaited them: a procession — led by the raja carried on a palanquin, flanked by his priests, his family, and his entire court, arrayed in all their finery and heraldic weapons — heading toward the Dutch troops. As the Balinese drew closer, they broke into a run, brandishing lances and daggers *(keris)*. The Dutch army opened fire on the procession. Among the first to fall was the raja; and at this, a frenzy broke out, and his followers began to kill themselves and each other. The massacre turned to plunder, and it is said that the Balinese threw their gold and their jewels at the invaders in contempt.

(2) For a Western perspective on the history of the conquest, see Hanna (1976), and for a Balinese perspective, Agung (1991).

The same scene repeated itself that afternoon before a neighboring palace, and again two years later with the sack of the *puri* of Klungkung, seat of the Dewa Agung, Bali's most prestigious raja. He was the final one to surrender (Wiener 1995) (3).

Thus the encounter between Bali and the West, begun under the best auspices, ended in the ritual of confrontational sacrifice - the "fight to the finish" *(puputan)* - by three of the island's leading royal houses, who chose to give themselves a glorious death rather than give themselves up to a foreign master.

The island of Bali was one of the last regions of the Indonesian archipelago to be subjected by the Dutch. Its conquest was not an isolated or incidental event: it was carried out in the course of a territorial expansion that, starting with the consolidation of Dutch power in Java, saw the transformation of what had been initially a mere commercial enterprise into a grand design of economic exploitation. This required the political domination of those regions still under native rule and the reinforcement of the colonial administration, which completed the formation of the empire of the Netherlands East Indies around 1910. It is significant that at the time it was consolidating its colonial empire and expanding its boundaries, the Dutch government adopted an "Ethical Policy", in which the Netherlands acknowledged a "moral obligation" toward the people of the Indies. This new policy was to entail a much deeper penetration of the local societies by the colonial administration, which felt both obliged and justified in acting to reform them in the cause of peace, order and welfare.

The Balinization of Bali

The Dutch government had been highly embarrassed by the agitation provoked in Holland and foreign diplomatic circles by the spectacular self-sacrifice of the Balinese nobility. To obliterate the memory of their brutal intervention, they tried to develop a more worthy image of their colonial policy in Bali — an image based on the preservation of Balinese culture and on its promotion through tourism (4).

The Dutch had discovered Balinese culture well before they finally incorporated the island into their empire. Indeed, they had begun to take an interest in the culture in the 19th century as they consolidated their position on the island. This interest was due especially to the studies of orientalists employed by the government, who held that Bali was a "living museum" of the Indo-Javanese civilization, the depository of the Hindu heritage of Majapahit that had been swept from Java by the arrival of Islam. In their view, the Hindu religion was the foundation of Balinese society, the guardian of its cultural integrity and the inspiration of its artistic works.

If the Dutch understood poorly the society over which they stretched their empire, they nonetheless had a certain notion of what it should be, and they set about

---

(3) For a romantic vision of the conquest of Badung, see Baum (1937).

(4) Thus writes Vicki Baum in the preface to *A Tale from Bali:*

> *I would like to believe... that the self-sacrifice of so many Balinese at that time had a deep significance, since it impressed upon the Dutch the need of ruling this proud and gentle island people as considerately as they have, and so kept Bali the paradise it is today.* (Baum 1937: x)

without delay making that society conform to their ideas. To them, Bali was a sanctuary, a world apart, fragile and unique, to be protected by the enlightened paternalism of colonial guardianship against pernicious foreign influences and the traumatizing impact of modernity. The following quotation by G.P. Rouffaer, a former director of the *Bali Instituut* founded in 1915, sums up the prevailing position of the colonial administration rather well:

> *Let the Balinese live their own beautiful native life as undisturbed as possible! Their agriculture, their village-life, their own forms of worship, their religious art, their own literature — all bear witness to an autonomous native civilization of rare versatility and richness. No railroads on Bali; no western coffee plantations; and especially no sugar factories! But also no proselytizing, neither by Mohammedan (by zealous natives from other parts of the Indies), nor Protestant, nor Roman Catholic. Let the colonial administration, with the strong backing of the Netherlands (home) government, treat the island of Bali as a rare jewel, that we must protect and whose virginity must remain intact.* (in Robinson 1995: 41)

To the Dutch, what this meant was not so much preserving the culture as they found it, as restoring it to what they thought was its original integrity. Thus, not content to merely shelter the Balinese from outside contacts, the orientalists and colonial officials undertook to teach them how to be authentically Balinese. This was the objective proclaimed in the policy effected in the 1920s known as "the Balinization of Bali" (*Baliseering*). Specifically, its aim was to make Balinese youth conscious of the richness of their cultural heritage through an education that emphasized the study of their language, literature and traditional arts, all the while actively discouraging any improper expressions of modernism (te Flierhaar 1941). The Dutch also duly collected and inventoried artifacts of Balinese culture, not only to put them at the disposal of scholars, but also to prevent them from being sold as souvenirs to tourists (5).

If this idea of a "living museum" was so willingly taken up by the colonial authorities, it is not only due to a genuine concern that the uniqueness of Balinese culture might be destroyed by indiscriminate contact with the wider world, but also because it fitted their political agenda neatly. In the early 1920s, the Dutch came to regard Bali as the cornerstone of their effort to contain the spread of Islamic radicalism as well as the various nationalist movements which had recently arisen in Java and Sumatra. And in this respect, it soon dawned upon them that the Balinese nobility, whom they saw as the vehicle of the Hinduization of the island and the pillar of its traditional order, was the best barrier against the threat of Islam and that of

(5) In 1928 the government chartered a foundation in Singaraja — the *Kirtya Liefrinck-Van der Tuuk*, named after two great tutelary figures of Balinese studies — dedicated to the collection and study of Balinese manuscripts, while a museum for the various forms of the material culture of the island, the *Bali Museum*, was opened in 1932 in Denpasar.

nationalism. Thus, despite the suspicion and low esteem in which they held the Balinese lords, the Dutch resolved to ensure their loyalty, first by entrenching and codifying the so-called "caste" system and legalizing its hierarchy, then by restoring the royal houses to their position of political and religious authority — this, of course, under the strict supervision of the colonial officials (6).

This conservationist policy — which in making Bali the showcase of enlightened colonialism earned the Dutch government its greatest claim to glory — nonetheless profoundly disturbed Balinese society. The enlistment of the former rajas in the colonial bureaucracy, the imposition of taxes and forced labor, the introduction of a monetary economy, and the access of a fringe of Balinese youth to a European form of education destabilized the relationships which had prevailed between the peasantry and the traditional elites. And in cultivating a class of Western-educated Balinese (essential to running the colonial administration), the Dutch created a native intelligentsia which would mediate between the Balinese and their new masters.

At the risk of somewhat simplifying a complex and ill-documented process, one can say that these Balinese intellectuals addressed themselves to making sense of the upheaval provoked by the intrusion of foreigners in their world (7). Their solution was to define the Balinese simultaneously as a religious minority — the ultimate bastion of Hinduism in a predominantly Islamic environment — and as an ethnic group, a people distinguished by their own customs. There were other processes going on as well. At the same time that the "Balinization" program was rousing the Balinese to new interest in their cultural heritage, the admiration of foreigners for certain aspects of Balinese culture affected the way the Balinese were beginning to see themselves. This admiration can be described as an "aestheticizing gaze"; and whether it was held by orientalists or the travelers that had begun to visit the island, this esteem must have been seductive to a newly colonized people, and it is not surprising that the Balinese were easily persuaded that they were "artists". Thus colonialism and nascent tourism helped launch a debate on the island about the relationships among religion, custom and art — a debate which continues in the same terms today as the Balinese are more preoccupied than ever with examining their cultural identity. This debate was provoked by the presence of foreigners, by the intrusive and admiring "Other" in their midst; and this, in turn, incited them to account for their culture in terms comprehensible to non-Balinese, and in a language, moreover, that was not their own — Malay, the lingua franca of the archipelago, adopted by the colonial government to run its empire and, ironically, soon to become the unifying mortar of the Indonesian nationalist movement.

Thus it is in the context of an identity crisis that one must consider the

(6) The cultural policy of the colonial authorities in Bali is still not well known, and its history cannot be reduced to the necessarily simplified account given here. A good presentation is furnished by Schulte Nordholt (1986) and by Robinson (1995).

(7) Balinese writings from that time refer to the pre-colonial era as "when the world was steady" (*dugas gumine enteg*).

effervescence of artistic and religious activity that followed the imposition of colonial rule. The renewal of art forms and the revival of rituals were generally interpreted by observers as a sign of Bali's "cultural renaissance", commonly attributed to the enlightened benevolence of the Dutch officials (with the help of a few foreign artists and scholars living on the island). This benevolence, however, was self-serving: if the colonial powers deliberately encouraged Balinese culture, they did so to more effectively stifle any inclination for political activity. Culture was to be the safeguard of "peace and order" (*rust en orde*) (8).

2. The opening of Bali to tourism

Such was the situation in Bali when the first tourists arrived. Yet before Bali could become a paragon of international tourism, it had to meet two prior conditions. First, the island of "plunderers" and "barbaric cults" had to be made attractive to travelers in search of the exotic. Second, those regions of touristic interest must be made accessible to visitors. Barely six years after its incorporation into the Netherlands East Indies, Bali fulfilled both these conditions.

The setting up of tourist facilities

One may trace the beginnings of tourism in the East Indies archipelago from 1908, a few weeks before the last Balinese raja fell under Dutch cannon fire. That year in Batavia (today Jakarta), representatives of commercial banks and rail, insurance and shipping companies founded the Association for Tourist Traffic in Netherlands India. Among these was the Royal Packet Navigation Company (KPM), which had a monopoly on shipping in the archipelago. In the same year, this government-subsidized association opened an Official Tourist Bureau which established relations with the principal tour operators of the time and installed representatives in Java as well as abroad. Initially limited to Java, its field of action extended, from 1914 onwards, to Bali, christened in the brochures as the "Gem of the Lesser Sunda Isles" (Picturesque Dutch East Indies, 1925).

After the military conquest, governing the island required the rapid development of infrastructures and means of communication. In 1914, deeming that the pacification of Bali was now complete, the government replaced the occupying army with a civil authority. Bali was then accessible by boat from Surabaya (Java), and travelers could get around the island by horse or by car and — space permitting —

(8) This is precisely what was denounced by a handful of Balinese intellectuals, freshly educated in Dutch schools, in a magazine launched in 1925 in Singaraja for the edification of their fellow-countrymen, whom they reproached for allowing themselves to be seduced by the glamour of their island abroad. They rejected the image of a "living museum" propagated by the orientalists and condemned the policy of cultural conservationism instituted by the colonial government. Zealots of progress, they wanted Bali to shake off its archaic reputation and become a place like any other, with nothing about it to arouse the curiosity of tourists in search of the exotic (Anonymous 1927).

stay overnight in the government resthouses (*pasanggrahan*) used by the Dutch officials on their tours of inspection around the island. But tourists did not begin to visit Bali in earnest until 1924, with the opening of a weekly service of sea connections linking Singapore, Batavia, Semarang and Surabaya to Buleleng (the port serving Singaraja) and Makassar (today Ujung Pandang) in the Celebes. This initiative came from the KPM, which had decided to carry passengers on the ships it sent to Buleleng to take on copra, coffee, cattle, and above all pigs. This line, called the Bali Express, soon earned the unflattering nickname "Babi Express" (*babi* meaning "pig" in Malay).

Soon after this, the KPM agent in Singaraja became the representative of the Official Tourist Bureau in Bali, on hand to help tourists hire a taxi with an English-speaking guide or reserve a room in the *pasanggrahan* of their choice. From the start, the KPM had to face the competition of several colorful characters, such as Jacob Minas, an Armenian entrepreneur who owned a traveling film-house and operated in partnership with André Roosevelt, an American adventurer, representing American Express and Thomas Cook on the island. And then there was "Princess" Patimah, a Balinese woman often mentioned in travelogues who claimed to have been married to the raja of Klungkung. Thanks to the tourists, she became the richest business-woman on the island, the owner of a fleet of taxis, goldsmith workshops, and weaving studios at Bratan on the slopes above Singaraja.

In 1928, the KPM opened the Bali Hotel, replacing the Denpasar *pasanggrahan* and built on the very site of the *puputan* of 1906. Next, it renovated the *pasanggrahan* at Kintamani, henceforth reserved exclusively for tourists who wished to enjoy the spectacular panorama over Lake Batur. Not long after this, Padang Bay in the south-eastern part of the island was outfitted to receive cruise ships. Maritime connections multiplied and by the end of the 1920s reached an average of four ships a week. In 1934, a daily ferry was running between Gilimanuk, at the western point of Bali, and Banyuwangi on the east coast of Java. Starting in 1933 an airline linked Surabaya to Bali, and by 1938, with the opening of the airport in Tuban near Denpasar, there were three flights a week.

While these services were being set up, the publications of the Tourist Bureau show how Bali's image as a tourist destination was developing. When the island was opened to tourism in 1914, the Bureau published an *Illustrated Tourist Guide to East Java, Bali and Lombok* (Official Tourist Bureau, 1914), striking for its sobriety and essentially practical nature. One searches in vain for information about the history of Bali or contemporary Balinese society, nor does one find the lyrical gushing about the beauty of the island and its inhabitants that later became the standard style. Instead, travelers are warned of the discomfort and difficulties of the expedition they are about to undertake, and of the inhospitable or frankly uninteresting character of certain regions. It was only with the publication in 1923 of a booklet entitled *Short Guide to*

Bali (Official Tourist Bureau, n.d.) that tourists were granted slightly more substantial information. A brief introduction describing Balinese society and its history, religious traditions and arts precedes the recommended itineraries. In 1927, the Tourist Bureau began publishing a monthly review entitled *Tourism: A Monthly Bulletin of Information Relative to Travel in the Dutch East Indies* which devoted several issues entirely to Bali. There one finds, among other things, announcements of Balinese religious festivals, as well as notice of cremations for which the Bureau will charter a ship if the event is likely to be especially spectacular. It was not until 1931 with the Colonial Exposition in Paris that the Bureau decided to provide its clients with serious information on Balinese society, entrusting to one of its foremost experts, the Dutch orientalist Roelof Goris, the editing of a small booklet entitled *Observations on the Customs and Life of the Balinese* (Goris n.d.), republished in a revised edition in 1939. Publications aimed at tourists multiplied during the 1930s. Among these, one notes in particular a guide edited by a Chinese from Java, written in Malay and aimed at travelers native to the archipelago, which describes the island and its inhabitants in a manner largely inspired by the Dutch guidebooks of the time (Soe Lie Piet n.d.).

The arrival of the first tourists

It is hard to know precisely how many tourists came to Bali during the time of the Netherlands East Indies because the available statistics do not distinguish tourists among the registered visitors. The first figures published by the Tourist Bureau announce 213 visitors in 1924, a number that increased regularly to 1,428 in 1929. After this, arrivals stagnated for several years because of the economic depression, and then began to rise again in 1934 to reach an annual average of some 3,000 visitors toward the end of the decade (9).

The first tourists came to Bali on a cruise ship that anchored at Padang for a day or two or, more generally, on one of the boats of the KPM line that moored in the harbor of Buleleng. Whether they came from North America or Europe, these long-distance voyagers had already either crossed the Pacific Ocean or traveled the coasts of Asia. This meant that they saw Bali as either the last of the Pacific islands or the most extreme point of Asia — giving Bali the concentrated perfumes of the mysterious Orient and the enchantment of a South Sea island paradise. Most tourists spent three days on the island, arriving at Buleleng on a Friday morning and leaving on the same ship when it returned from Makassar on the Sunday evening. More adventurous travelers could stay for ten days and catch the following boat.

The publications of the Tourist Bureau recommended a program of activities for

(9) Bali's hotel capacity before the war consisted of 70 double rooms (48 rooms at the Bali Hotel, 16 at the Satrya Hotel — a Chinese hotel in Denpasar built at the beginning of the 1930s — and 6 at the KPM Bungalow Hotel in Kintamani). 32 additional double rooms were made available to travelers in the 8 *pasanggrahan* on the island, as well as a few bungalows kept by some Americans in Kuta.

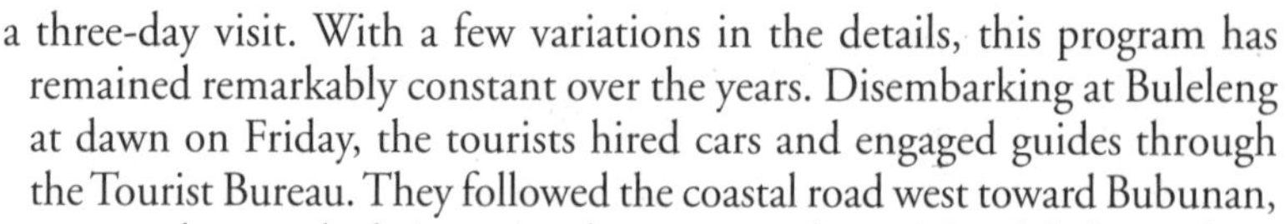

a three-day visit. With a few variations in the details, this program has remained remarkably constant over the years. Disembarking at Buleleng at dawn on Friday, the tourists hired cars and engaged guides through the Tourist Bureau. They followed the coastal road west toward Bubunan, then made their way to the *pasanggrahan* at Munduk from where they could explore the regions of the Tamblingan and Buyan lakes on horse back. In the afternoon, they descended to Denpasar through Tabanan and took a room at the Bali Hotel. After dinner, the hotel staged a program of "native dances".

On Saturday morning, the tourists could visit the Bali Museum, unless they preferred to watch another dance performance near the hotel. After this they hurried off to Bedulu to visit the "elephant cave" (Goa Gajah), then to Tampaksiring, making sure not to miss the "moon" of Pejeng, the "royal tombs" (Gunung Kawi), and the "holy spring" (Tirta Empul) along the way. After lunch at the *pasanggrahan* at Tirta Empul, they headed for Gianyar and Klungkung where they visited the "court of justice" (Kerta Gosa) and continued on to Kusamba to see the "bat cave" (Goa Lawah). At dusk they returned to Denpasar.

On Sunday morning they set off to discover the famous temple at Bangli and then headed for Penelokan to admire the panorama offered by the crater of the Batur volcano, the highlight of their trip to Bali. After lunch at the *pasanggrahan* at Kintamani, they returned to Singaraja, stopping on the way to visit the temples of Kubutambahan and Sangsit. The visit ended with the tourists boarding their ship at Buleleng in the late afternoon.

The role of the foreign residents

Among the visitors to Bali, one must give particular consideration to the small community of foreigners who lived there between the wars. For the most part artists and scholars — along with a handful of adventurers and traders — these foreign residents constituted an avant-garde as well as a cultural guarantee for the elite tourism of the colonial era, and in this role they mediated between Bali and the tourists (Spruit 1995). Not only did they certify and disseminate to the West the image of Bali as paradise, they also, and above all, identified Balinese society with its *culture* — which they saw mostly in terms of its artistic and religious activities. Their influence on the way in which tourism developed worked in several ways.

They helped to popularize the villages in which they lived — primarily Ubud, Sanur, and Kuta, which would later become the island's main centers of tourism. They brought a decisive energy to the renewal of Balinese arts by showing enthusiasm for art forms threatened with extinction, by popularizing techniques and aesthetic codes previously unknown to the Balinese, and by encouraging local artists to produce works that would appeal to foreigners and could be sold on the tourist market.

Above all, their writings and the paintings, photographs and films that they brought back from the island portrayed a paradisical image of Bali, an image that the promotional services of the emerging tourist industry quickly relayed (MacRae 1992). Thus it is that since the 1920s the island of Bali has been described to the point of exhaustion as a true Garden of Eden, the cradle of a traditional culture that has remained aloof from the vicissitudes of the modern world, whose exceptionally gifted inhabitants devote most of their time and wealth to staging sumptuous ceremonies for their pleasure and that of their gods — and now, for the greatest satisfaction of their visitors as well.

3. The Last Paradise

What is the source of this image that so seduced the West between the wars? More than a simple transcription fashioned from an existing reality, it is the product of a construction; indeed, one could almost say that it is the result of an objective complicity among the colonial government, cultural anthropology, and the tourism industry. The fact remains that before they became famous for the richness of their culture, the Balinese were known for the beauty of their women, and before that, for their ferocity as warriors and the cruelty of their princes. This implies that the image of the "Other" in the dominant discourse was fashioned in a self-serving way: before their conquest, the Balinese had to be perceived as savages to be *pacified;* once the conquest was accomplished, they could become an exotic curiosity to be *gazed at* (Urry 1990).

Although one could hardly call the first European travelers to Bali tourists, their accounts nonetheless already bear the mark of what would later become a touristic cliché. The term "Last Paradise" (10), which has greatly contributed to the promotion of Bali in the 20th century, carries a reverberating echo of the reported enchantment of the first visitors at the end of the 16th century. Or rather, it is the story surrounding the "discovery" of the island that retroactively establishes the first link in

(10) Title of the first book in English on Bali, published in New York in 1930 by the American journalist Hickman Powell (1930).

a long chain of images that Bali has generated during the turbulent history of its relationship with the West.

According to the chroniclers of our own century, the European sailors' encounter with Bali was love at first sight. Note, for example, the terms in which this event is described in a work still regarded as authoritative:

> *In 1597, a fleet of Dutch ships, headed by a former employee of the Portuguese, Cornelius Houtman, discovered Bali. He and his men fell in love with the island and made excellent friends with the king, a good-natured fat man who had two hundred wives, rode in a chariot drawn by two white buffaloes which he drove himself, and owned fifty dwarfs whose bodies had been distorted into resemblance of kris handles. After a long sojourn in the island, some of the Dutch returned to Holland to report the discovery of the new "paradise"; others refused to leave Bali. The news created such a sensation in Holland that in 1601 the trader Heemskerk was sent to Bali with presents of all sorts for the king, who in turn presented him with a beautiful Balinese lady.* (Covarrubias 1937: 29)

The truth is that the Hollanders' first visit to Bali lasted sixteen days and that only two of them stayed on, for reasons we do not know. This no doubt excited the imagination of the chroniclers, obviously tempted to attribute the defection of the young men to the irresistible allure of the Balinese women — an allure that the first photographers of Bali did not fail to exploit.

"The Island of Bare Breasts" (11)

Of the many image-makers of Bali, two among the earliest are of particular importance: W.O.J. Nieuwenkamp and Gregor Krause. It is to Nieuwenkamp — a Dutch artist who made several visits to Bali at the turn of the century — that we owe the first albums, abundantly illustrated with drawings by the author, describing for the general public the island of Bali, the daily life of the people and their artistic traditions. Above all, it was he who first called the attention of his compatriots to the beauty of the island that they had just conquered (Nieuwenkamp 1910).

But it was certainly Gregor Krause, a German physician in the service of the Dutch government posted in Bali between 1912 and 1914, who made the decisive first step in the touristic promotion of the island with the publication in 1920 of an album illustrated with nearly four hundred photographs. The success of this book, as its subsequent editions attest, is no doubt related to the great care with which the author emphasizes the physical beauty of Balinese bodies and to his enthusiasm for the photographic theme of Balinese women at their bath (Krause 1920, 1930, 1988). It was, especially, the seduction of these photos that induced the Mexican artist Miguel Covarrubias, as well as the Austrian novelist Vicki Baum, to make the voyage to Bali.

---

(11) Title of a novel by Edouard de Keyser (1933).

W.G. Hofker
ni made Toewi
april 1943 Taman

Their two books, later published in 1937, remain to this day the most celebrated of all that the island has inspired — *Island of Bali* and *A Tale from Bali* (Covarrubias 1937; Baum 1937; cf. also Williams 1994).

The breasts of Balinese women no doubt constituted a major attraction to the island during that time; but the text accompanying Krause's photographs gives us better idea of the European perception of Bali when the first tourists were beginning to arrive:

> *The inhabitants of Bali are beautiful and, incredible as it may seem, inconceivably beautiful. Anyone at all in Bali, seated by the side of the road or elsewhere, who bothers to simply look at what passes before him, will begin to doubt the reality of what he sees. Everything is beautiful, perfectly beautiful, the bodies, the clothing, the gait, each pose, each movement. How is such beauty possible? From whence comes such incredible harmony with the surroundings? The traveler's legs will never tire, his eye never cease to be charmed, as long as a lucky star allows him to escape from the confines of the officials, European traders and the tourist industry, whose sole preoccupation is to find out how one can gather up Bali as quickly as possible into the Moloch of civilization.* (Krause 1930: 9-10) (12)

This inconceivable beauty Bali owes primarily to its women:

> *Balinese women are beautiful, as beautiful as one can imagine, with a physiologically simple and dignified beauty, full of Eastern nobility and natural chastity.* (Krause 1988: 55)

It is also the charm emanating from a rich and happy country whose inhabitants have a genius for festive celebrations:

> *For these happy people, life on earth seems to be an almost uninterrupted festival, an ecstasy of overflowing joy in life and of gratitude and devotion to the Gods.* (Krause 1988: 89)

One understands how in such heavenly conditions our author comes to exclaim:

> *I was furious with God that I was not born in Bali!* (Krause 1930: 35)

---

(12) This seems far from the time when Elisée Reclus could write, in the *Nouvelle géographie universelle* which appeared in 1889:

The civilization of Bali displays great decadence... The use of opium, which is widespread among all the castes, the civil wars between provinces, the expeditions of slave traders, and finally the debasement of women, reduced to being nothing more than a piece of merchandise, are the causes of the backwardness of the Balinese civilization... In the mountainous regions, goiters are extremely common; in some districts more than half the population are afflicted with them, and one hardly finds a woman who is not deformed by these excrescences. (in Lombard 1990, Vol.1: 48-50)

To read Gregor Krause, and especially to glance through his photographs, one would think that Bali had succeeded Tahiti as the ultimate image of South Sea Island glamor. This, in any case, was the opinion put forward by Miguel Covarrubias:

> *The remote little island only became news to the rest of the Western world with the advent, a few years ago, of a series of documentary films of Bali with a strong emphasis on sex appeal. These films were a revelation and now everybody knows that Balinese girls have beautiful bodies and that the islanders lead a musical-comedy sort of life full of weird, picturesque rites. The title of one of these films, Goona-goona, the Balinese term for "magic", became at the time Newyorkese for sex allure. The newly discovered "last paradise" became the contemporary substitute for the nineteenth-century romantic conception of primitive Utopia, until then the exclusive monopoly of Tahiti and other South Sea Islands.* (Covarrubias 1937: 391-392)

The Island of Artists (13)

Persuasive as it appears, however, Covarrubias's argument only partially conveys Bali's seductiveness. And in any case, Margaret Mead challenged him on this, pointing out how much the image of Bali, elaborated during the 1930s, differed from that of the South Seas that prevailed in the 1920s. According to Mead, while the South Sea image crystallized the dreams of hedonistic idleness and erotic gratification of a West soured by war and its privations, the force of Bali's attractiveness lays, by contrast, in the obvious contentment its people found in a life entirely occupied with religious festivals, generating a profusion of art forms unknown elsewhere. Mead concludes:

> *Many Americans in the 1920s sought for an escape as single individuals from a society which denied them self-expression. Many in the 1930s sought for a formula by which we could build our society into a form which would make possible, on a firm economic base, both simple happiness and complexity of spiritual expression. Of such a dream, Bali was a fitting symbol.* (Mead 1970: 340)

---

(13) "Every Balinese, man or woman, is an artist" (Roosevelt, in Powell 1930: x). For some interesting comments on the often-repeated and romantic notion that "all Balinese are artists", see Kam (1993: 71-73).

By the early 1920s, Bali had found a place in Western imagination thanks to the beauty of its women, but it had yet to find someone to communicate to the world the profuse diversity of its cultural riches. That role would be filled by the German painter and musician Walter Spies. It was, incidentally, after having seen the photographs of Gregor Krause that the young Spies left in 1923 for the Netherlands East Indies. In 1927, he established himself in Bali from whence only the Second World War would force him to leave. During this period, his reputation as a connoisseur of things Balinese made him sought after by artists, writers and other celebrities traveling in the island, and his house in Ubud became a mandatory stop for visitors eager to distinguish themselves from the other tourists (14).

Most of the foreigners who lived in Bali during the 1930s acknowledged how much they owed to the competence and unselfish good-will of Walter Spies. It was his first recordings of Balinese music that made the Canadian composer Colin McPhee decide to establish himself there (McPhee 1947); it was Spies who inspired the novelist Vicki Baum and who guided Miguel Covarrubias in his approach to Balinese society; and it is to him that André Roosevelt as well as Victor von Plessen owe the enduring allure of their films *Goona-Goona* and *Insel der Dämonen*.

But it was not enough for Walter Spies to share his interest in Balinese culture and record its different manifestations. He is equally credited with the renaissance of Balinese arts that flourished during the 1930s. Not only was he the author of the first studies of Balinese dance and drama (Spies & Goris 1937; de Zoete & Spies 1938; Hitchcock & Norris 1995), he and his friends also helped to revive the enthusiasm of the Balinese for certain theatrical forms that had fallen into disuse, and they even incited the creation of new compositions.

It is in the domain of painting and sculpture that Walter Spies was most influential. Assisted by the Dutch painter Rudolf Bonnet, who had been living in Ubud since 1929, he helped to renew both the techniques and the thematic content of the plastic arts, encouraging painters and sculptors to explore the themes of daily life and to free themselves from their ancient conventions. Above all, he turned the Balinese into "professional" artists by helping them to direct their works toward the budding tourist market (15).

The Island of Gods and Demons

After the artists came the anthropologists. We should note that during the 1930s, Bali — which drew the majority of its tourists from the United States — had

---

(14) "Thanks to Walter Spies — Bali is, for me, the island of a hundred dances, of magic, of trances — without him I would have been one of a thousand tourists" (excerpt from Walter Spies's guest book, 1938).

(15) Other European painters settled in Bali during that time, among whom one should mention the Austrian Roland Strasser, the Swiss Théo Meier, the Belgian Adrien Jean Le Mayeur de Merprès (Ubbens & Huizing 1995), and the Dutch Willem Hofker (Carpenter & Hofker-Rueter 1993). But, unlike Spies and Bonnet, they had no influence on Balinese art.

particularly held the attention of American anthropologists of the "Culture and Personality" persuasion, the most prominent among them being Jane Belo, Margaret Mead, and Gregory Bateson (Belo 1970; Bateson & Mead 1942; Boon 1986; Jacknis 1988). Strongly influenced by Walter Spies, they found in Bali an island where culture and nature converged in subtle correspondences, the cradle of a stable and harmonious society periodically agitated by spectacular rituals.

Their writings reinforced the Dutch government in its policy of cultural protectionism by confirming the idea that Balinese society had not really been affected by colonization. To read them, it would seem that the Balinese were too busy celebrating their culture to be bothered by the presence of a foreign administration (Pollmann 1990). They provided anthropology's stamp of authority to the impressions of tranquil harmony reported by the visitors of that time, their analyses of the stability of Balinese society never suggesting that this may be due to its occupation by a colonial power (Bateson 1970). It is precisely this forced peace — imposed by the Dutch armies on an island hitherto known more for the fierce character of its natives than for their docility — that would soon be considered an inherent trait of Balinese society. In short, it appeared that from the moment matters of government were appropriated by the Dutch, the Balinese had nothing else to do but busy themselves with art and religion, elaborating their expressive culture to their hearts' content.

For Mead and Bateson, the ritual and artistic effervescence of the Balinese was a symptom to be interpreted through the grid of a culturalist psychology. In their view, Balinese culture became a mechanism for regulating impulses, causing a kind of cultural schizophrenia: while the Balinese normally appear quiet and well-adjusted, on certain occasions they let themselves be carried away by paroxysms of frenzy that, however spectacular and violent, remain culturally codified. Through these periodic outbursts, which take place in a state of trance, they relieve themselves of the oppressive weight of an excessively strict social control on their daily existence (Jensen & Suryani 1992; Suryani & Jensen 1993).

Following Spies, Mead and Bateson constructed a symbolism of two alternating states of the Balinese ethos — diurnal and nocturnal, Apollonian serenity and Dionysian seizures — in the contrasting figures of the dancer and the witch: behind the nymph-like figure of the young dancer lurked the hideous shadow of the old witch. The "Island of the Gods" was also the "Island of Demons" (16).

---

(16) Title of a film by Victor von Plessen, made in Bali in 1931 with the assistance of Walter Spies, as well as of a novel by Johan Fabricius (1941). On this point, one may refer to the penetrating analyses of Vickers (1989).

A Lost Paradise?

Whether as a vivacious bare-breasted village girl, a dancer in a heavy gilded headdress, or a witch in a terrifying mask, Woman is the major metaphor of Bali. But one must be aware that the power of this metaphor lies in its multi-faceted meaning, and, more precisely, in its capacity to combine the mystery of Asia with the seductiveness of the Pacific — as if Balinese harmony resulted from a rare alliance between the fecundity of a traditional culture and the fertility of a primitive natural world. Indic in its ceremonies and Polynesian in its way of life — such did the island of Bali appear to the first European sailors in 1597, and such does it remain in travelers' tales and tourist brochures nearly four hundred years later.

Furthermore, if Bali lends itself so easily to lyrical effusion — what the American anthropologist James Boon called a "romance" (Boon 1977) — it is not only because of its festive abundance, but perhaps even more so because the harmony it evokes seems threatened. For at the same time that the chroniclers of the 1930s conspired to present us with an image of Bali as a theater where the artistic and ritual genius of the inhabitants vies for splendor with the gorgeousness of its landscape, they never failed to emphasize the archaic character of Balinese society, which they described as a medieval relic, miraculously preserved from the corrupting outrages of modernity. Thus the fascination of Bali for visitors was heightened by fear of its imminent decline, as if the image it conjured was as evanescent as "the dream of an opium eater":

> *Bali is too near Java for security from the blight of European ugliness that will fall upon it; it is now like the dream of an opium eater.* (Clifton 1927: 130)

This is the impression one gets from reading travelers' accounts published between the Wars, a recurring scenario padded with preconceptions and clichés that acquired the force of truth by sheer repetition. Thus it was that so many travelers were amazed and enchanted by their discovery of the "real" face of Bali. Made mistrustful by so many unwarranted stories about so-called enchanting islands, they came to Bali warily, with a cynical skepticism that nonetheless bore a trace of hopefulness. One account among many, written at the end of the 1930s:

> *Since the day Gauguin first showed Parisians his canvasses of Tahiti, no island of original civilization has excited the spirit of artists and intellectuals sated by Europe like that "last paradise on earth" which we have known for three centuries by seductive descriptions, the island of Bali. Idealists, breaking all ties with their past, seek refuge in this "island of dreams". But alarming news has reached Europe of the utter sans-gêne of the hordes of tourists and the rapid decadence of Balinese "authenticity". Bali is finished, they say. It has become a fair-ground of souvenirs for globe-trotters. The "last paradise" has become a victim of its own fame. With what prudent skepticism, then, did I arm myself when I set off!* (Schuh 1954: 117)

As the tourists of the 1930s disembarked in Bali, their first impression — that of the port of Buleleng with its Chinese shops and roofs of corrugated tin — was inevitably disappointing, confirming in our visitors their fear of having fallen, yet again, into a tourist trap. And then, rounding a hill, leaving the main coastal town behind them, they would be seized with rapture, convinced that the tourist slogans are true after all — Bali is indeed the paradise it is vaunted to be, and surely the last:

> *In the last ten years this island has been written about, filmed, photographed, and gushed over to an extent which would justify nausea. I went there half-unwillingly, for I expected a complete "bali-hoo", picturesque and faked to a Hollywood standard; I left wholly unwillingly, convinced that I had seen the nearest approach to Utopia that I am ever to see.* (Gorer 1936: 42-43)

The travelers' wonder was that much more precious because of their conviction that the Balinese idyll was extremely precarious, menaced by an invasion from the West of which tourism was not the least harmful form. It was as if, since the "discovery" of the island by an avant-garde of travelers and artists during the 1920s, the very conjuring of the name of Bali suggested the imminence of a fatal fall from a Garden of Eden in which the Balinese could not expect to indulge indefinitely. Sooner or later, this "last paradise" was condemned to become a "lost paradise". So confided Margaret Mead in a letter:

> *There is not much hope for Bali ultimately because their social system is founded on religion and that is bound to crack before the Muslims, the Christians or the modern skeptics who worship industrialism.* (Mead 1977: 172)

Persuaded that they were the final spectators to witness the swan-song of an exceptionally creative culture, a few visitors tried to record what they discovered before it was too late. This was the case of Covarrubias in particular, who closed the introduction of his celebrated work with the following reflection:

> *The Balinese still retain their traditions and hold to their own manner of life, but they are only too willing to adopt every new idea, good or bad, brought into their island by merchants, tourists, unsuitable education, and missionaries. The only aim of this book, therefore, is to collect in one volume all that could be obtained from personal experience by an unscientific artist, of a living culture that is doomed to disappear under the merciless onslaught of modern commercialism and standardization.* (Covarrubias 1937: xxv)

Faced with the urgency of this threat, observers generally took one of two positions. The first is well represented by André Roosevelt, who undertook in the 1920s to develop the tourist market, although this did not deter him from suggesting measures to preserve the integrity of Balinese society and its culture:

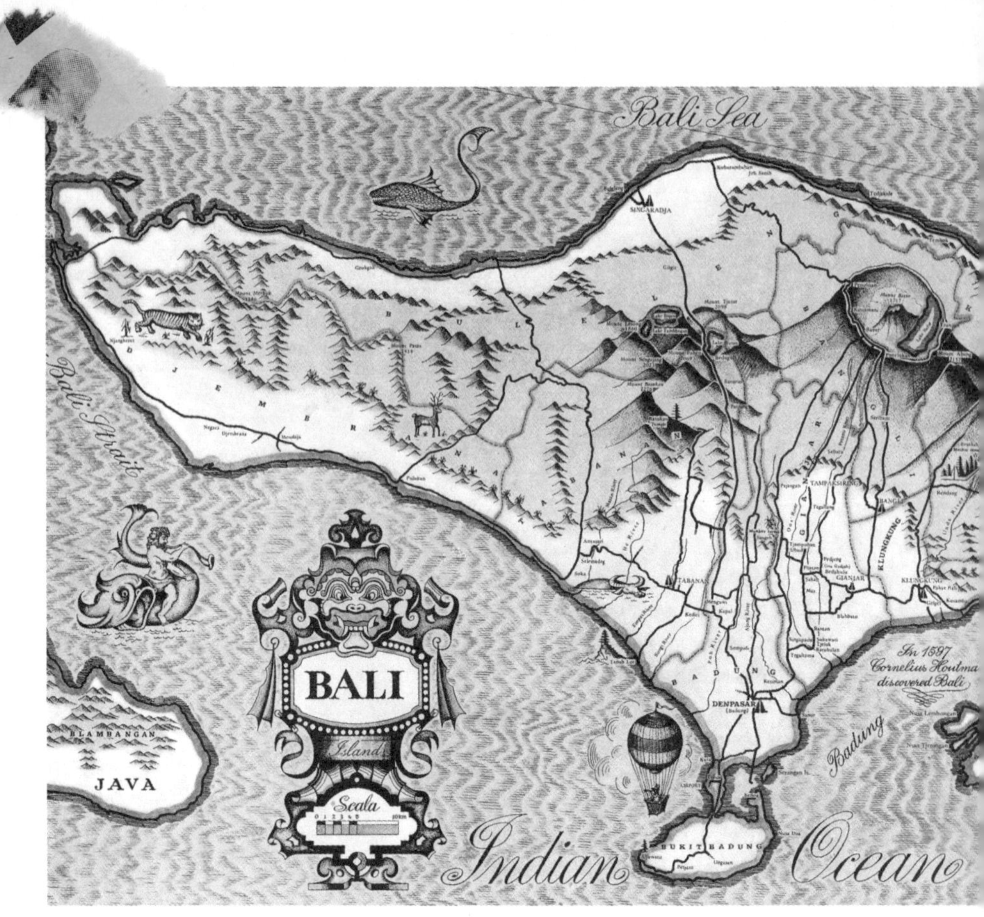

Having leisure, my friend Spies and I started a scheme which would tend to slow down the invading forces from the West and keep the Balinese in their happy, contented ways for a few decades longer... We want to make of Bali a national or international park, with special laws to maintain it as such. (in Powell 1930: xiv-xvi)

During the same period, Miguel Covarrubias believed that it would be in vain to try to prevent Westernization, and in particular to try to restrict tourism, which he nonetheless deplored for its corrosive effects on Balinese culture:

It would be futile to recommend measures to prevent the relentless march of Westernization; tourists cannot be kept out... To advocate the unconditional preservation of their picturesque culture in the midst of modern civilization would be the equivalent of turning Bali into a living museum, putting the entire island into a glass case for the enjoyment of hordes of tourists. (Covarrubias 1937: 402-403)

The controversy was echoed in the Tourist Bureau, whose spokesmen, since the installation of their representative in Singaraja in 1924, criticized the attitude of Western

artists and writers who, having helped to popularize Bali by extolling the beauty of the land and the richness of its culture, nevertheless wanted to forbid tourists access to the island. Now that the curiosity of the West was aroused, it was too late to back-paddle. It was for the Balinese to decide their future, and all the colonial administration could do was to prepare them by affirming its respect for their traditions and way of life (van der Kop 1924: 648-649) (17).

The tour operators were more cynical. While they paid lip-service to the enlightened paternalism of the colonial authorities, they used the argument of the imminent degradation of Bali to incite visitors to hurry and come before it was too late. A look at the pamphlets published by the KPM in the 1930s is revealing. One, entitled *Bali: The Enchanted Isle*, after assuring readers that Bali is not yet ruined by modernism and that "as yet it has not been invaded by hordes of ordinary tourists", warns them that "who knows — in another ten years, it may be spoiled by that insidious modernism". And the unsurprising conclusion follows, urging the elitist clientele to which the pamphlet is addressed, "Oh, do not wait too long to visit this extraordinary island" (Yates n.d.).

As for the colonial authorities, their attitude in regard to tourism showed a certain ambivalence. Convinced of the vulnerability of Balinese culture, the Dutch tried to save it from the irreparable degradation that threatened it. Now, among the perils lying in wait for the Balinese and their culture, the most insidious was none other than the tourists themselves (18) — so that, if the decision to conserve Bali as a living museum represented the best asset for tourism promotion of the island, it required some counter-measure to preserve the Balinese cultural heritage from the harmful influences propagated by the tourists. Thus the colonial authorities, who had

---

(17) In this regard, the promotional literature never missed an opportunity to praise the colonial administration, which in its great wisdom had resolved to let the Balinese live their life as they wished — as witnessed by this passage from a booklet published by the Tourist Bureau:

With characteristic insight into the requirements of the situation the Netherlanders have decided to rule Bali with as light a hand as possible. There was hardly any need to change the customs of the country, which lacked most of the abuses that had crept with time into the Hinduism of India. Here and there an innovation was brought about, an improvement in this direction, the removal of some abuse in that, mostly with the cooperation of the Princes and Priests of Bali, but as far as possible the Balinese have been left to themselves to live out their quiet lives in their own way. (Travellers Official Information Bureau, 1935: 3)

(18) This problem was already apparent to observers of the time, as may be seen in an article entitled "Tourists in Bali" which opens:

The Dutch Government is trying to keep the island of Bali free of modern influences — an impossible task. Missionaries are excluded to be sure — but tourists are admitted — and tourists bring to bear the most insidious modern influence of all. (Benson 1935: 261) already kept the Balinese from missionaries and traders, tried as well to protect them from any contact with tourists that might, in their eyes, be corrupting, in an attempt to control a quasi-monopoly on the tourism industry and to dissuade foreigners from living in the villages.

Judging by the exemplary status that Bali soon acquired in travel literature, it seems that they were fairly successful. The French travel writer Alain Gerbault, deploring what had already become of the islands of the Pacific, referred to the enviable lot of Bali:

> *I would have liked to make of Porapora a kind of Pacific Bali, for I have read a book about this island where the arts and indigenous customs are preserved, where tourists come but are not allowed to stay.* (Gerbault 1941: 216, in Urbain 1991: 61) (19)

So it was that *culture* became the brand image of Bali, the chosen common ground where the views of the Dutch orientalists and American anthropologists, the artists and tourists converged. As for the Balinese, it remains to be seen to what extent this idealization of their culture by foreigners has become part of their own views.

(19) The allegory of the Garden of Eden and the Fall is clearly not unique to Bali. In the course of a subtle analysis, Jean-Didier Urbain explains why the worlds described in travel literature are necessarily represented as menaced, while the discourse of the traveler, imprinted with nostalgia, presents itself as salvatory, when it does not abandon itself entirely to lament.

Chapter Two

THE SHOW WINDOW OF INDONESIA

There are compelling parallels in the way tourism in Bali was first developed under the Dutch and then again under the Republic of Indonesia. In the 1920s and '30s, tourism was initiated and controlled by the colonial authorities and foreign firms; since the proclamation of independence, the revival of international tourism has been the initiative of the central government and advised by foreign experts. The Balinese themselves were scarcely more consulted once they had become a province of Indonesia than when they were still a possession of the Netherlands East Indies. The decision to make Bali the "show window" of Indonesia was imposed upon them, just as in earlier times it had been imposed upon them that their island be conserved as a "living museum".

I will describe the circumstances in which the Indonesian government decided to make Bali a model for the development of tourism in the archipelago, reviewing their objectives and the considerations that shaped their policy. Then I will examine the orientations fixed by the foreign consultants for the planning and development of tourism on the island. To conclude, I will sketch a picture of the growth of tourism in Bali and of its contributions to the economic development of the region.

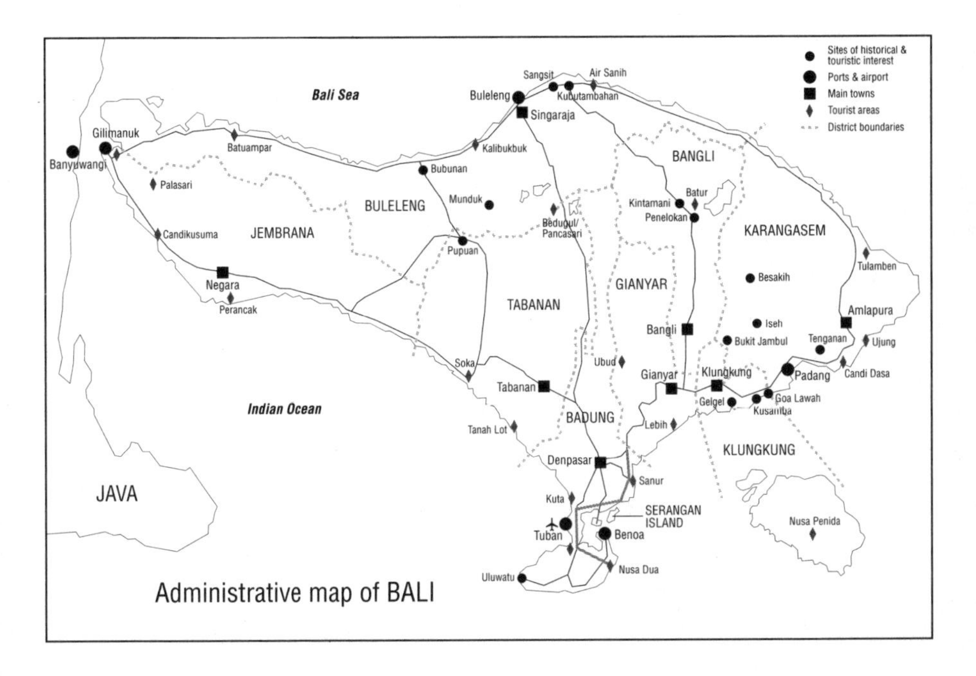

Administrative map of BALI

1. From the arrival of the Japanese to the return of the tourists

The landing of Japanese troops on Sanur beach in 1942 put a stop to the promotion of tourism in Bali. Still, the war did not completely stop tourism itself. Bali became a holiday spot for Japanese officers, thus confirming the island's "touristic vocation".

After the Japanese surrender and the proclamation of the independence of Indonesia on August 17th 1945, Bali found itself in the midst of a fierce struggle between the nationalists (partisans of the Republic established in Java) and the advocates of Balinese autonomy, still loyal to the Dutch. The Dutch were impatient to reoccupy Bali: because of its renown, they were afraid that the political turmoil there would draw international attention. That would be embarrassing. On the other hand, a quick restoring of order in Bali would reinforce their legitimacy in the rest of the archipelago. Despite their impatience, however, it was not until March 1946 that the Dutch were able to return to re-conquer the island — and then they had to overcome the resistance of the nationalist army. The nationalists were commanded by the colonel Ngurah Rai who, finding himself surrounded in the hills of Tabanan with less than a hundred men, led them in a fight to the death to the last soldier, another *puputan*. Once Bali was again under their control (thanks to the allegiance of a good part of the ruling aristocracy), the Dutch tried to re-establish the traditional order that had been disturbed by four years of military occupation and political conflict.

The Dutch seem to have been more preoccupied with questions of "culture" and "tradition" than with their immediate administrative and military problems. In their view, the present decline of Balinese culture, corrupted by the Japanese occupation, was mainly responsible for the troubles agitating the island, and they set about without delay restoring the traditional institutions with the goal of re-establishing political order. The artistic activities that had made Bali famous before the war were strongly encouraged with the idea — hardly crowned with success — of luring back the tourists, no doubt the best way of proving that things were back to normal.

Bali, province of the Republic of Indonesia

The intransigence of Sukarno and, especially, the diplomatic pressures exercised by the United Nations and the United States forced the Netherlands to recognize the sovereignty of their former colony in December 1949, and on August 17th 1950 it was proclaimed the Republic of Indonesia. But victory over the Dutch did not bring peace to Bali. Besides the conflict between "Republicans" and "Loyalists", there were rivalries among different nationalist leaders and intrigues in the royal houses, anxious to cover their backs (Last 1955; Pendit 1954; Robinson 1995; Vickers 1989). The Balinese people were exhorted to consider themselves full-fledged Indonesian citizens — although at the time, given their ethnic, religious, and customary peculiarities, this hardly went without saying. The island of Bali became a province of the Republic of Indonesia in 1958, under the authority of a Governor; and in 1960, the provincial seat was moved from Singaraja to Denpasar, which was deemed preferable because of its proximity to the airport. Not long afterwards, land reform undermined the foundations of the Balinese nobility's wealth and power which they had been able to preserve during the colonial occupation, considerably reducing their landed property and liberating the peasants from dependence on their former masters.

The province of Bali is divided into eight districts (*kabupaten*): Tabanan, Badung, Gianyar, Klungkung, Bangli, Karangasem, Buleleng, and Jembrana. The districts (governed by *bupati*) are divided into subdistricts (*kecamatan*) and subdivided further into administrative villages (*desa dinas*) made up of a number of neighborhood wards (*banjar dinas*). This hierarchical administrative structure, which describes the integration of Balinese society into the Indonesian state, is essentially a legacy of the colonial period. The division of the province into districts reproduces the divisions imposed by the Dutch administration, who more or less followed the boundaries of the old kingdoms, fixing permanently the hitherto shifting borders. It was also the Dutch who invented the distinction between an "administrative" domain and a "customary" one, creating alongside the *desa* and *banjar "adat"*, *desa* and *banjar "dinas"* (from the Dutch *dienst*, "service"), divided according to demographic and territorial criteria. The result of this duplication is that the respective attributes of the customary and administrative villages are clearly distinct and their boundaries very rarely coincide.

While the Dutch had sought to keep Bali at a safe remove from Western modernity, the Balinese nationalists strove to bring their people the benefits of progress and education, and they deplored the idea of treating their society as a museum for tourists in search of nostalgia and the exotic (Coast 1951). Significantly, among the first measures adopted were two aimed at dismantling a tourist image that many Balinese found embarrassing: the obligation of Balinese women to cover their breasts in public; and a rule forbidding visitors to photograph bare-breasted women (1).

But the island had plunged into economic depression, and the Balinese nationalists, despite their radicalism, were close to admitting that only tourism could rescue them from financial dependence. This, however, presented a dilemma. The nationalists were aware that to revive tourism, Bali must nurture the cultural particularity that had distinguished it before the war — but that contradicted the spirit of their movement toward national integration. This dilemma is well expressed by an American observer of the time:

> *Bali's artistic and cultural heritage, while it constitutes its greatest asset to Indonesia, constitutes also, at least from the point of view of the intensely nationalistic, its greatest liability. Other Indonesians, particularly the Javanese, tend rather to resent the fact that to the outside world Bali all too often represents Indonesia, and that Balinese music, dancing, painting and carving are the Indonesian accomplishments*

---

(1) Out of a concern for morality and decency, the colonial authorities had, long before, ordered that Balinese women cover their breasts in public, but this order was followed only in Singaraja and Denpasar. Already in 1939, the Balinese nationalists had urgently requested that the Dutch government take the necessary steps to prevent tourists from photographing the breasts of Balinese women and to forbid the circulation of pamphlets and postcards illustrated with photos of bare-breasted Balinese women.

> *which all the world knows. Whether to preserve Bali's unique charm and culture, whether to turn the island wide open to outside influences, including those of the Western tourist, or whether to guide Bali by easy stages to a preconceived Indonesian ideal, this is an understandably difficult decision to make.* (Hanna 1957: 8)

In any case, up to the end of the 1960s, international tourism to Bali, as to Indonesia generally, remained very limited: the rudimentary state of its infrastructure and the ruinous condition of the economy, as well as endemic political agitation and the xenophobic attitude of the regime, tended to discourage visitors. But the accession to independence had opened Bali to a new tourist clientele — the Indonesian governing élite. President Sukarno (whose mother was Balinese) adopted the island as his favorite retreat and made it an obligatory stop for his most distinguished guests.

The political and economic chaos in Bali, particularly severe at the beginning of the 1960s, was no doubt a factor in the decision of the island's religious authorities to carry out a solemn ritual purification at the temple of Besakih on the flanks of Mount Agung in 1963. This rite, called *Eka Dasa Rudra*, is in principle centennial, but its execution was considered propitious because the universe had been disturbed. The government took advantage of the circumstances by mounting a promotional campaign, inviting the participants of an international conference of travel agents in Jakarta to go to watch the ceremony in the company of President Sukarno himself. Scheduled to last two months, the ritual cycle was almost called off because of signs forewarning the eruption of Gunung Agung. Despite the unease of the religious authorities confronted with this deadly portent, the ceremony proceeded — because, it seems, of the national stakes it represented. The dreaded eruption took place during the celebration of the rituals, and it devastated the eastern part of the island, causing famines and epidemics (Mathews 1965). It is said that the government invited the travel agents to fly over Mount Agung to enjoy the splendid sight of an erupting volcano. Some Balinese declared that the cataclysm was a punishment from the gods, angry to see the ritual turned into a tourist show.

Soon after this, Sukarno, counting on Bali's former renown to attract foreign tourists, expanded the Ngurah Rai airport in Tuban to make it accessible to jetliners, and undertook the construction of a luxury hotel on Sanur beach, the Bali Beach Hotel, financed by Japanese war reparation funds (2). (Three other luxury hotels were built at the same time with the same money in Java: the Hotel Indonesia in Jakarta, the Samudra Beach Hotel in Pelabuhan Ratu, and the Hotel Ambarukmo in Yogyakarta.) But the tension that had been brooding in the country for some years exploded after the aborted "coup" of September 30th 1965 and unleashed a bloody hunt for "communists" and their sympathizers (or those supposed to be so). The massacres were

---

(2) By a probably unconscious irony, the airport was named after the nationalist hero who died trying to prevent the return of the Dutch. And one can hardly help wondering at the peculiar fate of the village of Sanur which, after witnessing three landings of foreign invaders, then paved the way — times having changed — for the tourist invasion of Bali.

particularly violent in Bali, where figures quote from 50,000 to 100,000 dead. The tragedy left deep scars that remain masked, with difficulty, under a façade of amnesia (Cribb 1990). The Bali Beach Hotel was nonetheless inaugurated in 1966, at a moment when the troubles following the coup had closed Indonesia to foreigners. It was only after the accession of General Suharto to the presidency in 1967 — and the reopening of the country under what he declared as the "New Order" (*Orde Baru*) — that the Indonesian government began to exploit Bali's tourism potential in a systematic manner. More precisely, we may date the resumption of Bali's tourism from August 1st 1969, the day of the inauguration of Ngurah Rai International Airport.

The New Order and tourism

Born of the 1965 crisis, the new regime succeeded in a few years, with the support of the army and of a team of technocrats educated in the United States — and above all with revenues from oil exports — to impose its authority and establish its legitimacy as it restored the political and economic stability of the country.

The New Order, established with a firm fist by President Suharto, set itself the goal of redressing Indonesia's catastrophic economic situation and called on the aid of foreign capital and experts. Simultaneously, it reinforced the authority of the State: the political agitation that had marked the Sukarno years was henceforth outlawed as an impediment to the country's march toward development and modernization.

The opening to the West found expression starting in 1966 with the formation of an Inter-Government Group on Indonesia (IGGI), made up of the principal industrialized nations, the World Bank (IBRD) and the International Monetary Fund (IMF). In 1967, a law was promulgated with the goal of attracting foreign investment and setting up control measures to protect Indonesia's interests. The following year, the World Bank group installed a permanent mission in Jakarta that played a decisive role in the economic policy of the new regime, both in its financing and in the shaping of its policies.

In 1969, a team of technocrats assembled in the National Development Planning Board (Bappenas) launched a program of Five-Year Development Plans (Repelita), intended to make the Indonesian economy "take off" in 25 years. At the time, the program was primarily concerned with attaining self-sufficiency in the country's rice production and establishing a mixed economy in which the state led and directed a strictly subordinate private sector.

The First Plan (1969–1974), elaborated with the help of experts from the IBRD and the IMF and financed for the most part by the IGGI, affirmed the importance of international tourism as a factor of economic development for Indonesia, and laid the foundations of a tourism policy (Department of Information, 1969: Vol.2B, Chap.VIII, pp.168–180; Prajogo 1985). This policy is under the jurisdiction of the President of the Republic, who is assisted by a National Advisory Council for Tourism (Depparnas), presided over by the Minister of the Economy and Industry. A Directorate General of Tourism (Direktorat Jenderal Pariwisata) is instituted within the Department of Communications. The Minister of Communications is assisted by a National Board for Tourist Development (Bapparnas), presided over by the Director General of Tourism.

The objectives proclaimed by the Indonesian tourism policy are as follows:

- to augment foreign exchange earnings and raise the national income, create employment, and stimulate priority sectors of the economy;
- to capitalize and promote the natural and cultural resources of Indonesia;
- to reinforce national and international solidarity.

While the arguments advanced in favor of the development of international tourism in Indonesia addressed mainly economic objectives — primarily to redress the national balance of payments, badly negative at the time — one should not underestimate the political objectives of the operation. Indeed, the country's leaders needed to dispel the memory of the massacres that had accompanied their rise to power if they wanted to affirm the legitimacy of the New Order. In this regard, there is a striking parallel between the situation of the Indonesian government and that of the colonial government some 60 years earlier: in both cases, tourism proved itself an opportune means of anesthetizing the trauma of the regime's ascent to power.

By promoting an image of social peace and political order, international tourism gave the country a more benign and sophisticated face to the outside world, attractive to the new business bourgeoisie, that would help Indonesia recover its place in the community of nations. Luxury hotels, an incontestable symbol of modernity, also constituted a privileged milieu where national and foreign élites met for conferences or society gatherings. One could almost say that, at the time, the influx of tourists and tourist money counted less than the prestige associated with international tourism, which was to help improve Indonesia's image.

The tourism policy drawn up by the First Plan was the outcome of a series of studies, conducted in 1967–68 at the request of the government, on the measures to take in developing international tourism in Indonesia. These studies were preceded by the Checchi Report, a seminal forecast on the future of tourism in the Pacific and Far East prepared in 1958 by Harry Clement for the United States Department of Commerce (Clement 1961). Although the report emphasized the promising nature of the archipelago's tourist potential — and especially its extraordinary cultural diversity — it was frank about the obstacles to developing that potential. Among those cited were precarious infrastructures and mediocre services, a negative attitude toward tourism, and a deplorable image due to the disorder and endemic instability that reigned in the country. Clement proposed a series of measures to ease the most flagrant deficiencies, but above all he insisted on the necessity of concentrating the development of tourism in Bali, whose main advantage was that its image was already world renowned.

Such, then, was the situation until the advent of the New Order, which in 1966 commissioned Pan American Airways to conduct a market study on the perspectives of international tourism in Indonesia (Pan American Airways, 1966). The conclusions were the same as the Checchi Report, notably in regard to the priority that should be given to developing tourism in Bali. It is on this point that the studies carried out by Indonesians in 1967–68 differ most markedly from the preceding ones (Lembaga Pariwisata Nasional, 1967a, 1967b; Purbo & Mulia 1968; Soeroto, Atiek & Hendro 1968). Contrary to the foreign experts, the Indonesians were generally partisan to the principle of developing tourism gradually and in a diffuse manner throughout the archipelago, in order to distribute more widely the economic benefits throughout the country. But behind this declared intention were power struggles among the representatives of various pressure groups — and most notably of ethnic groups — in the capital, eager to capture the manna of tourism and envious of Bali's privileged position. Furthermore, the Indonesian government was circumspect about the idea of developing Bali through tourism. It thought that the ensuing prosperity would further strengthen the position of this province and would only exacerbate the particularism of its population, already far too pronounced according to the Javanese, particularly Muslims, for whom the pork-eating Balinese are ever subject to insinuations of paganism.

Despite these concerns, however, the recommendations set forth by the First Plan coincided with the position of the foreign experts: agreeing that the country's best asset lay in the image of Bali as a "paradise" inherited from the colonial era, they proposed making the island Indonesia's *show window* and giving it priority in the development of international tourism. Moreover, the experience that Bali would gain in the process would make it a *model* for the future development of tourism in the archipelago. Since the decision to develop tourism in Bali was taken with a view to economic returns at a national level, the plan gave no consideration to the possible consequences for Balinese society and culture.

2. The Bali Tourism Development Master Plan

In March 1969, a month before the First Plan was issued, a delegation from the World Bank traveled to Indonesia at the government's request and recommended drawing up a Master Plan for the development of tourism in Bali. After inviting tenders from various international groups, the government engaged a French firm, the Société Centrale pour l'Equipement Touristique Outre-Mer (SCETO), to work on the Master Plan. SCETO's study, begun in April 1970, was financed by the United Nations Development Program (UNDP) and carried out under the auspices of the World Bank, the executive agency of the project. The firm delivered a report in six volumes in April 1971 (SCETO 1971).

The orientations of the Master Plan

Designed to come to term in 1985, the Master Plan was based on a market study forecasting that by that year, 734,000 tourists would visit Bali. They would stay an average of four days in luxury hotels and spend around $35 per day. To meet this potential demand, the consultants proposed building 9,500 rooms.

The analysis of the primary needs of this market — accommodation and seaside tourism — as well as considerations pertaining to the necessary protection of Balinese society and its culture from an overly-traumatic exposure to foreign visitors, led the consultants to propose that tourism be concentrated in one place that met the following conditions: removed from the local population; by the sea; near the airport; and not too far from the most attractive regions in the southern part of the island. It was clear that there would be limitations to developing the beach areas of Sanur and Kuta, so they proposed that 6,950 rooms be built at Nusa Dua, on the east coast of the Bukit Peninsula, leaving a free disposition of 2,550 rooms to be built in Sanur, Kuta and Denpasar.

The SCETO study proposed that the Indonesian state would acquire the land needed to build this new resort and develop it in such a way as to make it attractive to foreign and national investors, who would be allowed to lease parcels of land on which they could build and operate hotels and other tourist facilities. The cost of the infrastructure was estimated at $143.5 million. The development of Nusa Dua would be completed by 1976, so that the pressure of hotel construction that would surely be felt in Sanur and Kuta could be eased as quickly as possible.

The secondary needs of tourists — "discovery" and cultural tourism — would be met by the creation of a network of *excursion* routes giving access to the principal sites of the island. *Stopovers* would be installed along these itineraries, where tourists could spend the night. As to the encounter between the tourists and their hosts, this would be restricted to *tourism centers* run by Balinese. Conceived as a means of integrating tourism with Balinese society, these centers would involve local communities in their activities. Finally, to safeguard religious ceremonies and the various performances that adorn them — as well as to save tourists the discomfort and long waits characteristic of these performances, quickly tiresome for non-Balinese spectators — it was recommended that dance performances be organized especially for tourists, freely transposed from the traditional forms and adapted for a diverse foreign audience.

The dilemma of the French consultants

Before looking at the implementation of the Master Plan, it is useful to consider for a moment the thinking behind it — the conditions that governed its elaboration and the implicit conceptual model that shaped it.

First, none of the SCETO members engaged in designing the Master Plan had the slightest previous knowledge of Bali, nor indeed of Indonesia. Moreover, the presence on the team of a specialist in matters regarding society and culture — a sociologist or anthropologist — was not considered necessary. Most striking of all, the Balinese authorities had not been included in formulating the study's terms of reference, and they were consulted only as a matter of form on those orientations carried over into the plan. Indeed, local participation was limited to the addition to the French team of three Balinese "advisors".

Finally, the interviews I have had with the SCETO consultants convinced me that neither the Indonesian government nor the World Bank experts were concerned with the implications of tourism on Balinese society and culture. The guiding concern was to develop international tourism in Bali, with the primary objective of helping to redress the national balance of payments.

The determining element of the Master Plan — the factor that decided the form that tourism development in Bali would take — was the market study. For the foreign experts, logically as well as strategically, it was demand that determined what should be supplied. This naturally led to their seeing Bali as a tourist product — to be conceived, fabricated, and promoted according to market demands and endowed with a prestigious brand image tailored to give it added value and distinguish it from other products on the international tourist market.

Upon examination, the demand made on Bali appears to be composite. The potential clientele is composed of wealthy Westerners who purchase an organized tour with the idea of spending several days of vacation on a white sandy beach bordered with palm trees. In the tourist imagination, however, Bali is not a tropical island like the others — it is "the Island of the Gods", a magical place, abounding with temples and picturesque ceremonies, vibrant with exotic music and dance. But there is a problem: while the tourists hope to find a traditional culture in Bali still miraculously preserved from the corrupting ills of the modern world, they are themselves the harbingers of those ills: they are part of the wave of modernity rolling over the planet, and their arrival on the island could crush that which they would embrace. How, given these conditions, is tourism to be developed without spoiling Balinese culture in the process?

The problem is that much more delicate because the encounter between the visitors and their hosts is based on a mutual misunderstanding:

> *What happens is that the visitors arrive as individuals with a high standard of living who are more or less frustrated in their own culture and then attempt to idealize a civilization they can appreciate only superficially, identifying it with a Lost Paradise they hope to see preserved. The hosts, on the other hand, only see the exterior trappings of a foreign way of life and are tempted to think of the countries from which the tourists arrive as a sort of Promised Land they must make all efforts to emulate.* (SCETO 1971: Vol.2, p.97)

The French consultants treat this misunderstanding as a *dilemma*, which theoretically presents two extreme solutions, the first of which is as impractical as the second is undesirable:

- a *preservation* at all costs of the Balinese culture as it is, freeze-framing it in a sort of "living museum", testimony of a bygone past, a Utopian vision which would require, among other things, keeping out foreign influences, especially those propagated by tourists;

- a touristic *consumption* of the Balinese culture which would lead to:

> *introducing tourism to an area and considering the way of life and culture of a people to be a natural resource which can be exploited for a certain period of time, at the end of which time the culture will have ceased to exist as such.* (op.cit.: 97)

Should that be the case, faced with this threat to their culture, the Balinese would be tempted to close themselves off from foreign influences, which would hinder the full development of tourism. To avoid this troublesome outcome, a balance had to be found that allowed a preserved "paradise" for the tourists without denying the Balinese their legitimate aspirations to "progress".

The solution the consultants adopted was to protect Balinese culture as much as possible from the frontal impact of tourism by relegating the tourists to a safe distance from the local population. But since Bali's main attraction, which distinguishes the island from other exotic tourist destinations, lies in the promise of a contact, however fleeting, with a living traditional culture, the tourists must have an opportunity to see it, or at least to make limited incursions into the rural villages. Thus the "Bali product" becomes split into a *seaside tourism*, residential and concentrated, and a *cultural tourism*, itinerant and diffuse. It is, in fact, a classic example of tropical beach tourism — a residential resort space, with the added value of an excursionary space into the indigenous society, which confers the "plus" of a prestigious cultural image.

Hence, the objective to which the Master Plan responds is to guarantee a sustainable development of international tourism in Bali by protecting the resources that nourish it, mainly the island's abundant cultural riches. Nevertheless, its authors hardly seem to have any illusions about the outcome of the measures they prescribe, for they coolly predict that by the time the project is completed in 1985:

> *the cultural manifestations will probably have disappeared, but Bali can still retain its romantic image and still be thought of as a green and sumptuous garden.*
> (ibid.: 161)

The World Bank's evaluation report

The Master Plan was published in April 1971, adopted the following year by Presidential Decree and ratified by the Provincial Assembly of Bali in December 1973. During this period, foreign firms conducted a series of technical studies on the feasibility and modalities of the development of Nusa Dua (Pacific Consultants International, 1973). At the same time, the SCETO report was submitted to the World Bank for evaluation, with a view to obtaining its financial aid. The Bank engaged a foreign consultant, anthropologist Raymond Noronha, to assess the impact of tourism on Balinese society. His report was fairly critical, and it was kept confidential (Noronha 1973). Following Noronha's study, an evaluation team from the World Bank went to Bali and published its conclusions in May 1974 (IBRD/IDA 1974).

The World Bank was more reserved than SCETO regarding the perspectives for tourism development in Bali. Starting with an estimate of 95,000 foreign tourists in 1973, its report forecast 290,000 arrivals to 1978 and 540,000 in 1983, showing an annual rate of increase of 26% until 1978 and 14% afterwards. The tourists' average daily expenditure was estimated at $46 and their length of stay at 3.5 days.

The main lines of the Nusa Dua project were retained, but the first phase was limited to 2,500 rooms of international standard to be built by 1985. A site of 425 hectares was to be developed by public agencies, and parcels of land were to be leased to private hotel developers. The number of rooms to be built in Sanur, Kuta and Denpasar was limited to 1,600, making a total of 4,100 international-class rooms by 1985 rather than the 9,500 initially planned. Outside this priority zone for tourism development, the building of accommodations would be authorized with the condition that they be Balinese in style and have no more than 20 rooms. Employment created directly by the Nusa Dua resort was estimated at 6,000 jobs, plus 4,000 indirect jobs. As to net foreign exchange earnings, these were to reach $8.5 million by 1978 and $36.2 million by 1985.

The project included improving the road network and building an expressway bypassing Denpasar that would give direct access from Nusa Dua and the airport to the main tourist sites throughout the island. A training center for hotel staff was to be built at the edge of the resort area. The plan encouraged the use of local building materials and construction styles inspired by traditional Balinese architecture. Building height was limited to 15 meters — so as not to surpass the tops of the coconut palms — and the local population was to be assured access to the sea.

Technical assistance was to be provided for the development of Nusa Dua, whose cost was estimated at $36.1 million (of which $18.1 million in foreign currency). Credit from the International Development Association would cover $16 million, and the rest was to be financed by the Indonesian budget. The realization of the project would be entrusted to two recently created bodies: the Bali Tourism Development Board (BTDB) and the Bali Tourism Development Corporation (BTDC). Foreign experts would be engaged to advise and assist the officials of these agencies, to ensure that the plans were carried out in conformity with the proposed guidelines, and also to train Balinese specialists in their respective disciplines.

Finally, a chapter was dedicated to the socio-cultural impact of tourism in Bali, whose conclusions were founded in principle on Noronha's study. On reading this chapter, it becomes apparent that this version, which expresses the official position of the World Bank, omits most of the critical questions raised by Noronha — particularly those regarding the capacity of the Balinese to control and draw profit from international tourism. The only explicitly recognized problems concern the concentration of tourism in the southern part of the island and the risk that tourist revenues be appropriated by professional operators to the detriment of the local population. Consequently, it was recommended that the BTDB try to effect a balance between the seaside resorts in the south and the necessary diffusion of tourist activities in the rest of the island, and that it influence market structures in such a manner that the Balinese receive an equitable portion of the benefits derived from tourism.

3. The growth of tourism in Bali

Once the Master Plan had been adopted by Presidential Decree and ratified by the Provincial Assembly, tourism officially became the island's second economic priority after agriculture. Nevertheless, the volume of tourism activity in Bali — as in the whole of Indonesia — long remained behind the forecasts of the foreign consultants and the technocrats in Jakarta.

Yet the beginnings of international tourism in Indonesia were highly promising. In the course of the First Plan, foreign visitor arrivals went from 51,000 in 1968 to 270,000 in 1973, an average increase of 40% per year. This initial success greatly surpassed the target of 150,000 fixed by the First Plan. Starting in 1976, though, the archipelago's tourist frequentation stagnated for ten years. Only since 1987 has the situation improved markedly, with an annual increase in tourist arrivals to Indonesia of more than 20%: from 1 million in 1987 to 4 million in 1994 (3). These visitors brought $4.7 billion in foreign exchange earnings, amounting to an expenditure of $1,150 per person for an average stay of 12 days.

If one compares Indonesia's performance with that of the other member countries of the Association of South-East Asian Nations (ASEAN), generally cited as a frame of reference, one notices that Indonesia remained in last place for a long time. And it took the fall of the Marcos regime and the instability that followed for Indonesia to move up past the Philippines. But it has progressively gained market share over the years, moving up from 6% of foreign arrivals in ASEAN in 1980 to more than 10% in 1990 and nearly 15% in 1993, as indicated in the following table.

Table 1: ASEAN tourist arrivals (in thousands of visitors)

	1980	1985	1990	1993
Indonesia	500	700	2,100	3,400
Malaysia	2,200	2,900	6,100	6,300
Philippines	1,000	800	1,200	1,400
Singapore	2,600	3,000	5,300	6,400
Thailand	1,900	2,500	5,300	5,500
ASEAN	8,200	9,900	20,000	23,000

Source: Directorate General of Tourism

Tourist arrivals in Bali

Disconcertingly enough, we do not know how many tourists visit Bali each year, be they foreign tourists, called *wisatawan mancanegara* (shortened to *wisman*) or domestic tourists, called *wisatawan nusantara* (*wisnu*). The only precise figures given by the Bali Government Tourism Office (Diparda) concern foreign visitors entering

(3) Entry to Indonesia is made primarily through its three international airports at Jakarta, Denpasar and Medan (Sumatra), and increasingly through the island of Batam, recently outfitted to draw visitors from Singapore. The 4 million foreign visitors to Indonesia in 1994 were distributed as follows among the main ports of entry: Jakarta (32%), Denpasar (26%), Batam (22%), Medan (5%), and others (15%). They came from the following regions: Southeast Asia (42%) — of which Singapore (27%) — Europe (19%), Japan (12%), Australia (9%), North America (5%) (Source: DGT). A large part of these visitors, especially those coming from Southeast Asia and Japan, was composed of business travelers and excursionists whose stay in Indonesia was mainly limited to Jakarta or Batam.

Indonesia through Bali on direct international flights, registered by the provincial immigration services. These numbered 1,032,000 in 1994 (4). This figure, therefore, does not take into account Indonesians or foreigners arriving on internal flights, or arrivals at Gilimanuk by the ferry coming from Java, or even tourists from cruise ships mooring at Benoa or Padang.

The fact is that the arrival of foreign tourists in Bali on international flights indicates less about the island's volume of tourist activity than about the airline policy at the time. And the fluctuation of arrivals attests to the hesitation of the Indonesian government in the matter. With the aim of promoting tourism in Bali, the First Plan decided to grant landing rights liberally to foreign airlines. Visitor arrivals at the Denpasar airport increased rapidly — nine-fold between 1968 and 1973, while entries to Indonesia increased by five. But in 1973, under joint pressures from the national airline Garuda and the hotel industry in the capital, this liberal policy was revised to the more restrictive "one gate policy", which limited the landing rights of foreign airlines to Jakarta unless they were willing to offer two ports of entry in their own country. Direct arrivals of foreign visitors declined noticeably in 1973–74. This led to protests from the Balinese tourism industry and foreign tour operators, and in 1975, the government adopted a "multiple gate policy" authorizing certain foreign airlines to land in Bali. The Indonesian airline policy fluctuated until 1986 when the government decided to open the airport in Denpasar to foreign airlines (5).

Proceeding from the figure of direct arrivals of foreign visitors, the Tourism Office establishes an estimate of the total number of foreign visitors to the island, based on statistics published by the airport services as well as figures from the forms filled in by the hotels. According to this procedure, more than 1.5 million foreigners visited Bali in 1994 — almost 40% of all visitor arrivals to Indonesia that year — each spending around $800 in the course of a stay of approximately 10 days (6).

Bali's international tourist market is composed of two quite clearly distinct segments. The majority of foreign visitors are tourists traveling in a group, on a package

---

(4) The 1,032,000 foreign visitors entering Indonesia directly via Bali in 1994 were divided by nationality as follows: Europe (38%) — of which UK (9%), Germany (8%), Italy (4%), France (3%) — Japan (20%), Australia (15%), Taiwan (8%), North America (8%), Southeast Asia (6%) (Source: Diparda Bali). During the 1980s, Europe's share in the Balinese market has grown, while Australia and North America have seen their relative importance diminish. In the past few years, it is the Asian market that has shown the greatest increase.

(5) In 1994, of the thirty or so foreign airlines allowed to land in Indonesia, 15 airlines served Bali with 45 flights per week, to which should be added some 80 flights by Garuda. The total capacity is of more than 40,000 seats per week.

(6) The surveys conducted by the Bali Government Tourism Office concern only visitors arriving on international flights, among whom 95% are recorded as coming to Bali on holiday, compared with some 70% of all visitors to Indonesia. Nearly 30% of these visitors were not on their first trip. Finally, one should mention that seasonal variations have tended to lessen, to the point where the monthly distribution of foreign visitors to Bali is quite regular, with noticeable increases, nevertheless, in August and around the year-end holidays.

Table 2: **Increase of foreign visitor arrivals in Indonesia and Bali (in thousands of visitors)**

Year	Foreign visitors to Indonesia/ %		Foreign visitors direct to Bali/ %		Airport arrivals in Bali/ %	
1965	30					
1966	19	*-36.6*				
1967	26	*36.8*				
1968	51	*96.2*	6			
1969	86	*68.6*	11	*83.3*		
1970	129	*50.0*	23	*100.1*		
1971	179	*38.7*	34	*47.8*		
1972	221	*23.5*	47	*38.2*		
1973	270	*22.2*	54	*14.9*	149	
1974	313	*15.9*	57	*5.5*	167	*12.1*
1975	366	*16.9*	76	*33.3*	202	*20.9*
1976	401	*9.6*	115	*51.3*	268	*32.7*
1977	433	*7.9*	119	*3.5*	290	*8.2*
1978	469	*8.3*	133	*11.7*	321	*10.7*
1979	501	*6.8*	120	*-9.8*	356	*10.9*
1980	561	*11.9*	147	*22.5*	404	*13.5*
1981	600	*6.9*	159	*8.2*	455	*12.6*
1982	592	*-1.3*	152	*-4.4*	432	*-5.0*
1983	639	*7.9*	170	*11.8*	424	*-1.8*
1984	701	*9.7*	189	*11.2*	497	*17.2*
1985	749	6.8	211	*11.6*	526	*5.8*
1986	825	*10.1*	243	*15.2*	615	*16.9*
1987	1,060	*28.5*	309	*27.2*	751	*22.1*
1988	1,301	*22.7*	360	*16.5*	882	*17.4*
1989	1,626	*25.0*	436	*21.1*	1,038	*17.7*
1990	2,177	*33.9*	490	*12.4*	1,176	*13.3*
1991	2,569	*17.9*	556	*13.5*	1,287	*9.4*
1992	3,064	*19.2*	738	*32.7*	1,514	*17.6*
1993	3,400	*11.0*	885	*19.9*	1,848	*22.0*
1994	4,007	*17.6*	1,032	*16.6*	2,070	*12.0*

Sources: Directorate General of Tourism and Bali Government Tourism Office trip purchased from a tour operator, and for whom Bali is but a three- to five-day stop, usually staying in international-class hotels. To these may be added businessmen passing through Jakarta, whose Indonesian trips frequently include an excursion to Bali. On the other hand are independent tourists, with a more limited budget, for whom Bali is either a stop in the course of a long voyage or a principal vacation place. Their stay may last several weeks, and they often use the services set up for the needs of the local population. A growing portion of these are young vacationers from Australia and Japan, who tend to make Bali a more or less regular vacation place, which is also the case of foreign residents in Indonesia.

To the foreign tourists one must add Indonesian tourists, whose number is very difficult to estimate. The only available data on this matter rest, on one hand, on information furnished by the hotel forms, and on the other, on the number of arrivals and departures of passengers counted at the airport in Denpasar and the ferry at Gilimanuk. Airport arrivals on both international and domestic flights rose to more than 2 million in 1994, and in the same year, some 2.5 million passengers entered Bali by the ferry coming from Java. The arrivals at Gilimanuk are comprised mostly of Indonesians, and the proportion of "tourists" among them is obviously impossible to determine. As to the hotel forms, aside from the fact that they are not regularly filled in and that they give no information on the motive for the visit, they do not allow one to take into account Indonesians staying with relatives or friends during their sojourn in Bali. Despite these uncertainties, the Tourism Office estimates that Indonesian tourists in 1994 numbered some 1 million, a figure that is probably under-estimated. Be that as it may, according to official estimates, the total number of tourist arrivals to Bali in 1994 was about 2.5 million visitors, on an island of less than 3 million inhabitants (7).

Whatever the real number of domestic tourists visiting Bali, the fact is that they constitute a rapidly developing market. For the most part, they are members of the new Indonesian middle class living in the large cities of Java. Among these we find two sub-groups: a growing portion of students, increasingly inclined to travel during their school breaks; and representatives of the business bourgeoisie, accustomed to traveling by plane, who gladly take several days' holiday in Bali from time to time. In this regard, it is interesting to note the influence exercised by foreign tourists on Indonesians' choice of place and vacation activities. Although holidays in Bali became fashionable with Sukarno in the 1950s, it is only since Bali became a destination for international tourism in the 1970s that it became preferred by wealthy Indonesians to the hill stations made fashionable by the colonial Dutch (Withington 1961).

Table 2 summarizes available information on foreign visitor arrivals to Indonesia,

---

(7) I must emphasize the very uncertain nature of the figures for tourist arrivals. Some Balinese observers hold that the number of foreign indirect arrivals is equal to the direct arrivals, while the number of Indonesian tourists is equal to that of foreign tourists. According to this calculation, one would have a total figure of tourist arrivals in Bali of nearly 4 million in 1994.

direct arrivals of foreign visitors in Bali, and international and domestic arrivals registered at the Denpasar airport.

The Indonesian tourism policy

How can one explain the relative stagnation of tourist arrivals in Bali, and more generally in Indonesia, from 1976 and its clear resurgence since 1987? Indonesian and foreign analysts generally agree that if Indonesia's figures were long disappointing — especially in comparison to its immediate competitors, who are less richly endowed with touristic resources —it is not so much because of the world's economic recession (as the Indonesian government would have it), as because the government did not give itself the necessary means to attain the goals proclaimed in its tourism policy. In support of this argument, they cite the insufficiency of the budget for promoting Indonesia abroad, poor coordination of tourism authorities at the national and regional levels, lack of professionalism in the Indonesian tourism industry, and the protectionist nature of the airline policy. And if the situation has improved in recent years, it is because the drop in the price of raw materials — most especially of oil products — drastically reduced the country's foreign exchange earnings, finally forcing the Indonesian government to take international tourism seriously.

During the 1970s, the Indonesian economy registered strong growth, financed largely by its oil revenues. But beginning in 1982, the drop in the price per barrel brought about a slowing of the economy, followed by a serious decline in 1986. The government responded vigorously by launching a program of reforms that stopped the growing deficit in the balance of payments and boosted economic growth. The model of state-run development that had been in place since the First Plan was revised dramatically in favor of deregulation and a more open policy toward foreign capital. The government encouraged the export of non-oil products and facilitated private investment; the Indonesian currency (rupiah) was sharply devaluated in 1983 and again in 1986; and international tourism moved into the limelight.

In 1983, the President of the Republic declared that tourism must be intensively promoted in order to pass from seventh to third place as a source of foreign exchange earnings for the country, after oil and timber products (8). The same year, the institutional position of tourism was strengthened by the creation of a Department of Tourism, Post and Telecommunications (Departemen Pariwisata, Pos dan Telekomunikasi), which quickly adopted a series of measures intended to stimulate the development of international tourism. Among these were the exemption of visas

---

(8) In 1983, Indonesia drew more than 70% of its revenues from oil and natural gas, while receipts from international tourism comprised only 3% of its exports. In 1993, tourism ranked third among the country's sources of foreign exchange earnings, after oil and wood products and before textiles, accounting for 10% of total exports, while oil products represented only 19%. Analysts generally agree that tourism will be the main source of foreign exchange earnings for Indonesia by the end of the decade. On the development of tourism in Indonesia and its implications, see Booth (1990) and EIU (1991).

for tourists, the opening of new ports of entry to the country, and facilities accorded to foreign firms in order to attract investment in the tourism industry. The devaluations of the rupiah made Indonesia more competitive on the tourist market; and Garuda modernized its fleet, strengthened its network, and launched an aggressive promotional policy toward new markets. Most importantly, and after long equivocation, in 1986 international flights of foreign airlines were authorized to land in Bali and Medan (in Sumatra) without having to land first in Jakarta.

Meanwhile, campaigns to increase the population's awareness of tourism were intensified, with the aim of generating a hospitable atmosphere that would attract visitors. To this end, in 1981 the Director General of Tourism launched a slogan calling for "the Socialization of Tourism and the Touristification of Society" (*Memasyarakatkan Pariwisata dan Memariwisatakan Masyarakat*). It called on Indonesians to take on tourism as a means of development and also to become tourists in their own country. According to official statements, the objective of domestic tourism was to integrate the different ethnic groups of the archipelago into the Indonesian nation. But it was also intended to dissuade the wealthier classes from traveling abroad in order to stem the outflow of precious foreign currency. This dissuasion was made more convincing by the imposition in 1983 of a tax of 150,000 rupiah — about $200 for a GNP per capita of less than $500 per year at the time — on every Indonesian citizen leaving the country. Before this measure was introduced, expenditures on international voyages had been higher than receipts, mainly owing to frequent trips to Singapore by the Jakarta bourgeoisie. The situation has improved markedly since then, and starting in 1985 the Indonesian tourist balance has become positive.

While Bali has remained the best known destination for international tourism in the archipelago, other regions have progressively been developed for tourists. As early as 1978, the Directorate General of Tourism made ten provinces "Tourist Destinations" (*Daerah Tujuan Wisata*) and launched slogans — such as "Bali Plus Nine" and "Bali and Beyond" — reminding tourists that Indonesia was not limited to Bali. Since 1993, all of the 27 provinces of the country have become Tourist Destinations. Thus, each province is urged to make an inventory of its natural sites and cultural traditions, with a view to promoting them as tourist attractions that could become the trademark of the region. But for now, the destinations most popular among foreign tourists — apart from Jakarta, Batam and Bali — remain those regions that enjoy a well-established reputation for cultural richness, such as Yogyakarta in central Java, the Batak country in Sumatra, and the Toraja country of Sulawesi (the Celebes).

After the Fifth Plan, implemented as of 1989, the government intensified its promotional efforts, starting with the launching of a Tourism Awareness campaign (*Sadar Wisata*), aimed at making Indonesians conscious of the benefits of tourism for their country and encouraging them to show their visitors the Seven Charms of Tourism (*Sapta Pesona*): "peacefulness, orderliness, cleanliness, verdancy, beauty, hospitality, and happy memories". The goal of this campaign was to prepare the population to work toward the success of the Visit Indonesia Year, slated for 1991, after Thailand in

1988, Singapore in 1989, and Malaysia in 1990. After Visit Indonesia Year would come Visit ASEAN Year in 1992, the Year of the Environment in 1993, and finally the Visit Indonesia Decade from 1993 to 2000.

In view of all this, Bali's role — apart from being the show window of Indonesia and the model for its tourism development, as defined by the First Plan — is that of a lure as well as a point of entry for foreign visitors into the rest of the archipelago: "Let's go Archipelago", proclaimed the official slogan of Visit Indonesia Year. In anticipation of the crowds of tourists, Bali's airport was enlarged, 20 years after its inauguration, and its runways lengthened to permit the landing of Boeing 747-400s. The new international Ngurah Rai airport was inaugurated in 1992, and is presently the second busiest airport in the country, after that of Jakarta.

The Fifth Plan initially forecasted that the increase in tourist arrivals in Indonesia would continue at an annual rate of 15% to achieve a total of 2.5 million visitors in 1993 — a figure that was amply surpassed. Since then, projections have been reviewed and are now estimated at some 7 million visitors by the end of the Sixth Plan in 1999. Foreign analysts generally think that as far as the tourism potential goes, these projections are entirely realistic. But they are unanimous in believing that Indonesia is not yet ready to receive the number of tourists it is trying to attract because of its endemic deficiency in infrastructures and lack of qualified manpower. They particularly blame the shortage of available plane seats and the lack of superior-class hotel rooms outside of Bali and, to a lesser extent, of Jakarta.

4. The economic contribution of tourism to Bali

The growth of tourism in Bali is obvious, if only in the transformation of the landscape, which is especially dramatic since the recent upsurge in tourist arrivals on the island and the frenzy that seized the tourism industry at the announcement of Visit Indonesia Year. Nevertheless, it is difficult to evaluate tourism's actual contribution to the Balinese economy, because available figures are unreliable — at once imprecise, inadequate, and contradictory. In the first place, one may reproach the rudimentary nature of procedures for gathering statistics. But the confusion is aggravated by the multiplicity of government agencies, each occupied with collecting and interpreting data according to different methods and in different frameworks. Thus, just as there is still no way of knowing how many foreign and domestic tourists visit Bali each year, we do not know precisely how much they spend or how they spend it, nor do we have any better idea of the revenues or the number of jobs created by tourism. As a result, most of the available information on this matter is the product of more or less chancy extrapolations drawn from surveys. In these conditions, the provincial government is unable to ascertain the effective contribution of tourism to the island's development.

The reports published annually by Bali's Statistics Office indicate a strong increase in the province's Gross Regional Domestic Product (GRDP) since 1969. This is above the national average — 10% per year in adjusted prices for the First Plan, 12% for the Second Plan, 9% for the Third Plan, 8% for the Fourth Plan, and 8.4%

for the Fifth Plan. In 1994, the GRDP exceeded $2 billion, and the average income per capita reached $900 (a little more than the national average). During this period, the structure of the Balinese economy underwent a considerable transformation, marked by a rapid decline in the relative importance of agriculture, an increase in the importance of industry, construction and administration, and more recently, a large increase in trade, transportation and the hotel industry. Indeed, according to the Regional Capital Investment Board (BKPMD), private investment in tourism related facilities have ranged from 55% to 95% of all investment in Bali during the first five Regional Plans.

Two already-dated studies by Balinese economists give an idea of the economic importance of tourism — which, because of its multi-sectorial character, has no specific category in the province's accounts. While the value added by tourism was estimated in 1983 at 10.3% of the GRDP, it reached 32.8% in 1987, the year that tourism really took off (Bappeda Bali 1985; Nehen et al. 1990). The authors of this last study concluded from this remarkable progression that tourism's contribution would soon surpass that of agriculture. And in fact, according to the Regional Development Planning Board (Bappeda), in 1994, tourism accounted for 42.2% of the GRDP while agriculture barely reached 28%. Furthermore, according to the estimations of a Balinese economist, the tourism income multiplier went from 1.2% in 1984 to 1.5% in 1994, about average compared with island destinations in the Caribbean and the Pacific (Erawan 1994).

More generally, a recent study carried out for the Indonesian government by foreign consultants under UNDP technical assistance attributed to tourism the merit of the Balinese economy's growth in the 1980s based on a number of indicators: a strong growth of the GRDP; lower unemployment; wide distribution among the population of the revenues of growth; and a redressing of the island's trade balance (Hassall and Associates 1992; see also Daroesman 1973; Bendesa & Sukarsa 1980; Jayasuriya & Nehen 1989).

The hotel industry and the travel agencies

The tourism industry in Bali underwent an evolution parallel to that of visitor arrivals: that is, a rapid increase up to the mid-1970s followed by a decline that required restructuring the whole industry, and finally an accelerated recovery in recent years. This restructuring has been partly in response to national and provincial objectives to promote a form of tourism that contributes to greater capital accumulation within Indonesia, and partly the result of global economic and social changes that have transformed the structure of the tourism industry worldwide.

This process is most evident in the spectacular boom in hotel investments. The large international hotel chains have recently settled in Bali, enticed by deregulation of the banking system and solicited by Asian investors, most of them backed by Jakarta-based conglomerates. While the SCETO report counted fewer than 500 rooms in 1970, there were more than 3,000 in 1975, 4,000 in 1980, and 10,000 in 1985. From then on, Bali's hotel capacity grew at an annual rate of 7%, and leapt 64% in 1990 in anticipation of Visit Indonesia Year (9). Thus in 1990 there were some 50 starred hotels operating on the island, with 8,500 rooms, as well as 900 unstarred hotels and homestays with 12,500 rooms, giving an overall hotel capacity of 21,000 rooms, compared to 13,000 the previous year. In 1994, hotel capacity exceeded 30,000 rooms, with close to 17,000 in some 90 starred hotels and the rest in more than 1,200 unstarred hotels and homestays (10). That same year, there were more than 500 restaurants in Bali, which amounted to about 34,000 seats.

Because tourist arrivals lagged behind projections until 1988, hotel occupancy rates remained lower than the 70% predicted by the Master Plan. Only after 1988 did the average rate of occupancy in starred hotels pass this figure, while the unstarred hotels and homestays, most of them owned by Balinese, registered a much weaker rate — barely 35%. But the following year, the hotel building boom caused an over-capacity, bringing about a rapid fall in occupancy rates, which dropped to 51% and 25% respectively for starred and unstarred hotels in 1990. The situation was judged serious enough that, on the eve of Visit Indonesia Year, the Director General of Tourism decreed a year's moratorium on hotel construction on the island's south coast, already threatened with saturation. But besides being provisional, this measure was unabashedly dodged by certain investors, obviously covered by their contacts in the capital. And the fact remains that two years after the moratorium was established, more than 20,000 rooms were under construction or being planned, which brought the already projected hotel capacity of Bali to more than 52,000 rooms. As the difference between the respective rates of hotel capacity and tourist frequentation continues to worsen, to the extent that over-capacity has induced a price war, it is the small Balinese hoteliers who are the first to bear the costs. In 1994, occupancy rates hovered around 60% for starred hotels and 35% for unstarred hotels.

As with the hotel industry, travel agencies also followed the fluctuations of the island's tourist frequentation. The first Indonesian agency, Natour, opened in 1956, but it was not until after 1969 that agencies began to proliferate, many of them doomed to an ephemeral existence: from 42 in 1970, their number dropped to 29 in 1980. This forced downsizing of the industry, due especially to bankruptcies, hurt the Balinese, who gradually lost their ownership of agencies. In recent years, many new agencies have opened, totaling 178 in 1994 — not counting some 30 undeclared agencies. Too numerous, hampered by constant cashflow problems and by an undeniable lack of professionalism, the position of most of these agencies remains weak in relation to their foreign partners who are able to lower their prices competitively.

Many of the agencies operating in Bali are regional branches of firms based in the capital. Their activities consist mainly in taking charge of the tour groups sent to

---

(9) In 1989, investments in hotel constructions exceeded four-fifths of the total investments effected in the province.

(10) By comparison, for the whole of Indonesia the Directorate General of Tourism counted in 1994 more than 600 starred hotels with a capacity of about 60,000 rooms, to which are added some 6,000 unstarred hotels with a capacity of around 110,000. It forecasted some 100,000 additional rooms in starred hotels by the end of the Sixth Plan in 1999.

them either by their office in Jakarta or by foreign tour operators with whom they are associated. The travel agencies also organize dance performances and excursions around the island. To this end, they employ nearly 3,000 duly licensed guides and maintain a fleet of buses, minibuses and taxis, numbering 3,200 vehicles by 1994. In addition to these are some 1,600 rental cars available to tourists.

Tourism revenues

The only data permitting an evaluation of foreign exchange earnings from tourism concern the volume of transactions registered by the regional branch of the Bank Indonesia in Denpasar. These transactions have undergone a spectacular increase, from $2.13 million in 1970 to $1.22 billion in 1994 — accounting for more than a quarter of tourism revenues for all of Indonesia. But however great this figure is, it offers only an estimate of the gross foreign exchange earnings attributed to tourism. It gives us hardly any information on the net foreign exchange earnings that tourism brings to the province, which depend in particular on the amount spent on imports directly related to tourism. Presently, no reliable study exists on this subject, and the estimates are highly variable.

Furthermore, to appreciate fully the importance of gross receipts attributable to tourism, one must take into account foreign exchange earnings generated by the exportation of goods, which went from $3.94 million in 1970 to $295.56 million in 1994. During this period, the structure of the exports changed radically. In 1970, coffee accounted for 81%, livestock for 14% and handicrafts for 1.5% of export receipts. In 1994, clothing represented 49%, handicrafts 28% and coffee barely 1%, while livestock was no longer exported at all. The table below summarizes the respective evolution of receipts from tourism and the export of goods.

Table 3: Receipts from tourism and the export of goods (in millions of dollars)

	1970	1975	1980	1985	1990
Tourism receipts	2.13	21.86	82.63	98.11	458.84
Exports of goods	3.94	7.18	17.03	42.03	190.80
:Handicrafts	0.06	0.29	2.25	5.71	35.32
:Clothing	-	-	1.83	15.81	114.90

	1991	1992	1993	1994
Tourism receipts	546.34	744.43	1,049.67	1,221.87
Exports of goods	225.12	239.36	264.42	295.56
:Handicrafts	42.84	54.22	59.68	82.08
:Clothing	138.07	139.15	140.78	145.23

Source: Statistical Office of the Province of Bali

A glance at this table shows that during the 1970s, tourism receipts widely exceeded the total value of the exports. One also notices that the main export receipts are provided by clothing and handicrafts — primarily wood and silver — two branches of activity that, although they owe their spectacular rise to tourism, have become somewhat independent of it in recent years. One can, besides, group together clothing production with sculpture and jewelry, since they comprise, in fact, an industry of handicrafts.

Handicrafts

For many Balinese, handicrafts is a secondary occupation, made necessary by the shortage of farmland and the poor income to be earned from working the land. But the fact is that an ever greater number of craftsmen work full-time for the tourist and export markets. With the exception of a handful of well-known painters, sculptors and goldsmiths, the craftsmen are heavily dependent on entrepreneurs and merchants. Indeed, they are faced with a double problem of capital and outlets. First of all, they generally do not have the means to purchase the materials with which they work and which have become increasingly costly — especially wood: several varieties have to be imported from Kalimantan (Borneo), Sulawesi (the Celebes) or Timor. Second, they only rarely have access to the market because of their inability to meet tourists, and this reduces both their autonomy and their income.

Among the craftsmen, some — mostly painters and sculptors — work at home and are paid for each piece by an employer who furnishes them with raw materials. This employer may be the owner of a shop, or a wholesaler in hand-crafted goods. Others are employed as salaried workers in the workshop adjoining a boutique, where they are generally paid by the day. The income that craftsmen earn from their work depends on their degree of autonomy. While a craftsman working from home may receive up to 60% of the selling price of his work, one who is employed by a shop will receive barely 20%. But in both cases, the specifications of the finished product are set by the employer, and production is undergoing increasing standardization. Similarly, the process of manufacturing tends to be more production-oriented, with the master-craftsman making the general form or sketch which is then finished by his assistants, often apprenticed children.

Tourist crafts are sold through "artshops", which besides selling souvenirs to tourists take orders from overseas dealers. The largest artshops have established permanent relations with travel agencies and guides who regularly bring them contingents of tourists. In exchange for their patronage, the agencies — and even more so the guides and drivers of taxis and tour buses — collect a commission on the total sales made by the shops and sometimes even on the number of tourists they bring, whether or not they buy anything. From this position of power, they put the artshops in competition with one another, which produces the double effect of raising the commissions — between 40% and 60% of the selling price — and penalizing small shops which are unable to pay the commissions that are asked of them. This has the effect of consolidating the economic position of the most prosperous artshops, since they are able to draw ever-larger numbers of tourists.

Another way by which tourist crafts are sold is through street peddlers who, having no capital, borrow goods from craftsmen, wholesalers, or artshops and sell them to tourists with a varying profit margin. This practice is old: pre-war travelers mention the persistence of peddlers who came even onto the terraces of their hotel rooms to sell "antiques" and other "typically Balinese" souvenirs. But the situation has become considerably aggravated, and today tourists, wherever they go, are followed relentlessly by peddlers. At the entrance of their hotel, on the beach, and at each stop on their excursions, they are harried by local peddlers thrusting souvenirs at them. These peddlers are commonly referred to as *dagang acung* (11).

The spread of this phenomenon finally alarmed the provincial government, concerned about the good name of the island and worried about the bad impression that the *dagang acung* make on the tourists. Indeed, tourists give frequent signs of exasperation under these assaults and sometimes go as far as complaining to their guides or even to the Tourism Office. The guides, by the way, are the peddlers' fiercest adversaries, since they can extract no commission on these hit-and-run sales to their clients. The attitude of the authorities was initially limited to ordering periodic raids by the police on the beaches of Sanur and Kuta as a means of dissuasion. More recently, "art markets" (*pasar seni*) have been set up in the resorts and kiosks built at the tourist stops, with the aim of regrouping the peddlers. But, aside from the shortage of available places, a lack of capital more often forces peddlers to persist in their trade. For some, though, after years of assiduous peddling, their dreams come true when they finally have the means to open a shop of their own.

These days, a growing proportion of sculpture and jewelry is destined not for tourism but for export. These mass-produced goods are made in workshops located for the most part in the district of Gianyar — in Tegallalang, Pujung, Sebatu, Kemenuh and Mas for woodcarvings and in Celuk for silverwork. These workshops practice a very intensive division of labor, but mechanization remains limited. The finished products — made to the specifications ordered by foreign buyers — are sent to the district of Badung, where an exporter packs them and forwards them to their consignees.

---

(11) *Dagang* means "merchant" and *acung* is an Indonesian word describing the action of lifting something up; and this term no doubt comes from the peddlers' lifting their wares up to the windows of the tour buses, where the tourists "sit on high".

The garment industry in Bali owes its initial impulsion to the presence of tourists, who provided it with both a market and entrepreneurs. Some early visitors, seduced by life in Bali, decided that it would be nice to settle there, and they looked about for a way of supporting their life style. Among the various commercial opportunities that occurred to them, jewelry and clothing proved to be the most promising, because of the availability of raw materials and the willingness of skilled Balinese labor to work for very low pay. The manufacture of clothing for export did not really take off until the late 1970s when Balinese and Indonesian businessmen took over organizing the work. Foreign stylists pass their orders to export firms, based mostly in Kuta, Sanur and Denpasar, which have them made by contractual workers disseminated in the villages to whom they provide all the necessary materials and equipment. Thus today tens of thousands of Balinese — mostly women — are employed in the dyeing, sewing, and embroidering of miles of cotton and rayon imported from Java. These become clothes that are "Handmade in Bali" and sold in boutiques all over the world.

The creation of jobs

According to the projections made in the SCETO report, tourism was to create 78,500 jobs, directly or indirectly, by 1980. This figure has proven far too high, owing among other things to delays in the realization of Nusa Dua. In 1980, the Tourism Office estimated at 7,500 the number of jobs created directly by tourism, including 4,500 in the hotel industry. In 1987, just when tourism activity moved into high gear, Diparda estimated direct jobs at slightly over 18,000, with 11,000 in the hotel industry, 2,300 in the restaurant business, and 1,700 in travel agencies and transportation. In 1994, jobs directly created by tourism were estimated at 47,000, of which 32,000 were in the hotel industry, 8,300 in the restaurant business, 1,800 in travel agencies, 1,900 in transportation and 3,000 employed as guides. To this number must be added the artists and craftsmen working in a more or less permanent way for the tourism market or for export (whose numbers are difficult to estimate) as well as workers employed in the garment industry. In this respect, the previously mentioned study conducted under the aegis of the UNDP estimated that in 1989, 310,000 people were employed in tourism-related activities, that is, about 20% of the active population (1.5 million) (Hassall and Associates 1992: 67).

As to revenues drawn from having a job in tourism, they are of course extremely variable, depending on whether the job is that of craftsman or gallery owner, chambermaid or director of a travel agency. Wages for unskilled labor, as well as in handicrafts, presently range from 120,000 to 300,000 rupiah ($50–130) per month — about twice those for similar labor in Java (12). It is important to mention here that — apart from several hundred foreign nationals employed in tourism — the majority of skilled jobs are filled by non-Balinese Indonesians, mostly Javanese. And it is workers from Java who provide most of the labor on construction sites. Balinese

(12) In 1994, the daily minimum wage for the province of Bali was officially established at 3,900 rupiah — barely US$1.80.

recriminations are frequent against Indonesians who come to their island lured by the "gold mine" of tourism. In this regard, intending to guarantee priority in employment to the Balinese, the Governor issued a decree in 1973 forbidding any non-Balinese to come work on the island unless assured in advance of a job and lodgings. But this measure has proven impossible to enforce, and today it is not known how many immigrant workers are presently in Bali, although they certainly number more than 100,000.

The distribution of tourism revenues

One of the fortunate consequences of tourism and of the economic activities that it generates has been to put a brake on the rural exodus. This is particularly true of the district of Gianyar, where the handicraft industry has been able to accommodate a population that subsistence farming can no longer support — to the extent that Bali's success in the production of clothing, sculpture and jewelry is today presented by economists as an example to be imitated in other regions of Indonesia and more generally in the Third World, with a view toward absorbing the over-abundance of rural manpower.

On the other hand, tourism has indisputably aggravated regional imbalances. The concentration of seaside resorts in Badung — which has nearly four-fifths of the island's hotel capacity (13) — has accelerated urbanization and consolidated the wealth of that district, already favored as the administrative and commercial center of the province. Indeed, according to the BKPMD, during the first five Regional Plans, over 90% of all private investment has been concentrated in Badung. Thus Badung's GRDP per capita is nearly twice that of the rest of the island. In an attempt to remedy this imbalance, since 1972 the Governor has required that Badung re-distribute 30% of its revenues to the other districts. In spite of this measure, the budget of Badung accounts today for half of the total budgets of all the districts.

Furthermore, tourism tends to accentuate social inequalities, determining more and more who in Bali is rich and who is not. While a sizable portion of revenues from the tourism industry are spread out among the population, the gap is deepening between those with direct access to tourist money, and the others. The increasing difference in the prices of goods destined for the local market, including the price of

---

(13) In 1994, the distribution of accommodations and rooms among the districts was as follows: Badung, 600 and 23,400; Gianyar, 370 and 2,500; Bangli, 25 and 220; Klungkung, 28 and 200; Karangasem, 150 and 1,800; Buleleng, 120 and 1,600; Tabanan, 34 and 380; Jembrana, 25 and 260 (Source: Diparda Bali).

labor, and those to be sold to tourists, provides opportunities for the rapid enrichment of those privileged to play both markets at once. The newly rich — real estate speculators, hoteliers and restaurateurs, travel agents and art dealers, guides and taxi drivers — accumulate ostentatious symbols of their social rise, and these days the Balinese most favored by the manna of tourism go about in BMWs or in Mercedes Benzes and build themselves houses that would not be unworthy of Hollywood.

Yet the newly available consumer goods have not dethroned ceremonial expenses as a source of prestige and sign of status: the money earned from tourism feeds a competition for status that is expressed in the staging of ever more sumptuous and spectacular ceremonies — much to the delight of the tourists. Thus, despite what some may say, traditional Balinese values are far from being sacrificed on the altar of commercial consumption. Indeed, the nouveaux riches use their extra money in a most traditional way: to affirm their newly acquired social position and to display their rank according to ancient codes. On the other hand, they also contribute to the subverting of the traditional social hierarchy by competing with the nobility in the realm of conspicuous spending on ceremonies.

The fact is that the development of the monetary economy — by fostering the emergence of a business bourgeoisie and of a salaried middle class, and by diverting a part of the population from its traditional economic occupations — is bringing profound changes to Balinese society. The organization of agricultural activities is breaking up as Balinese employed in the tourism industry no longer participate in the rice harvest, which now tends to be confided to specialized groups who work for cash. And the monetarization of the village economy is blamed for inciting individualistic behavior that loosens social ties and weakens the systems of obligatory co-operation within the *banjar*. Land speculation brings a double-barreled stress to the social order: it makes land a matter of individual property; and it turns it into a commodity — one whose price, moreover, has grown by heretofore unimaginable proportions. This provokes conflicts that undermine the *banjar* and break up families (14).

But above all, tourism perturbs Balinese society with its capital — specifically, with the national and international capital that penetrates the Balinese social space. While it is difficult to identify the economic agents that control the tourism industry in Bali — they do not always operate openly — it is a matter of public notoriety that Indonesian generals and Chinese tycoons based in Jakarta have carved out strategic positions for themselves — not to mention the entourage of President Suharto, who are openly accused of having bought up much of the land in the southern part of the island. But most of the capital is of multinational origin, and the Indonesian businessmen serve as obligatory intermediaries to their foreign partners, while the Balinese generally serve as mere title-holders. Thus, according to the BKPMD, between 1969

(14) Not to mention the resulting psychological disturbances. The Indonesian national press recently noted a series of cases of Balinese peasants treated in psychiatric hospitals for being unable to adjust to their sudden wealth following the sale of beachside land to developers.

and 1994, investors from Jakarta and other Indonesian or foreign sources accounted for around 75% of investments in hotels and tourism related activities, and over 55% of the total number of investments in Bali. As to the provincial government, it receives only indirect revenues from tourism by way of local taxes, building permits, and development funds. In 1994, these revenues accounted for less than 20% of the province's budget, the rest of which being mostly financed by subsidies from the central government.

The province of Bali thus seems ever more tightly enmeshed in the webs of international tourism and the state apparatus, even though the promotion of their island as the "show window" of Indonesia has considerably augmented the prestige of the Balinese, while the growing importance of tourism in the Indonesian economy has correspondingly strengthened their bargaining position with Jakarta.

Chapter Three

THE TOURIST DEVELOPMENT OF THE ISLAND

Although it is relatively small, the island of Bali is still far from "overrun" by tourists, as it is often said. The great majority of tourists are concentrated in a very limited zone from which they disperse along quite strictly defined itineraries. Nonetheless, as tourism develops, it makes itself felt on an ever more extended portion of Balinese territory.

One may distinguish three kinds of tourist regions, which differ according to their functions: the resorts where the tourists stay; the sites they visit and the routes that take them there; and finally the villages specializing in tourist handicrafts.

Most tourists stay at the beach resorts of Nusa Dua, Sanur and Kuta — to which now must be added the new resort area of Jimbaran — in the southern district of Badung. Besides these, two coastal zones have been gradually built up that cater to a clientele wishing to escape the crowds of vacationers — the first on the north coast around Lovina, west of Singaraja, and the second in the east at Candidasa, between Padang and Amlapura. Finally, those visitors more interested in cultural matters than in the pleasures of the beach generally choose to stay in Ubud, in the district of Gianyar.

This rather neat delineation of tourist resorts is undergoing a profound upheaval with the steady increase of tourists in recent years and the concomitant explosion of hotel investments stimulated by the prospect of the Visit Indonesia Year in 1991. In 1988, invoking the necessity of disencumbering the southern coast, the Governor undertook to revise the island's tourist map, announcing a "Spatial Arrangement Plan for Tourist Areas". This new plan created 15 "tourist areas" (*kawasan wisata*) and lifted the restrictions hitherto imposed by the Master Plan, which confined hotels of more than 20 rooms to the Nusa Dua-Sanur-Kuta triangle. In 1993, the number of tourist areas went from 15 to 21; they presently cover 1,437 square km, a quarter of the total surface of the island — which many Balinese opinion leaders have denounced as frankly excessive (1). The fact remains that the districts previously less favored than Badung have competed frantically for a bigger share of tourism wealth, scurrying to discover and exploit the rich deposits of natural and cultural heritage that lie slumbering beneath the memory, or the interest, of the population. And this

(1) The tourist areas are distributed among the districts as follows: Badung (Nusa Dua, Kuta, Tuban, Sanur); Gianyar (Ubud, Lebih); Tabanan (Tanah Lot, Soka); Buleleng (Bedugul/Pancasari, Air Sanih, Kalibukbuk, Batuampar); Jembrana (Gilimanuk, Candikusuma, Palasari, Perancak); Bangli (Kintamani); Klungkung (Nusa Penida); Karangasem (Candi Dasa, Ujung, Tulamben). To this should be added the non-classified 4,800 hectares on Serangan Island in Badung slated for resort development.

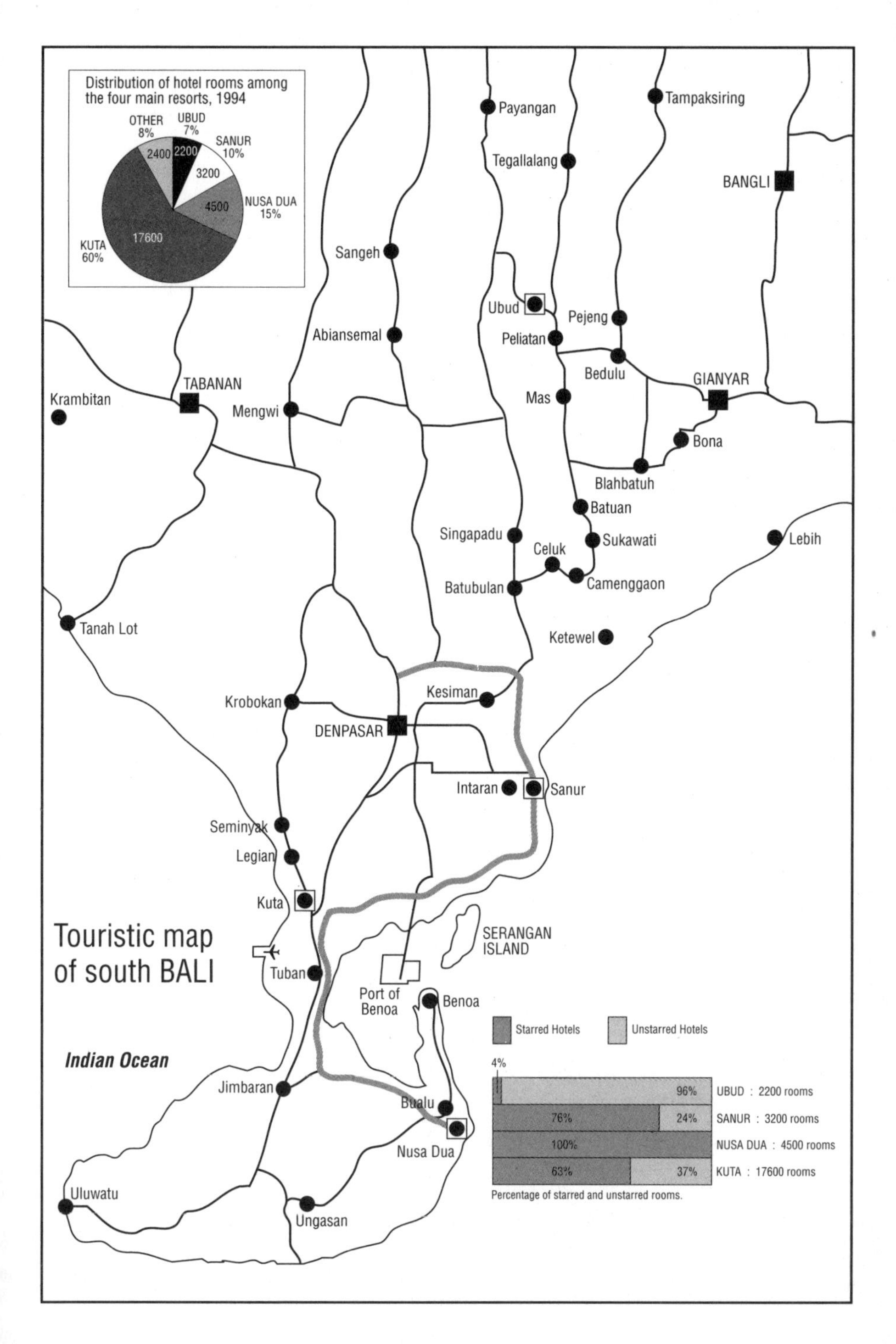

Distribution of hotel rooms among the four main resorts, 1994
OTHER 8%
UBUD 7%
SANUR 10%
NUSA DUA 15%
KUTA 60%
2400
2200
3200
4500
17600
Payangan
Tampaksiring
Tegallalang
BANGLI
Sangeh
Ubud
Pejeng
Abiansemal
Peliatan
Bedulu
GIANYAR
TABANAN
Krambitan
Mengwi
Mas
Bona
Blahbatuh
Batuan
Singapadu
Celuk
Sukawati
Lebih
Batubulan
Camenggaon
Tanah Lot
Ketewel
Kesiman
Krobokan
DENPASAR
Intaran
Sanur
Seminyak
Legian
Kuta
Touristic map of south BALI
SERANGAN ISLAND
Tuban
Port of Benoa
Benoa
Starred Hotels
Unstarred Hotels
Indian Ocean
4%
96%
UBUD : 2200 rooms
76%
24%
SANUR : 3200 rooms
100%
NUSA DUA : 4500 rooms
63%
37%
KUTA : 17600 rooms
Percentage of starred and unstarred rooms.
Jimbaran
Bualu
Nusa Dua
Uluwatu
Ungasan

frenzy reverberates among the villagers who, caught up in the ambient business fever, wonder what, indeed, they can do to get the tourists to visit them (2).

It is in this context that an agreement was signed in 1990 between the Directorate General of Tourism (DGT) and the United Nations Development Program (UNDP) with a view to revising the Master Plan, whose term had expired in 1985. Making note of the increasing stress on the environment and the incapacity of the provincial authorities to regulate the construction of tourist facilities — and seeing a decline in the quality of Bali's tourism product in the 1980s —, the UNDP undertook a study of the island's carrying capacity, as well as a plan for the development of tourism by 1995 and 2010 (Office for Project Services, 1992; Hassall and Associates 1992). During the same period, a project of scientific collaboration — the Bali Sustainable Development Project, financed by the Canadian International Development Agency and associating Canadian and Indonesian scholars — was launched with the aim of helping the province of Bali to formulate its Sixth Regional Plan (1994-1999), while setting guidelines for a sustainable development of tourism in Bali (BSDP 1992; Martopo & Mitchell 1995).

Emanating from the resort areas, a network of excursion routes was built giving access to the main sites of natural or cultural interest. Along these itineraries, the rice fields have progressively given way to ever more monumental and ostentatious souvenir shops and art galleries. The anarchistic proliferation of these buildings — often embellished with the most garish signs — has seriously degraded the beauty of the surrounding landscape, even though most of the tourist excursion routes have been classified as "green belts" (*jalur hijau*), where no construction is permitted. Moreover, the growing number of tourists visiting the island has led to traffic jams on the main roads, and this is further aggravated by the rapid increase in the number of private and commercial vehicles on the roads.

Tourists make an average of two to three excursions around the island during the course of their stay (3). These short trips, by bus or by car, are arranged by the travel agencies and the hotels, and some are written into the package price of organized tours. Besides these, the rental of individual cars and motorcycles allows the more adventurous visitors to explore the countryside beyond the regular routes, which is leading to an ever deeper and more diffuse penetration into the island's interior.

---

(2) This competition between districts and between villages is expressed in an urge for distinction, as attested in recent years by the vogue for monumental statues built at the edge of villages situated on a tourist route. While some of these signify the artistic reputation of the particular village (a dancer for Peliatan, a *Barong* for Batubulan, etc.), the relevance of others — the giant baby at Sakah, for instance, or the elephant lying by the road to Klungkung — is truly enigmatic, and visitors wonder why they are there.

(3) The most popular are the following:
- "Ubud Tour": Batubulan, Celuk, Mas, Ubud, Pujung, Sebatu.
- "Kintamani Tour": Batubulan, Celuk, Mas, Bedulu, Pejeng, Tampaksiring, Penelokan, Kintamani, Bangli, Gianyar.
- "Besakih Tour": Batubulan, Celuk, Gianyar, Bangli, Besakih, Bukit Jambul, Klungkung.
- "Tanah Lot Tour": Sangeh, Mengwi, Alas Kedaton, Tabanan, Tanah Lot.

Since 1975, some 180 sites have been classified by the Bali Tourism Office as official "tourist objects" (*obyek pariwisata*). The "objects" distinguished as such are overwhelmed by adjacent tourist facilities, cut off from their surroundings to become a series of interchangeable elements and robbed of the particular charm that drew the attention of tourists in the first place (4). The most frequented sites have been equipped as stopovers, whose usual amenities include a parking lot, toilets, refreshment stalls and souvenir "kiosks" (5). Besides these stopovers, the Master Plan had prescribed the construction of tourism centers with the aim of integrating tourism into Balinese society by incorporating local communities into their activities. The fact is that only two centers were built by the Directorate General of Tourism: Samuan Tiga in Bedulu and Taman Ayun in Mengwi. They were practically never operational, however — partly for lack of adequate funding, but mainly because of the boycott inflicted on them by the tourism industry and a lack of interest on the part of the Balinese, who were not associated with their creation.

Among the island's tourist regions, we must mention certain villages of craftsmen. It is in fact traditional in Bali for village communities to specialize in various crafts, whether forging musical instruments, chiseling silver containers, wood-carving or stone-carving, or even extracting coconut oil or palm toddy. Some of these villages adapted to the new tourist market, while others, envious of their success, imitated them by launching into the mass production of souvenirs. Tourist handicrafts — sculpture, painting, jewelry, weaving, basketry and so forth — are today a specialty of the district of Gianyar (6). Among the craft villages are those that tourists visit during the course of their excursions and whose roadsides are lined with shops, while others are somewhat removed from tourist routes and sell their wares in the resorts or at nearby stopovers.

Of these three sorts of tourist regions, the most affected by tourism — those whose landscapes bear the most visible marks of the presence of tourists — are obviously the resort areas. Their development testifies to the evolution of Bali's

---

(4) As the sites and curiosities of the island, duly mapped out and equipped by the Tourism Office, were designated as tourist attractions, they rapidly underwent the stages of site sacralization conceived by Dean MacCannell and ended up being covered over by the proliferation of their markers (MacCannell 1976: 43-48). Brochures, postcards, guidebooks and road maps proliferated, and old travel books were republished, stirring up nostalgia for "the last paradise", whose myth continues to attract more tourists than ever before, while the reality of Bali's tourist product becomes increasingly removed from its promotional image.

(5) Among the most visited sites are the coastal temples of Tanah Lot and Uluwatu, the temple of Taman Ayun in Mengwi, the Sangeh "monkey forest", the Goa Gajah cave in Bedulu, the funerary monuments of Gunung Kawi and the temple of Tirtha Empul in Tampaksiring, the "hall of justice" Kerta Gosa in Klungkung, the "bat cave" of Goa Lawah, the "mother temple" of Besakih on the flanks of Gunung Agung, the crater lakes of Bedugul and Batur, and finally the Bali Museum in Denpasar.

(6) The most famous villages are Batubulan (stone sculpture), Celuk (jewelry), Batuan (painting), Mas (wood-carving), Peliatan and Ubud (painting), Gianyar (weaving), Tampaksiring (ivory- and bone-carving), Bona (basketry), Tegallalang, Pujung and Sebatu, and more recently Kemenuh (wood-carving).

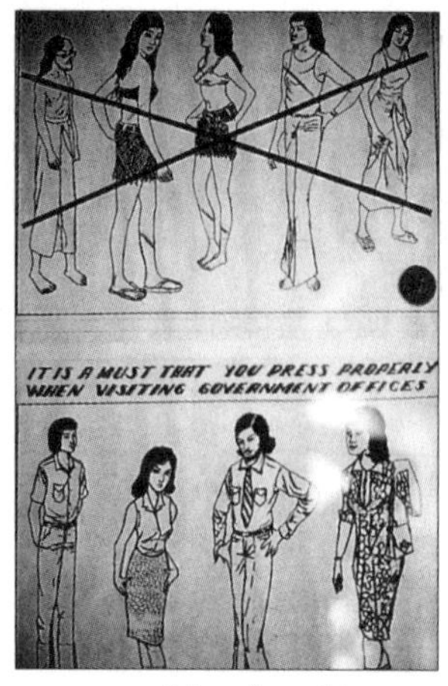

tourist market — a market that has proved to be much more diversified than the experts anticipated.

The projection studies carried out in the 1960s with a view to planning the development of tourism on the island considered only international luxury-class tourism, and it was with this market in mind that the Master Plan was conceived. At the beginning of the 1970s, however, Bali became an obligatory stop for the Western hippie travelers who were beginning to plow through Asia. Their non-conformist ways made them unpopular with the authorities, who were anxious about the pernicious influence that these hippies might exercise on the youth. As for the local population — who were more pragmatic — they rapidly seized the commercial opportunities that this new clientele represented, and adapted themselves ingeniously to their requirements.

Toward the end of the decade, however, the hippie travelers, having become more respectable with time, were viewed more positively — as a supplementary market to that of deluxe tourism, which was slowing down. Certain Balinese officials spoke of the "new tourists", whom they presented as a young, educated clientele with a limited budget, less concerned about comfort than with local color, and keen to mingle with the Balinese. They advocated responding to this demand by encouraging the construction of small hotels integrated into village life, which offer the advantage of requiring only modest cash investments and no import of equipment (thus no foreign currency spending) and could therefore be more easily owned and run by Balinese. The provincial government, for its part, deliberately pushed up the rates on goods and services for this market with the intention of rendering the tourist enterprise more profitable for the population.

In spite of the undeniable size of this market, the official position in Jakarta as well as in Denpasar continued to grant priority to deluxe tourism, which was clearly more prestigious, easier to standardize, and was considered more viable in terms of foreign exchange earnings. Nevertheless, a number of Balinese economists argued that the international hotel industry remains beyond the reach and control of the Balinese, that it has only a slight effect on the regional economy, and that it is expensive and requires considerable imports (Erawan 1994). Foreign analysts had differing opinions as to the respective advantages and drawbacks of these two markets. Some held that the small enterprises offered a better chance of profit for the Balinese and also fitted better into the island's physical and socio-cultural environment (Rodenburg 1980). Others asserted that the decline in expenditures per visitor — noticeable since the beginning of the 1980s because of the increase in the number of low-budget tourists — was not compensated by the lower content of imports in their spending (Gibbons & Fish 1989). The fact is that these differences of opinion do not merely bring out the respective merits of both sorts of tourism development. They are also expressions of conflicting interests — between foreign operators and the Indonesian tourism industry, between the investors in Jakarta and those in Denpasar, between the entrepreneurs and the Balinese population who wish to reap the fruits of tourism.

This diversification of the Balinese tourist market may be seen clearly in the different resort areas. Reviewing the most important — Nusa Dua, Sanur, Kuta and Ubud — one goes from large-scale, capital-intensive tourism, financed and operated by foreign agencies and relatively isolated from the host population, to small-scale, labor-intensive tourism, financed and operated by local agencies and relatively integrated into Balinese society.

1. Nusa Dua

This beach resort, conceived by the authors of the Master Plan, is located 20 kilometers from Denpasar, near the village of Bualu on the east coast of the Bukit peninsula at the southern extremity of the island. The choice of this site responds, as we have seen, to the decision to isolate tourists from the population, and this area is both peripheral and sparsely populated because of the aridity of the soil. In its revised version, the Master Plan proposed the development by the state of 425 hectares, divided into 12 lots to be leased to private hotel investors, and the construction of 2,500 international-class rooms by 1985.

Begun in 1974 under the aegis of the Bali Tourism Development Corporation (BTDC), the realization of the project ran considerably behind schedule. Completion of the infrastructures, forecasted for 1976, required three more years. The expressway giving access to Nusa Dua was opened only in 1981. Forty kilometers long, it serves the airport in Tuban — and the resorts of Jimbaran, Kuta and Sanur — and joins the road to Gianyar that leads to the main tourist sites on the island.

In 1978 the Bali Hotel and Tourism Training Center was inaugurated. This is a professional training school conceived by the International Labor Organization and financed by the United Nations Development Program, equipped to receive 450 students. The following year a 50-room training hotel was added, owned by the BTDC and serving as staff accommodation as well.

But investors were slow to appear — made hesitant by the global economic recession, finding the conditions imposed on them too restrictive, and manifestly uncertain about the future of tourism in Indonesia. Thus it was a subsidiary company of the national airline Garuda that took the initiative in 1980 to build the first hotel destined for tourists. The 450-room Nusa Dua Beach Hotel was solemnly inaugurated in 1983 by the President of the Republic, having first been properly consecrated by a Balinese priest. This is incontestably the showcase hotel of the island, designed expressly to impress visitors with its ostentatious luxury and the profuse ornamentation intended to create a "typically Balinese" atmosphere. The super-abundance of decor signifying the Balinese character of the place is in fact absolutely necessary, in that, having isolated the clients of Nusa Dua from the Balinese, it gives them the impression that they are, after all, in Bali.

In any event, Garuda's initiative created a climate that was encouraging to investors, now reassured by the upsurge of tourism in Bali and by the relaxing of Indonesian legislation regarding the repatriation of profits. By 1990 five hotels were in operation, totaling 2,200 international-class rooms. The following year three more hotels opened, bringing the resort's capacity to 3,800 rooms in April 1991 at the time of the Pacific Asia Travel Association (PATA) Conference, the highlight of the Year of Indonesia. In 1996, with the 12 lots by then occupied, the resort will have ten five-star hotels with a capacity of 4,585 rooms (around 15% of the total hotel capacity) and will employ nearly 10,000 persons (7).

If one refers these figures to the Master Plan, one can see that the 2,500 rooms projected for 1985 were not available until five years later. Moreover, the projections corresponded to forecasts of Bali's tourist frequentation that proved to be greatly overestimated. This error in estimates is apparent in the occupancy rates of the Nusa Dua Beach Hotel which stagnated below 50% during its first year of operation. The situation has improved noticeably since then, reaching 80% for the Nusa Dua hotels in operation in 1990. But with the opening of the second wave of hotels in 1991, the occupancy rate fell to around 60%, rising again to 75% in 1994.

Isolated as the resort is, its development nonetheless affected the surrounding population. In 1974, the inhabitants of Bualu were forced to cede their land to the authorities for a price that was considerably under-valued. Some of them believed that they had been wronged, and they sued, unsuccessfully. Moreover, the Master Plan called for giving job priority to the inhabitants of Bualu and Benoa; but, given the required qualifications and the recruitment procedures that were applied, most of the jobs were filled by people from outside the area (8). In 1978, following a number of incidents in Bualu, the BTDC commissioned a professor of psychology from the university in Jakarta to study the project's impact on the region's inhabitants. The conclusions of the study insist on the need to consult with the villagers and inform them of the consequences arising from the resort's development, with the aim of calming their fears and taking into account their legitimate aspirations.

Thereafter, the declarations of the BTDC and of the provincial government have not failed to call for the participation of the local people — but the concept of the resort itself inhibits any inclination for initiative on the part of the villagers. The site is, in fact, an enclave, physically cut off from the exterior by fences, and entry is forbidden to Balinese who are not employed there. And even when they are authorized, peddlers or small tradesmen selling their wares between the

---

(7) Of these ten hotels, two were financed with public-sector capital; the others sought private capital in Indonesian and foreign joint ventures. These are operated by seven foreign hotel chains: Melia-Sol, Club Méditerranée, Sheraton, Hilton, Hyatt, Westin and Pacific Island Club. The resort also includes the Bali International Convention Centre, an immense complex with state-of-the-art facilities, as well as the Bali Golf and Country Club with an 18-hole championship golf course, and an 80,000m2 shopping village with a performing arts theater (Darling & Helmi 1995)

(8) According to a recent Balinese study, 25% of the jobs at Nusa Dua are occupied by inhabitants of the region, 58% by Balinese from other regions, 15% by other Indonesians, and 2% by foreigners.

luxury hotels are frowned upon. The hotels — islets set in the heart of a vast and carefully maintained park — are actually residential complexes conceived in such a way as to provide absolutely everything their clients could possibly need during their stay in Bali, from swimming pools to "folk dances", and including every kind of shop and service imaginable.

The development of the site and its growing fame have created a magnet that Indonesian and Balinese businessmen have been quick to profit from. Unable to establish themselves within Nusa Dua, they have opened hotels, restaurants, boutiques and other tourist services along the beach connecting Nusa Dua to the village of Benoa — situated three kilometers to the north — which has become an unforeseen extension of the resort conceived by the French consultants. Moreover, the bay of Jimbaran has recently begun to be developed, and its luxury hotels already compete with those of Nusa Dua and other hotels around the Bukit.

The fact remains that the Nusa Dua experiment is considered an indisputable success by the Directorate General of Tourism, and it is thus destined to serve as a model for the development of some sixteen other resorts soon to emerge in other regions of the archipelago.

2. Sanur

At the time that Nusa Dua was still in the planning stages at SCETO, Sanur was the island's only beach resort area, and as such it received the majority of visitors — but it was apparent even then that its location would not be able to withstand the anticipated growth of international tourism in Bali.

The municipality of Sanur is situated six kilometers southeast of Denpasar, and comprised of two *desa adat*, Sanur and Intaran. The inhabitants are mainly farmers, with a large minority occupied in fishing, handicrafts, and the raising of livestock. Literary and artistic traditions have long flourished there, no doubt due to the large presence of *Brahmana* in the population. After witnessing the landing of the Dutch war fleet in 1906, Sanur began to take in a few foreign artists in the 1930s: the American dancer Katharane Mershon and her husband Jack, a photographer; the German brothers Hans and Rolf Neuhaus, who opened an aquarium and an art gallery; and the Belgian painter Adrien-Jean Le Mayeur de Merprès, who married a Balinese dancer famous for her beauty.

At the time, most tourists stayed at the Bali Hotel in Denpasar, from which they visited the island by taxi. It was only after the independence of Indonesia, in 1956, that the KPM — still the proprietor of the Bali Hotel and still holding a near-monopoly on the maritime links in the archipelago — built a complex of pavilions by the sea, the Sindhu Beach Hotel. It is said that this astonished the Balinese, who simply could not comprehend how one could live next to the sea in the company of all the demons that infest it (9; overleaf).

After the nationalization of the Dutch enterprises by the Indonesian government in 1957, the Sindhu Beach Hotel — as well as the Bali Hotel in Denpasar and the Kuta Beach Hotel in Kuta — were entrusted to the Indonesian national tourist agency,

Natour. Sanur then became the island's beach resort area, and hotels slowly began to open there. But it was only after the inauguration of the 300-room Bali Beach Hotel in 1966 that Bali was finally able to offer services of an international standard.

Built by Japanese at the initiative of President Sukarno, the new hotel was the symbol of Bali's opening to the outside world and the proof of its rise to modernism. It was also a controversial symbol, ever reproached for the gigantism of its ten stories, totally inappropriate to the character of the island — all the more so since the hotel flouted the Balinese architectural canon that forbids building anything higher than the temples. Since then, the provincial government has explicitly prohibited the construction of buildings rising above the tops of the coconut palms — that is, about 15 meters (10). This encouraged the fashion for bungalow-style hotels, in the form of small pavilions clustered around a central building in a garden by the beach. The Bali Beach Hotel nonetheless continues to exercise a certain fascination for the Balinese, to the point that for a long time the management organized guided tours of the hotel designed specifically for them.

At the end of the 1960s, the announcement of tourism development projects unleashed a wave of real estate speculation on beachside property left vacant by the Balinese (11). The coast was rapidly urbanized and the resort area underwent accelerated development in anticipation of the PATA conference in 1974 that was to mark the "Year of Tourism" in Indonesia. Around 30 new hotels were built between 1969 and 1974, raising Sanur's hotel capacity from 400 to 1,800 rooms. Building momentum slowed considerably thereafter, mainly due to competition

---

(9) In this regard, one may point out that this fear that the Balinese held for the sea encouraged the implantation of seaside resorts, in that the villagers settled at a respectful distance from the beach, leaving the coast vacant. This explains the particular physiognomy offered today by the urbanization of Sanur and of Kuta, where a road several hundred meters from the sea separates the Balinese settlements from the coastal fringe abandoned to the tourists.

(10) The fire that ravaged the Bali Beach Hotel in 1993 provided an unhoped-for occasion to gauge the resolution of the provincial government on this matter. In fact, the Governor took advantage of the opportunity to declare that the hotel must be restored in keeping with the Balinese norms in force. But the Minister of Tourism decided otherwise, stipulating that the Bali Beach Hotel would be rebuilt as it had been. At this, the Governor went back on his word, conceding that the restriction applied only to new buildings, that this was only a matter of reconstruction...

(11) The price of beach land in Sanur multiplied by ten between 1968 and 1973. Because Indonesian law forbids the sale of land to foreigners, a good number of transactions were effected by Indonesians from Jakarta taking the role of title-holder for foreign investors. Today, more than half of the beach land is held by non-local people.

from Kuta and Nusa Dua. In 1981 Sanur's hotel capacity was 2,100 rooms, and by 1994, 3,200 rooms (of which 2,450 are distributed among 19 starred hotels, and the rest among some 60 unstarred hotels and homestays). This represents around 10% of the island's hotel capacity.

This development occurred in an unplanned way, independently of the measures written into the Master Plan, which had left the development of Sanur — and of Kuta as well, whose growth was barely beginning — to private initiative, considering that the imminent opening of Nusa Dua would quickly absorb the tourist pressure. The only restriction imposed by the plan concerned the number of international-class rooms to be built outside Nusa Dua — limited to 1,600 by 1985 — but this limit was not respected. In an attempt to control the proliferation of tourist facilities, the provincial planning agencies devised master plans for the development of Sanur and Kuta that came into effect only in 1980. The projection for Sanur was a total capacity of 5,000 rooms over 100 hectares by the year 2000.

Confronted with this movement of rampant capitalism, the municipal authorities undertook to turn tourism to their advantage, and as early as 1969 they worked out a plan for the development of Sanur. Among the projects related to tourism is the Sanur Beach Market, inaugurated in 1971. Favorably situated on the beach close to the major hotels, it offers sailing trips, presents exhibitions of painting and sculpture as well as dance performances, and runs a cafe-restaurant. The enterprises that participate in the Beach Market are organized in *seka* (12), and each pays rent and donates a portion of its profits to the municipal administration. Following this, three other restaurants, art and souvenir shops, a bank, a laundry, and a service garage were opened at the initiative of the municipality. Funds from these various enterprises — which employ several hundred people — have been used to build a health clinic, a library, a primary school and a kindergarten; to open a new market; to mend the streets and restore temples; to organize English courses for the villagers; and to buy television sets for each *bale banjar* (Warren 1993: chap. 7).

Supervision of all these activities is entrusted to a body headed by the mayor of Sanur and comprising representatives of various administrative and customary organs of the village, as well as private interests. The result is that in Sanur local participation in tourism has developed under the auspices of the municipal administration. Despite this initiative, however, the population has generally remained removed from tourism and its revenues. That is the picture that emerges from a study carried out in 1974 by a Balinese academic, which shows that 60% of the inhabitants of Sanur remained indifferent or hostile to the presence of tourists, in that they drew no profit from them. Furthermore, 40% of the people interviewed stated that they did not

---

(12) Most collective activities in Bali are traditionally carried out by voluntary associations, *seka* (literally, "to make one") — collectives of mutual aid or cooperation organized around specific functions. Thus each Balinese is generally a member of several *seka* which may be of widely varying sizes, of a temporary or permanent nature, and dedicated to the greatest variety of activities, economic, artistic, or religious.

want to establish relations with the tourists, considered too different from the Balinese.

In fact, tourist development in Sanur has remained generally inaccessible to local initiatives because of its massive, luxurious, and exclusive character. International hotels tend to want to provide in-house all the services that might be sought by their clients, who do not often leave the hotel, and when they do, they are duly enclosed in tour buses or taxis. And the great majority of hotels, restaurants, travel agencies and boutiques in the area are owned by Indonesians established in Sanur or by Balinese from other regions, when they are not controlled by foreign capital.

As for jobs created by tourism, the skilled positions are usually occupied by non-Balinese. Moreover, the hotel industry employs a number of Balinese from outside Sanur, with the result that very quickly the problem arose of the social insertion of immigrants, for whom the mayor created in 1970 a new *banjar dinas*, Banjar Pangastian. Composed in the majority of non-Balinese, the *banjar* also accepts Balinese residents from other regions, who maintain their ties to their villages of origin and who are obliged to return home for important religious ceremonies (13).

The fact remains that modern professional occupations, of the sort afforded by administration or tourism, generate social tensions, in that they entail a logic that is difficult to reconcile with traditional community obligations. Employers are understandably reluctant to let staff members return to their villages for every ceremony to which they are called. Very often, employees who are not permitted to leave their posts are obliged to fulfill their customary responsibilities by paying a fine, and tourist businesses prefer to hire personnel from outside the island to avoid disturbances in the work caused by the absenteeism of the Balinese.

Among the conflicts that arise between the respective demands of custom and tourism is the fact that the Balinese are particularly sensitive to changes in the ritual use of certain spaces. This includes the beaches, where numerous purification ceremonies take place, during which the presence of curious and scantily clad bathers has proven to be a source of exasperation for the Balinese. They also complain that their access to the sea is often blocked by the hotels, whose management show no hesitation in closing off the beaches in front — in flagrant violation of the rules.

A particularly significant scandal rocked Sanur in 1971 regarding a small temple by the sea unfortunately located on land destined for the extension of the Bali Beach Hotel. The *Bupati* of Badung, backed by the Governor and the Provincial Assembly, ordered the demolition of the temple and offered monetary compensation. But the temple's priest and its congregation sought the advice of the gods. It is said that all the participants in the ceremony fell unconscious and that the gods declared, through the voice of a medium in trance, that they were opposed to the demolition. The *Bupati* decided to proceed nonetheless, and it was then that the

(13) The Balinese who, for professional or other reasons, temporarily leave their village remain subject to the obligations incumbent upon members of the *banjar* from which they originate. When they are unable to fulfill them, they are compelled to pay a fine. When their change of residence is permanent, they become members of the *banjar* where they live.

priest in charge of overseeing the religious aspects of the operation was struck with paralysis. His wife died suddenly two days later. The press then seized upon the affair, and numerous protests arose over what became a symbol of the sacrifice of religious values on the altar of profit. Faced with the vehemence of the reaction, the services of the *Bupati* let it be known soon thereafter that the temple would not be demolished (Lovric 1986: 73-74).

This scandal has receded in people's memories, and today Sanur is a quiet place. This beach, once the island's foremost seaside resort, has become its most sedate, mantled in an elderly charm (and sometimes referred to by expatriates as "Snore"). Whereas almost everywhere else tourist development projects exert a visible pressure, development in Sanur seems to have settled, and its growing urbanization is due more to its proximity to Denpasar than to tourism. Since the end of the 1970s, the center of gravity of tourism in Bali has shifted toward Kuta.

3. Kuta

More so even than in Sanur, the tourist development of Kuta took place in response to a pressing demand for accommodations and services and long remained anarchistic, without control or direction of any sort.

Located some ten kilometers to the southwest of Denpasar, the municipality of Kuta is composed of three *desa adat*: Kuta, Legian and Seminyak. Unlike Sanur, Kuta was until not long ago a poor region and bereft of artistic traditions. Its inhabitants were mostly *jaba*, struggling to subsist on fishing and agriculture.

If Sanur saw the Dutch war fleet land in 1906, it was in Kuta that the first Dutch ships landed in 1597. But the region has stayed in the annals mainly for having been the island's principal slave market, a trade which flourished between the 17th and 19th centuries to the greatest profit of the princely houses who controlled it. To the unsavory reputation earned by this specialty, Kuta added that of a place of exile: here was tossed the refuse of society — Balinese expelled from their villages for serious crimes, fugitives escaping the extortion of some prince, or people afflicted with an ignominious disease, like leprosy. This trading zone also welcomed foreigners, Chinese or European, who were confined to the indispensable role of intermediaries between the Balinese rajas and the neighboring powers.

Under the colonial occupation, Kuta was a miserable and dusty village situated near a magnificent beach. It was not until 1936 that Kuta's vocation emerged, when a couple of American artists, Louise Garrett and Robert

Koke, discovered the beach in the course of a bicycle ride. Seduced by the beauty of the site, they decided to build several bungalows there in the local style, catering to tourists bored with Denpasar and the urban comfort of the Bali Hotel. Thus was born the Kuta Beach Hotel (Koke 1987). This version of the facts is contradicted by the account given by Vannine Walker, alias K'tut Tantri, who became famous as a propagandist for the Indonesian revolution under the pseudonym Surabaya Sue (Tantri 1960). It seems, in fact, that after having participated in the launching of the Kuta Beach Hotel, K'tut Tantri then built her own hotel nearby, the *Suara Segara* (the Sound of the Sea), and that the two hotels were in fierce competition until the war ended it all, leaving only a vacant lot.

To make things even more confusing, in 1955 the KPM built a hotel on the same site to which it, too, gave the name of Kuta Beach Hotel. But tourist frequentation of the place remained insignificant until, toward the end of the 1960s, the hippie travelers (who at the time preferred staying in Denpasar rather than Sanur which they considered too expensive) began to pass their days on Kuta beach, famous for the splendor of its sunsets as well as for its hallucinogenic mushrooms. It was then that certain villagers put guest rooms at their disposal (14), while several food stalls adapted their dishes to European taste. It did not take long for Kuta to earn a reputation as the cheapest and most alluring stop between India and Australia.

After this initial impulsion, due to the presence of growing numbers of long-term travelers and to the population's desire to draw some profit from them, one can detect three stages in the launching of Kuta as a tourist resort. The first ran from circa 1970 to 1973, and it entailed a spontaneous local movement propelled by individual or family initiatives. Villagers built pavilions (*homestays*) for tourists in their family courtyards, and several inexpensive guesthouses (*losmen*) appeared. Restaurants, clothing shops and souvenir stalls opened everywhere, as well as services such as tailors and bicycle rentals. Most of the local entrepreneurs, who had neither capital nor special skills, considered their participation in the rise of tourism a secondary activity which brought additional income to that earned from farming and fishing. During this period, the tourist frequentation of Kuta went from less than a thousand in 1970 to nearly 15,000 in 1973.

It was in 1973 that Kuta truly became a beach resort area. Its success drew the attention of Indonesian investors, stimulated by the prospect of the PATA conference the following year, and they anticipated a bright future. Land prices by the beach soared and hotels sprang up along the coast. The urbanization of the area accelerated with the proliferation of boutiques, travel agencies, motorbike rental shops, and restaurants.

Development emerged along two parallel markets. One was dedicated to the growing tourist clientele lured by Kuta's laid-back image and low prices — a market that

(14) The modular lay-out of the traditional Balinese house, composed of an ensemble of pavilions set out around an interior courtyard, greatly facilitated the decision to take in paying guests.

The Puputan Badung as seen by a French weekly magazine of the time
(Le Petit Journal, Supplément illustré, *14 October 1906).*

W.O.J. Nieuwenkamp's "Funeral procession in Sangsit" (1922)
(R. Spruit, Artists on Bali, *Amsterdam: The Pepin Press, 1995).*

Walter Spies' "Road on Bali" (undated) (Spruit 1995).

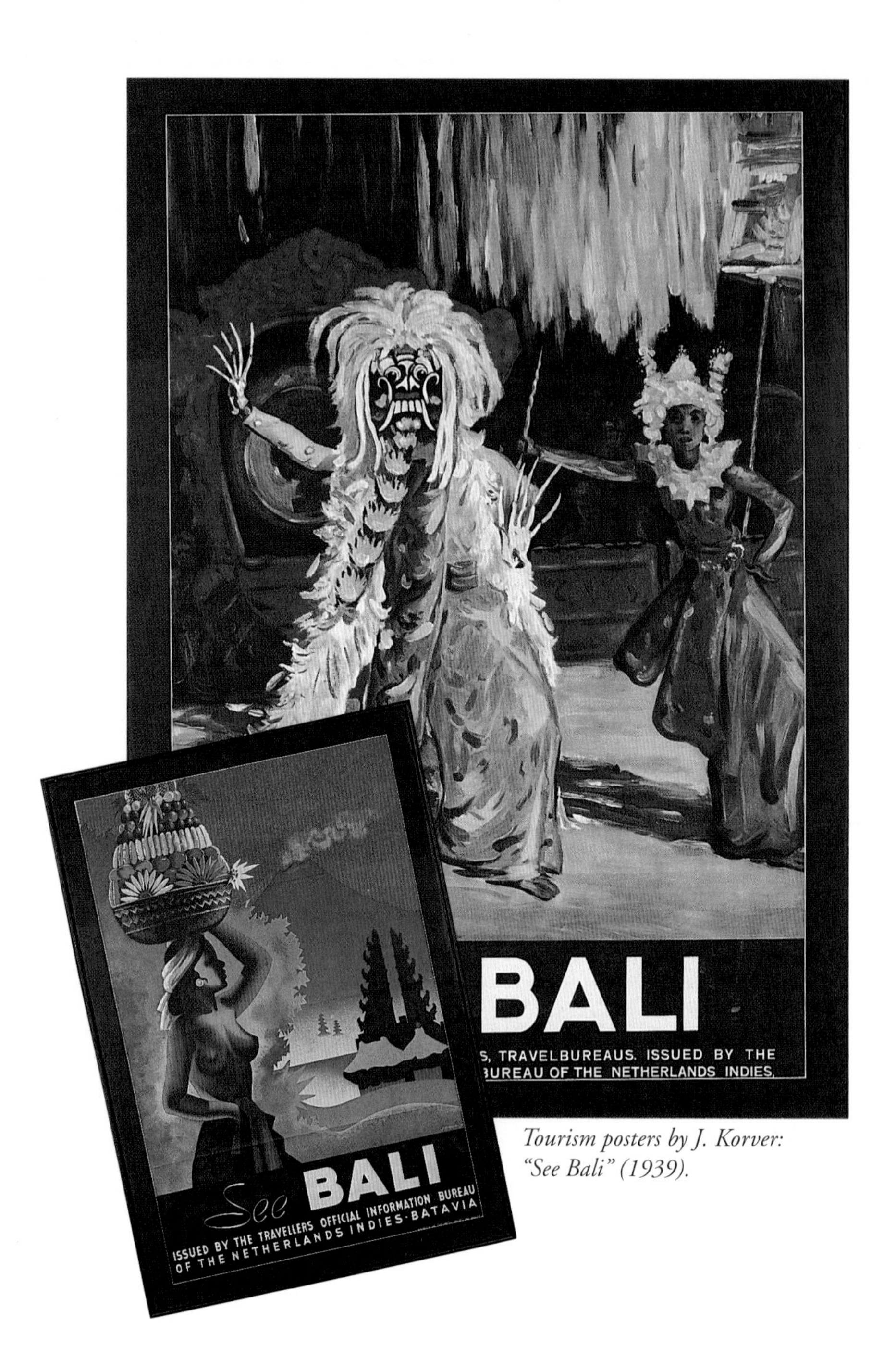

Tourism posters by J. Korver: "See Bali" (1939).

Left: "Atmosphere & Enchantment. Bali". Below: "Grace & Charm. Bali".

Posters by Willem Hofker for the Bali Hotel (1948) (B. Carpenter & M. Hofker-Rueter. Willem Hofker, Schilder van Bali/ Painter of Bali. *Wijk en Aalburg: Pictures Publishers. 1993).*

TAHUN
SADAR WISATA
1989 - 1990

SAPTA PESONA

1. KEAMANAN
2. KETERTIBAN
3. KEBERSIHAN
4. KESEJUKAN
5. KEINDAHAN
6. KERAMAHTAMAHAN
7. KENANGAN

The charming face of a Legong *dancer used in 1989 by the Bali Government Tourism Office in the campaign aimed at encouraging Balinese to show their visitors the Seven Charms of Tourism (see Chapter 3, §3).*

The threatening figure of Rangda used in 1989 by the government of the Province of Bali in a campaign aimed at eradicating the consumption of drugs among tourists.

A writing pad from the 1970s, illustrated with Janger *dancers in front of the Bali Beach Hotel.*

An advertisement for the Nusa Dua Beach Hotel in the 1980s.

was becoming institutionalized, financed and managed by professionals from outside the region. The other was controlled by the villagers and starting to feel the competition from Indonesian investors; but they continued nonetheless to provide survivors of the hippie wave — augmented now by American and Australian surfers — with the services they expected, and did their best to adapt better to the evolving situation. Over the years, the hippie-traveler clientele tended to move north, settling around Legian, which was considered less "touristic" and where a development took place that was analogous to Kuta a few years earlier, but at a much more rapid pace. In 1973 there were some 60 pensions and hotels in the area; in 1976, this number had tripled, giving a capacity of 1,500 rooms.

Starting in 1976, the local entrepreneurs' position was strengthened by the interest some of the early travelers showed for the pleasures of life in Kuta, and who sought a way of setting up there by going into business. In a number of cases, they formed partnerships with their former host, whether in upgrading his *losmen* or in opening a shop or restaurant under his name. They also went into selling traditional textiles from various islands around the archipelago, or more generally, in producing jewelry or clothing for export, of which a sizable remainder would be sold in Kuta to tourists. Some of them married local girls who officially looked after their businesses. And they built houses for themselves in Legian and Seminyak, which became ever more luxurious as their business prospered. Most often, their activities were not declared and they survived on scams and bribes — but eventually some of these former hippies managed to obtain work permits and form their own companies.

The Balinese seem to have an ambivalent attitude toward these foreigners. The local entrepreneurs understood very quickly the advantages they could derive from them in the face of their Indonesian competitors in terms of capital, know-how, and an understanding of the markets — but this does not stop them from considering their foreign partners as parasites hampering their own expansion. As to the provincial authorities, although they periodically denounce the presence of these foreign businessmen, they tolerate them to the extent that they know them to be indispensable, and profitable to them as well. It is of course difficult to guess the number of these new entrepreneurs, since their situation is often illegal, but one may estimate that it includes several thousand people of all nationalities, who maintain permanent ties among themselves that mix the old solidarity of the road with growing business competition.

As the hippies gave way to businessmen, and marijuana to beer, luxury hotels grew among the homestays and *losmen.* The urbanization of the coast kept up at a steady pace through the 1980s, and today the resort area extends from Tuban to Krobokan, beyond Seminyak, now covering nearly 10 kilometers. In 1981 there were 7 starred hotels and 230 unstarred hotels and homestays, totaling 2,900 rooms, a hotel capacity already higher than that of Sanur. This predominance has been further accentuated since then: in 1994, there were 46 starred hotels and 380 unstarred hotels and homestays, bringing the area's capacity to 17,600 rooms (of which 11,130 in starred hotels) — almost 60% of the island's hotel capacity. The master plan for Kuta, which in 1980 forecasted 7,000 rooms on 150 hectares by the year 2000, had become obsolete by the end of the 1980s.

Kuta's clientele is comprised in a great majority of young tourists, many of them Australian, who come to taste the pleasures of a low-cost beach holiday. Many spend their days surfing, and this has seduced a number of young Balinese who, forgetting their ancestral fear of the sea, have become virtuoso surfers. In the wake of the surfers came young Australian girls in search of amorous adventures with the natives. The presence of these youthful hordes, dedicated to solar hedonism and nocturnal amusements, has given the resort a dubious reputation that attracts Balinese and other Indonesians for various reasons (15).

There are the domestic tourists, and most especially students from the large cities of Java, for whom the very presence of foreign tourists constitutes the major attraction in Kuta. On Saturday and Sunday afternoons, their ranks are swelled by the bourgeoisie of Denpasar who have acquired the habit of strolling with their families along the beach, after shopping at one of Kuta's supermarkets and having lunch at a seaside restaurant — and today it is the Balinese, dressed from head to foot, who come to contemplate the generously exposed breasts of the foreign women.

Besides domestic tourists, the development of the resort has attracted a labor force from other parts of Bali and other regions of the archipelago. More specifically, a number of young Balinese and Indonesians have drifted to Kuta in search of an exciting life and easy money far from the constraints of home. Some find work in the local tourism industry or even manage to open their own businesses, while others launch into dubious, barely legal activities. Thus the resort has witnessed the emergence of a type of young Indonesians called "Kuta cowboys", with Western mannerisms and Australian accents, composed of failed artists, gigolos, pimps, traffickers of all sorts, or more generally, scammers ever in search of a new ploy. This more-or-less marginal youth readily affixes itself to the company of Western tourists, sought after for their money and their reputation for

(15) According to the Lonely Planet guide book: "Kuta is a good place to get a suntan, definitely a good place to get pissed and supposedly a good place to get laid" (Cummings et al. 1990: 355).

promiscuity, and assiduously frequents the fashionable night spots, including the always-crowded parties of foreign residents. Finally, for the less fortunate among the Indonesians tempted by the tourist manna, there still remains the possibility of becoming a street peddler, tirelessly walking the beach and soliciting each bather in the hope of selling refreshments, souvenirs, postcards, or a massage.

The cohabitation of all these diverse populations — tourists, migrants, Balinese — animated by different ambitions has made Kuta a heterogeneous, almost urban place, much more so than Sanur, in that the interactions are more diffuse and the control mechanisms less efficient. And yet one must beware of exaggerating retrospectively the degree of upheaval induced by tourism in the 1970s. According to a survey conducted by the Bali Tourism Development Board in 1976, residents from outside the municipality comprised 8% of the local population, and tourism activities concerned directly only 17% of the villagers, who drew revenues nearly three times higher than those in traditional activities — around $50 per month. Finally, while the majority of the hotels were owned by non-Balinese, 67% of the pensions belonged to inhabitants of Kuta, 28% to Balinese from other regions, and 5% to other Indonesians; the proportions were approximately the same for the restaurants and shops. By 1994, the situation had changed radically: according to a study by the Faculty of Economics in Denpasar, 90% of the tourist enterprises in Kuta are now owned by persons from outside the municipality, whether Balinese from other regions or Indonesians from other provinces. The entrepreneurs among Kuta's inhabitants have become landlords, finding it more profitable to lease their land by the beach or along the roads to outsiders than themselves to invest in a tourist enterprise.

The 1976 survey also provides interesting information on the villagers' perceptions, at the time, of tourism and its impact on their community. Contrary to the prevailing opinion in Sanur, a strong majority declared themselves in favor of the presence of tourists and willing to establish personal relationships with them. Nonetheless, the tourists' behavior was judged to be entirely contrary to Balinese moral values and seemed to carry a risk of acculturation with dreaded consequences. In other respects, the liabilities imputed to tourism were recognized as disquieting. The study cited, pell-mell: the rise of delinquency and prostitution; the bad example given by the open immorality of the hippies (whom they reproached mainly for the use of drugs and "free sex") and their pernicious influence on young people; the high cost of living; competition dividing members of a community which in earlier times had been cohesive; and the appearance in their midst of individualistic and materialistic attitudes. On the other hand, the villagers gave credit to tourism for raising the standard of living and creating jobs, introducing a command of English, and promoting the performing arts.

It is also revealing that the majority of people interviewed during this survey were in favor of a stronger intervention by the communal authorities, in particular concerning security and the regulation of activities related to tourism. In effect, and unlike what happened in Sanur, the participation of the population in Kuta's tourism industry first took the form of a multitude of private initiatives, without the slightest involvement of the administrative or customary institutions. Later the *banjar adat* most affected by tourism intervened, principally in two domains: the regular presentation of dance performances for tourists; and the reinforcement of social control on their territory.

This last matter deserves some elaboration because it long polarized the attention of the local population and that of the provincial authorities as well. Delinquency had soon become a worrying issue among the villagers, who condemned the drug traffic, burglaries, organized rackets, and prostitution (16). The situation deteriorated progressively during the 1970s, and at the end of the decade there was a dramatic worsening of crime, marked by armed aggression against tourists, which sometimes led to killings. An explosion of anger, strongly laced with xenophobia, broke out against the non-Balinese migrants, and the fever spread rapidly to other regions, where suspects seemed to multiply. It was then that the *banjar*, backed by certain youth movements, organized night patrols. On several occasions this improvised police force applied a hasty justice, killing on the spot the thieves that fell into their hands. Following these incidents, the provincial government stripped Kuta's *banjar* of their customary authority to maintain public order, enjoining them to turn malefactors henceforth over to the police. This raised tensions between the local population and the authorities, openly accused of laxity and corruption.

This atmosphere of violence was promptly quieted by the Governor, who appealed to the population for more restraint, reminding them of the damage to Kuta's image — and to that of Bali on the whole — that would be wrought if word of this troublesome affair should get out and frighten the tourists. One can cite other analogous examples as well, where the disciplinary responses of the authorities were tempered by considerations of a promotional nature and finally blocked in the course of their enforcement. So, too, with the campaign against nudism and even the attempt to control the night clubs — issues that, after having been on the front page of the local press for some months, were discreetly abandoned for fear that measures thought to be too harsh would adversely affect the tourist frequentation of the island.

It is difficult to assess the situation of the resort today, for everything concerning Kuta turns out to be controversial. It is at once a bauble and a sewer. Its power of seduction for young Westerners is equaled only by the fascination it exerts on those Balinese and Indonesians out to make their fortunes there. The fever of commerce is rampant, and prosperity is visible everywhere. The recent study by the Faculty of Economics concluded that the average income per capita in 1994 reached $2,500 — about three times the Balinese average — which makes the population of Kuta, with that of Jakarta, the richest of all of Indonesia. Land prices there have become the highest on the island outside Nusa Dua, around $3,000 per square meter in the

(16) Contrary to the legend that the Balinese do not prostitute themselves, tourism in Kuta has in fact brought about the appearance of Balinese prostitutes, generally based in Denpasar. That said, the phenomenon remains marginal, and the prostitutes operating in Bali are for the most part from the neighboring islands of Java, Madura or Lombok — and their clientele is mainly Indonesian.

center of town. But if the agglomeration evokes a frontier-town in its dynamism, the disorder is one of a mushroom-city — the aggressive ugliness of buildings piled one on top of the other, the quasi-permanent traffic jams, the galloping erosion of the shore, not to mention the trash strewn everywhere, especially on the beach (17).

Kuta is continually in the news and fills the Indonesian press with deliciously scandalized stories, while the authorities try to effect a semblance of order in a proliferation that seems beyond control. In this regard, although the construction of luxury hotels may eventually modify Kuta's clientele, it has not yet altered its dubious image. For some, Kuta is nothing but a disfiguring sore on the face of "the island of the gods", hardly less embarrassing than when it was a slave market and a leper colony. Others see it as a necessary evil, a localizing abscess with the prophylactic advantage of isolating the tourists in a cordon sanitaire as efficient as the deliberate seclusion practiced at Nusa Dua. But all agree that it is certainly the least "Balinese" place in Bali, even though behind the tourist facade it seems that Kuta's people have preserved their way of life, their customs and their beliefs to a remarkable extent, and that the money earned through tourism is spent generously on the religious ceremonies prescribed by tradition, more splendid now than they have ever been (Mabbett 1987).

What is certain is that Kuta's future depends to a large degree on the social control that the *banjar* will be able to maintain: first, among the villagers themselves, for whom the pursuit of lucrative businesses tends to take priority over communal obligations — often considered a constraint that they are tempted to elude by paying a fine (18); and second, in regard to the administrative authorities — at local as well as regional level — who, in dealing with the problems engendered by the development of tourism, tend to encroach ever further on the prerogatives traditionally held by the *banjar*.

4. Ubud

Unlike the beach resorts, Ubud is at once a place to stay and a tourist destination in itself. The area attracts tourists for whom Bali evokes arts and ceremonies rather than sex and surfing, those who want to discover an "authentically Balinese" village still preserved from the "tourist invasion" and which, according to the guidebooks, has kept its charm of yesteryear. Besides these, hundreds of tourists from Nusa Dua, Sanur and Kuta descend from their buses every day to visit "the village of painters", after making a few purchases in "the village of goldsmiths" (Celuk) and "the village of wood-carvers" (Mas) conveniently located along their excursion route around the island.

Situated 25 kilometers northeast of Denpasar, Ubud is nestled in the green folds of a countryside carpeted with terraced rice fields and carved by deep river gorges. The inhabitants are traditionally farmers and — increasingly, these days — mer-

(17) To be fair; I must say that in recent years the municipality has made a worthy effort to improve Kuta's image, especially in tackling the problem of garbage treatment.

(18) In 1990, a survey conducted by Balinese academics on the participation of the inhabitants of the resort areas in *banjar* activities showed a rate of absenteeism of 40% in Kuta, 33% in Sanur, 28% in Bualu (Nusa Dua) and only 3% in Ubud.

chants and "artists". Toward the end of the 19th century it was the seat of a powerful princely house, and today it is a municipality in the district of Gianyar, composed of six *desa adat.* Unlike many princely houses which were reduced and weakened by the colonial occupation, the *puri* of Ubud managed to maintain most of its power and wealth, thanks to a dexterous policy of allegiance to the island's new masters. And these days, the nobility — *Satria* for the most part — continues to play an eminent role in local affairs. The presence of numerous secondary *puri* also attests eloquently to the tight network of alliances and patronage that the princes of Ubud have woven in the region.

It was at the invitation of Ubud's lord, Cokorda Gede Raka Sukawati, that the German painter and musician Walter Spies made his first visit to Bali in 1925, and it was in the *puri* that he set up house — with his piano, bicycle and butterfly net — when he decided to establish himself in Bali two years later. Soon thereafter, he built a house with a swimming pool at the edge of the village, on land belonging to the *puri.* Fascinated by all that he discovered on the island, he quickly became the most ardent admirer of Balinese culture, and his reputation as a connoisseur made him the obliging host of many of the island's most distinguished visitors. He was joined in 1929 by the Dutch painter Rudolf Bonnet, who also elected to reside in Ubud.

At that time, the region was known more for its performing arts than for its painting and sculpture, which had fallen somewhat into neglect. It was dancers and musicians from Ubud and the neighboring village of Peliatan, led by Cokorda Gede Raka Sukawati, who were to represent Bali at the Colonial Exposition of Paris in 1931. But painting and sculpture were to undergo a spectacular "renaissance" with the flowering of new styles at the beginning of the 1930s.

Traditionally in Bali, painting and sculpture, like music and dance also, had a religious rather than artistic function. It is, in fact, incorrect to speak of "art" in this regard, if only because there exists no term in the Balinese language to designate "art" or an "artist". That which we call art had until then been a functional task, a "service" (*ayah*) rendered to the gods and ancestors, to princes and the community, rather than the expression of individual creativity. And the "artist" was still an anonymous "artisan" (*tukang*) who only by a greater mastery in the techniques of representation — pictorial or plastic, musical or dramatic — was distinguished from his neighbors.

Painters and sculptors were organized in family guilds around the *puri,* who supported them in exchange for their services; and the subjects they treated were primarily inspired by mythological themes, rendered according to orthodox codes. After the colonial occupation, which considerably reduced the patronage exercised by the *puri,* painting and sculpture underwent a certain decline. On the other hand, the recent infusion of modern Western ideas found expression in the blossoming of a new artistic sensibility, tuned more toward the realities of everyday life, and Balinese painting slowly disengaged itself from the grip of old conventions. Foreign observers tended to credit Rudolf Bonnet and especially Walter Spies with these developments, sometimes going as far as to speak of teachers and disciples. The fact is that the European artists furnished the Balinese with the necessary materials to exercise their talents, and bought the paintings and sculptures they produced. By encouraging the Balinese artists in a quest for innovation that was at once technical, stylistic, and thematic, Spies and Bonnet actually only accelerated and legitimized a movement that was already germinating when they arrived on the island.

Whatever their exact influence in the contemporary evolution of Balinese arts, it is undeniable that Spies and Bonnet played a decisive role as patrons and cultural mediators, first in selling the works of their protégés to rich collectors, and then in opening the budding tourist market to Balinese artists. At the beginning of the 1930s, the arrival of the tourists and their need to buy typical works of art with which to remember their visit to Bali amounted to a new form of art patronage. This brought radical changes, not only to the form and intent of art works, but also to the social status of their creators. Where previously there were only anonymous artisans, willingly offering their talents in a collective labor, "artists" began to appear, selling "works of art" of which they are the individual creator — although today, these works are most often the collective labor of apprentices under the direction of a master-artisan.

Even as they encouraged the Balinese to sell on the tourist market, Spies and Bonnet were conscious of dangers inherent in commercialism and mass production, and they strove constantly to control the artistic quality of the works they marketed. In this endeavor, they had recourse to the Bali Museum — opened in 1932 in Denpasar to safeguard the island's cultural heritage — where they exhibited contemporary works destined to be sold to tourists. They were well-placed to do so: Spies was the curator and Bonnet the sales director. Then, in 1936, with the support of the new lord of Ubud, Cokorda Gede Agung Sukawati, they founded an association dedicated to the promotion of the Balinese fine arts. Called *Pita Maha* (referring literally to the "great ancestors" under whose spiritual authority its members placed themselves), this association was constituted as a *seka* and had some 150 members. It remained active until the war (Djelantik 1986; Eiseman 1988; Kam 1993; Rhodius & Darling 1980).

Up to this point, Ubud was not yet on the tourist map — indeed, it was barely mentioned in the guidebooks of the time — and the paintings and sculptures that came out of *Pita Maha* were sold through the Bali Museum, as well as several galleries that had opened in Denpasar and Sanur. But the fame of Walter Spies brought tourists to Ubud in ever greater numbers, and in 1937, disturbed by the growing crush of visitors, Spies rented out his house in Ubud and moved to Iseh, at the foot of Mount Agung. He was interned by the Dutch in 1940 because of his German origins, and died during the sinking of a ship bearing prisoners of war, torpedoed by a Japanese shell off the coast of Sumatra.

After the war, Rudolf Bonnet returned to Bali and suggested to Cokorda Gede Agung Sukawati that he receive paying guests in his *puri*. Guests were accepted (by recommendation only) starting in 1947. In the 1950s, other foreign painters came to settle in Ubud, among them Arie Smit, Han Snel, and Antonio Blanco. In 1956, thanks to the joint efforts of Bonnet and Cokorda Agung, the old dream of the founders of *Pita Maha* was realized with the opening — on land belonging to the *puri* — of Ubud's Museum of Modern Balinese Arts (*Puri Lukisan*). Soon after this, private galleries began to open, selling the works of regional artists to tourists.

Ubud now figured among the sites regularly visited by tourists, and at the beginning of the 1970s there were four hotels, a homestay, and a dozen art galleries. Significantly, three of the hotels were situated in *puri*, and the fourth, built on the site of Walter Spies's house, belonged to the lord of Ubud (who admitted that it was largely thanks to the revenues earned by his hotel that he was able to maintain the numerous pavilions in his *puri* and to sponsor the incessant ceremonies incumbent upon him — in short, that he could still hold onto his rank and thereby conserve the good repute of the village).

It was in this era that Ubud became a residential resort, catering to two types of clientele: first, tourists on a tour of the island who stayed for a night or two; second, and increasingly, young travelers wishing to encounter the Balinese cultural scene, for whom Ubud represented an ideal contrast to Kuta, a sojourn in the hills after a stay on the beach. It was for this clientele that villagers decided to build homestays in their house compounds — reproducing, in effect, the same movement already described in regard to Kuta, but on a much smaller scale and at a slower pace — while others built bungalows at the edge of the village, generally situated in rice fields that had been drained and dried especially for this purpose.

Some of these young travelers undertook, with more or less perseverance, to become initiated in the arts for which the region was famous, be it music or dance, sculpture or painting. Only too glad to be able to respond to this new demand, well-known artists offered to take foreign students in residence. And the most popular among them made agreements with tour operators who were then able to offer courses of instruction with Balinese artists to a clientele no longer satisfied to bake themselves silly on the beach.

Ubud's specialization as the "village of painters" was born out in the flourishing of art galleries and, more generally, "artshops" — that is, souvenir shops where tourists could find nearly the entire gamut of Balinese arts and handicrafts. And as the vocation of painter spread among the villagers, the commercial middlemen strengthened their grip on the distribution of artworks, despite laudable efforts by the museum to organize the artists in cooperatives. In recent years, there seems to be a growing portion of the painting market that has been captured by Javanese "artists" settled in the area, whose inexpensive canvasses respond more to the taste of foreign visitors.

Tourism in Ubud did not really get under way until 1976, when the region found itself at last supplied with electricity. And it took off fully at the beginning of the 1980s, with the opening of homestays and restaurants, boutiques and galleries, banks and travel agencies along the back streets as soon as they became paved, one after another. Before long, one saw a dissemination of *losmen* and homestays, cottages and bungalows, as far as the neighboring villages of Peliatan, Andong, Pengosekan, Campuan, Penestanan, Sanggingan, Sayan, and Kedewatan. The hotel capacity went from 450 rooms in 1981 to around 2,200 in 1994 (of which 80 were in three starred hotels, the rest being distributed among 350 unstarred hotels and homestays — around 7% of Bali's hotel capacity).

The hotels built in the region are small in scale, rarely surpassing 20 rooms, in keeping with the regulations restricting the construction of large luxury hotels to beach resorts. This disposition has allowed Ubud to conserve until recently the intimate character upon which its image is built, and above all to avoid, to a certain extent, the glaring errors of taste so flagrant in Kuta. But it is certain that the lifting of this restriction will convulse the landscape of the region, and in fact several large hotels are already under construction, to the great distress of lovers of Ubud, who are starting to wonder where they will be able to take refuge from the tourists. Their fears, unfortunately, are only too well founded, to judge by the patent degradation of the area's environment. Besides an extreme commercialism, the visitors are starting to complain about the dirtiness of the place, and especially about the traffic jams, aggravated by the narrowness of the streets and the lack of parking — to the point that the local authorities finally decided in 1994 to remedy the situation for fear of seeing Ubud's image irreparably damaged.

So far, the region's tourism development remains mainly a matter of local initiative, and interference by outsiders is still rare. But these are individual enterprises, with the exception nonetheless of dance performances presented to tourists (27 every week in 1994), that are organized in *seka*, as well as a few painters' cooperatives that are trying, with varying degrees of success, to wrest their works from the grasp of the art dealers. The customary institutions, whether the *banjar* or the *desa adat*, play practically no role, and the communal administration restricts itself to exercising only routine control. Nevertheless, there is one initiative that is interesting in several respects: the creation in 1982, at the instigation of two homestay owners, of a foundation called *Bina Wisata* (literally, "to cultivate tourism") whose aim is to organize villagers involved in tourism, artists and craftsmen included. Its objective, as it is formulated in the foundation's brochure, is to "protect, foster and promote the Balinese culture with the aim of assisting the government to develop cultural tourism in the region of Ubud".

The initial objective of what was to become *Bina Wisata* (also known as Ubud Tourist Information) was, in the spirit of its promoters, rather modest: to persuade Ubud's population of the importance of decorating the streets with greenery. Over the course of several weeks, the project grew from protecting nature to defending the culture — both considered the key touristic assets of the area, in danger of being spoiled by their thoughtless exploitation.

Conceived as a militant enterprise based on voluntary service, the foundation set itself the task of providing information to visitors and inculcating in them a respect for local customs. Its founders appeared very anxious to distinguish Ubud from Kuta, and to this end they issued numerous declarations reminding tourists that they were not at the beach, recommending that they therefore behave properly and dress with modesty if they wanted to feel welcome in the village. Operating from an information office open to the public, *Bina Wisata* has published several maps and a guide to the surrounding region, and for a short time it published a magazine in English (somewhat grandly called the "Ubud Post") giving its readers information on the "cultural events" of the area and urging them to attend "not as tourists but as villagers" — only to warn them "that the religious ceremonies are not tourist attractions and that their participants are not there simply to provide a colorful décor for exotic photographs".

The composition of *Bina Wisata*'s board of directors is a sign of the importance accorded to tourism by the Ubud *puri*, whose members fill the post not only of president, but also of all the "advisors". One cannot help seeing in this endeavor to control tourism a prolongation of the role of patronage that the *puri* traditionally exercised in the village, but which is now in a novel situation where a good number of its members are involved in the tourism industry. The nobility managed to use its network of influence and clients to regain, thanks to tourism, part of the fortune that land reform had taken from them; and with those material gains they once again found the means to fill the ceremonial obligations of their rank. But a prince does not become an entrepreneur with impunity: as the *Satria* accumulate bases of new material power by opening their *puri* to tourists and profiting from the tourism industry, they derogate from their position and consequently risk losing their spiritual power, the "charisma" (*wibawa*) by which they traditionally commanded the respect and obedience of the Balinese.

Be that as it may, Ubud flourished with success during the 1980s. In 1983 — thanks to *Bina Wisata*'s campaign on the importance of their village presenting a neat and pleasing appearance to visitors — Ubud won the coveted title "Best Village of Bali". This competition (*Lomba Desa*) is organized by the Indonesian government with the intention of stimulating the development and modernization of rural villages (19). The choice of Ubud for this distinction was manifestly due to the privileged place it occupies on the island's tourist map, a place it holds mainly because of the region's cultural reputation, although the beauty of its landscape also contributes to this. Capitalizing on the prestigious memory of Walter Spies and a few other artists of lesser importance, Ubud found itself designated by the Balinese authorities as a "storehouse of the arts" (*gudang kesenian*) and henceforth has been presented as the living emblem of tourism with a cultural vocation.

It is revealing that Ubud's tourist image is acclaimed by visitors and Balinese alike. It is current not only among the tourists anxious to distinguish themselves from the

(19) In 1995, Ubud underwent a dramatic face-lift, frankly acknowledging that it has become a town. Sidewalks were laid; the graveyard was spruced up with landscaping; and the market enlarged with new two-story buildings designed in what appears to be a consciously postmodern idiom. The instigation for all this activity comes from the pursuit of the *Adipura* trophy, a national program of village development incentives. Similar in intent to the *Lomba Desa* program but more comprehensive in its requirements, the *Adipura* aims to instill more modern patterns of civic behavior, such as regular trash collection. (One measure that is less likely to be noticed by tourists is the institution of afternoon aerobics for the married women of the *banjar* — a response, perhaps, to the accusation that prosperity is ruining the figures of Balinese women: not only is food abundant, but now that water is piped into the villages, women no longer have to carry buckets of water from the river on their heads. In the Ubud of the 1990s, rich ladies wear sweatsuits and do gymnastics at the *wantilan* - the "town hall").

hordes who frequent the beach resorts, but also among Ubud's inhabitants — ever proud to display its qualities to foreigners — and even among Balinese from other regions, who are generally convinced of the cultural eminence of Ubud. Thus we have here a prime example of a place initially distinguished by Western fantasies and whose promotional image, confirmed by its touristic success, has ended up imposing itself on the local population as a reality (20). Conforming to the image that the Balinese like to give of their culture and of tourism, Ubud is presented as a model resort area, constantly cited as an example of tourism development harmoniously integrated into village life.

In this regard, the Balinese situate Ubud at the opposite pole to Kuta, which from their point of view is perfectly logical since Ubud is inland, upstream, toward the mountains (*kaja*) — associated with the gods and ritual purity — while Kuta is in the lowlands on the coast, downstream, toward the sea (*kelod*), associated with demons and pollution. In this cosmic perspective, it is appropriate that the tourists — who, like the demons, are perceived as stupid, red-faced, hairy, and crude — are for the most part installed by the sea.

(20) A recently published novel sketches an ironic description of the cultural promotion of Ubud through tourism — with the problems that ensued —, in which the village is thinly veiled under the pseudonym of "'Tumbensugih', which is Balinese for nouveau riche" (Darling 1992).

PART TWO

Balinese Culture under the Challenge of Tourism

While tourism is unquestionably responsible for much of Bali's spectacular recent economic growth, and especially for the accelerated physical transformation of the island, the question of its consequences for Balinese society and culture continues to haunt observers, who anxiously ask, "Will Balinese culture survive the impact of tourism?" The answers are emotionally charged and differ sharply. Some accuse tourism of corrupting Balinese culture by selling it off like a piece of common merchandise, while others insist that, to the contrary, the Balinese are perfectly capable of protecting their cultural heritage from whatever assaults it might undergo in the course of thoughtless touristic exploitation.

According to a rumor that is becoming more and more insistent, Bali is ruined — that is, almost... in any case, it's not what it used to be. The authentic traditions that made the island famous in the West have been altered to suit the tourists, the celebrated artistic creativity of the Balinese is a thing of the past, and the religious ceremonies have been turned into commercial shows. In short, the Balinese have let themselves be corrupted by the lure of profit, and everything on the island is for sale. Money has got the upper hand over culture, irreversibly. And although the hordes of tourists have not yet completely submerged the Island of the Gods, it won't be long. Excellent sales slogan for the travel agent dream-peddlers who whisper in your ear: "Hurry and go while there's still time! Next year it may be too late."

Thus an article that appeared in the early 1980s in a travel magazine opened with these words:

> *Bali is losing its soul. This wondrous and luxuriant island of 10,000 temples and a thousand festivals is polluted. It has been struck with a deadly disease: mercantilism. And the offending virus is called international tourism.* (Froment 1981: 75)

Other observers, believing themselves to be better informed, are pleased to reply that this alarmist talk is hardly new. As we have seen, the island of Bali had scarcely been discovered by an avant-garde of travelers and artists in the 1920s before travel accounts began to warn of the imminence of its inevitable ruin. After the war and Indonesia's independence, the few travelers to visit Bali had other reasons to fear the worst, in view of the nationalist zeal of the country's new leaders:

> *This anachronistic relic of the Hindu soul is, after ten centuries, about to lose its exceptional traits. Let us hurry while there is still time, and contemplate it closely before it gives in to the contagion of modern Indonesia.* (Durtain 1956: 21)

After the launching of the New Order, many perceived the Indonesian government's decision to develop mass tourism in Bali as the final knell for Balinese culture. A travel magazine in the 1970s warned:

> *Bali is still only at the dawn of pollution — but it seems imperative to me to sound a cry of alarm because, in reality, the gangrene is already there, ready to devour the marvelous edifice of one of the purest civilizations in the world.* (Millau 1974: 106)

And today — with the airport of Denpasar enlarged to receive even more tourists, and luxury hotels rising in the middle of the rice fields — the prophets of doom find even more reason to worry, as in this excerpt from a recent guidebook to Bali:

> *How much more tourism can the island take? How much more traffic? How many more craft shops? How many more Kutas? How many more jets? The answer is that it never stops, the roads are widened, the hotels multiply, the direct flights increase. Commercialism has crept into every aspect of Balinese life... It is now clear that the unbelievably complex social and religious fabric of the Balinese is at last breaking down under the tourist onslaught.* (Dalton 1990: 35-36)

However, no doubt for fear of dissuading his readers from trying nonetheless to make the journey, the same author adds:

> *If you get away from the commercial strips of Sanur and Kuta, there are still literally hundreds of villages which haven't changed since Covarrubias's book was written in the 1930s.* (Op.cit.: 38)

Thus, to each new generation of visitors, Bali seems to be on the brink of ruin, holding out by a reprieve from the good fairies. And so it is that by being so continuously repeated, this cry of alarm not only loses its edge, but it appears to confer a certain immunity to the Balinese culture. Inasmuch as fear of its imminent destruction continues into the present day, and the fall is thus continuously postponed, this fear gives way to the conviction that the Balinese have survived greater disasters in the course of their history and that consequently their culture has become more resilient than one might think after a hasty observation of the changes that have occurred on the island since the first tourists arrived. Indeed, the Balinese are unanimously credited for their capacity for selective assimilation, for their soundness of judgment in adopting only what is appropriate for them from outside influences and never ceding what is intrinsic to their identity (1).

---

(1) Shortly after her arrival on the island in 1936, Margaret Mead echoed this opinion in her first letter from Bali:

Bali seems to have learned through a couple of thousand years of foreign influences just how to use and how to ignore those influences. Accustomed to an alien aristocracy, accustomed to successive waves of Hinduism, Buddhism, and so on, they let what is alien flow over their heads. (Mead 1977: 161).

This commonplace supports the argument of many observers who maintain that the Balinese have adjusted to the tourist invasion of their island as they have adjusted to other circumstances of their past, that they have been able to make use of the attraction that their cultural traditions hold for foreign visitors without sacrificing their cherished values on the altar of commerce. The following quotation is a clear example of this conviction:

> *Has the tidal wave of tourism sweeping over the East Indies washed away the idyllic culture that enchanted earlier visitors? With its hamburger joints, discotheques and Kentucky Fried Chicken outlets, has Bali succumbed to the gritty homogenization of the modern world? The short — and definitive — answer is: By no means! Beset by invaders for millenniums, the Balinese are responding to the latest incursion, as they have to past incursions, by becoming even more like themselves. The fabric of Balinese society is too strong and too flexible to be rent by easy money.* (Elegant 1987: 9)

How can one make sense of such categorically contradictory opinions? First, one may note that while the responses differ, the question remains the same — whether they are confident or alarmist, all ask in unison whether the Balinese culture is able or not to withstand the impact of tourism. Now this question is not innocent. Beyond the legitimate concern it shows, its formulation rests on certain preconceptions that, if one is not careful, lead to a particular vision of tourism and its implications — that is, that tourism in Bali presents itself as a dilemma: Bali's success as a tourist destination depends on tourists having access to the exotic manifestations of Balinese culture, while the commercial exploitation of these cultural manifestations risks provoking their degradation (Francillon 1990). In short, while tourism is nourished by Balinese culture, it may kill the culture (2).

Confronted with such a dilemma, those charged with managing tourism in Bali have been striving to stimulate its development while at the same time limiting as much as possible its undesirable consequences. We may recall that the colonial authorities had an equivocal attitude towards tourism. While the decision to conserve Bali as a living museum in effect constituted the best tourist promotion, the protection of the Balinese cultural heritage from the fatal attractions of modernity

---

(2) It is precisely in the terms of a dilemma that commentators presented the decision to open Bali to international tourism at the end of the 1960s. As an example, one may refer to the article by Howard Taubman, "The Island of the Gods Faces an Earthly Dilemma", which opens with this question:

> *Will success spoil this remote corner of the globe, which likes to call itself the Isle of the Gods?* (Taubman 1968: 55).

Two decades later, the travel writer Pico Iyer poses the problem raised by tourism in analogous terms:

> *Say Bali, and two things come to mind: tourism and paradise. Both are inalienable features of the island, and also incompatible. For as fast as paradises seduce tourists, tourists reduce paradises... Hardly has a last paradise been discovered than everyone converges on it so fast that it quickly becomes a paradise lost.* (Iyer 1988: 30)

required a strict control of the tourist frequentation of the island.

Some 40 years later, the consultants charged with drawing up the Master Plan faced a similar dilemma: how to develop tourism in Bali in order to fill the coffers of the Indonesian state without in the process ruining Balinese culture, the island's principal tourist attraction? Like their predecessors, they sought to resolve the problem by isolating the Balinese, as much as possible, from the corrupting contact with tourists. It seems, however, that they had no illusions about the effects of their proposed measures, for they recognized that:

> *The actual economic benefits of the operation will go to too small a minority to compensate for the social nuisances caused by the project.* (SCETO 1971: vol.1, p.17)

This pessimistic conclusion was rejected by the World Bank experts charged with revising the Master Plan, who for their part affirmed:

> *Assuming that the negative effects can be controlled, it is expected that the positive effects — in terms of increased employment, incomes and foreign exchange earnings — will result in an overall impact which, on balance, is desirable.* (IBRD/IDA 1974: 25)

As to the recent study of tourism's contribution to the Balinese economy, published by Balinese academics in a work devoted to regional development in Indonesia, the authors prudently dodged the question of the social and cultural effects of tourism by alleging that it did not lie within the expertise of economists:

> *And whether the alleged negative socio-cultural effects of tourism are outweighed by its economic benefits is a question beyond the scope of this chapter.* (Jayasuriya & Nehen 1989: 347)

What is important here is not so much that the views of the World Bank experts contradict those of the SCETO consultants, but that both sides are in agreement with the Balinese economists in considering that an evaluation of the impact of tourism on a receiving society comes down to a compensation of its sociocultural costs by its economic benefits. As long as the problem to be dealt with is formulated in terms of the negative and positive effects of tourism, it can only lead to a cost-benefit analysis, which is expected to be resolved through optimization, by way of a trade-off. Now before even asking whether the benefits of tourism development are greater than its costs, the question remains whether this kind of approach will in fact allow one to understand what is involved in the touristification of a society.

For my part, rather than impale myself on the horns of a dilemma, doing my utmost, like so many others, to determine whether or not the Balinese culture has proved capable of withstanding the impact of tourism, I have set myself the task of trying to understand what this "Balinese culture" is that inspires as much solicitude among the experts as it excites admiration among the tourists. And to do this, I will put into perspective the presentation of their culture that the Balinese offer to tourists and the representation of their culture that they make to themselves when they speak of tourism.

Chapter Four

The Sociocultural Impact of Tourism in Question

When the Indonesian government undertook to rescue the country's economic situation in 1969 with the launching of a program of five-year plans, the promotion of international tourism might have seemed like an obvious solution. At the time, tourism was unanimously recognized as a factor of economic development, particularly for Third World countries, with their wealth of natural and cultural resources. The doctrine of development through tourism was touted as a panacea, but not for long. It soon came under critical fire when it was found that the economic benefits expected from tourism development projects had been over-estimated and that the costs had not been taken into account — be they consequences for the host society or repercussions on the environment. It was then that analysts became preoccupied with the "impacts" of tourism, differentiated as economic, physical and sociocultural according to the sector affected in the receiving milieu.

Concern for the sociocultural impact of tourism — which has arisen progressively among not only researchers but also governments, international organizations and the tourism industry — is generally presented as an appropriate response to the development of international tourism and to its increasingly obvious repercussions on host societies. It is important, however, to ask what such a response implies, because it is not certain that one should necessarily:

- apprehend the consequences of tourism for a society in terms of impacts on a receiving milieu;
- classify these impacts in terms of costs and benefits for the milieu;
- consider the economic impacts as benefits and the sociocultural impacts as costs;
- compensate the sociocultural costs with economic benefits.

I will relocate these questions in the context in which they arose, situating them within a convenient frame of reference provided by two inter-governmental conferences on tourism, held in Rome in 1963 and Manila in 1980. From Rome came the doctrine of tourism as a factor of economic development; Manila was devoted to the priority of tourism's sociocultural aspects over its economic returns. Meanwhile, the question of the sociocultural impact of tourism had been raised, in particular during an international seminar convened in Washington in 1976 under the auspices of the World Bank and UNESCO. We shall see that Bali played an important role there in the way the questions were formulated and in the elaboration of the responses.

1. From the Glorification of International Tourism to its Indictment

International tourism had not always been thought of as a factor of economic development. It was only after WWII that the governments of Western Europe, confronted with the demands of economic reconstruction, became actively engaged in the touristic promotion of their countries, seeing foreign visitors as bearers of precious hard currencies. They were encouraged in this by the International Union of Official Travel Organizations (IUOTO), founded in 1946 as a replacement of the defunct Union Internationale des Organes Officiels de Propagande Touristique, which pushed for the increase of international tourist exchanges. And when the idea of development started to be applied to the countries born of de-colonization — what Alfred Sauvy had recently called the "Third World" — international tourism naturally appeared to be a factor of development (Baretje 1987: 52).

In 1961, the Economic and Social Council of the United Nations decided to hold a conference on international travel and tourism, which took place in Rome in 1963. The resolution formulated at the conclusion of the conference officially affirmed "the fundamental role that tourism plays in national economies and international trade, as well as its social, educational and cultural influence, and the contribution that it can bring to the cause of friendship and understanding between peoples" (United Nations 1963: 3). In the belief that tourism could work in a significant way toward the objectives of the United Nations' "Decade of Development", the resolution recommended that the governments of the Third World countries give priority to tourism development projects, and asked the agencies of the United Nations and other concerned bodies to lend their assistance to these projects.

Tourism as a factor of economic development

The recommendations of the Rome conference and the considerations that motivated them were backed up by a report by Kurt Krapf entitled "Tourism as a Factor of Economic Development" (Krapf 1963). Krapf, a Swiss economist who had been the first tourism expert for the World Bank, had published an article two years earlier in which he presented international tourism as an aid to developing countries, calling on tourism experts to promote the idea that tourism was particularly suited "to start up and accelerate the process of economic growth" (Krapf 1961: 88). As it was exposed by Krapf, the thesis of development through tourism is based on a two-fold argument.

Starting with the fact that most rich countries spend more than they earn on travel, Krapf infers that the more developed a country is, the more its citizens tend to spend their earnings on travel outside the country. And since their trips are generally to less prosperous countries, their expenditures contribute to redressing the deficit in the latter's balance of payments. In these conditions, international tourism appears as a mechanism that could help correct the endemic imbalance of terms of trade suffered by the Third World, by distributing in the regions that receive tourists the surplus wealth of the countries that emit tourists. Moreover, by financing the receiving countries' import of goods and services, the income generated by tourism contributes to the expansion of international exchanges and finally to the economic growth of the emitting countries themselves:

> *Among all economic activities, tourism is without doubt that which is likely, through the expenditures of foreign tourists, to procure most quickly for the countries in question the foreign currency necessary for the import of consumer goods and for investment.* (Krapf 1961:87)

In addition, tourism also capitalizes on resources, which developing countries have in abundance, be they riches created by nature and the climate or those bequeathed by their history and civilization:

> *Without the foreign tourists, all these riches would lie fallow, they could not be exploited and the country would miss a unique opportunity* to help itself.
> (Krapf 1961: 87 [emphasized in the text])

This last argument was developed by UNESCO, which presented a report at the Rome conference on "The Cultural Factors in Tourism". Besides the usual declarations about the role of tourism as a medium of understanding, peace and co-operation among nations, the report emphasized the importance of a country's natural and cultural heritage in its economic development and thus called on governments to preserve and promote their heritage.

The capitalization of a cultural heritage for touristic ends was endorsed by the United Nations Conference on Trade and Development (UNCTAD 1967), and its consequences were theorized by the Italian economist Alberto Sessa in a study commissioned by UNESCO (Sessa 1970). For this author, insofar as tourism allows a country's cultural heritage to be introduced into the economic circuit, it contributes to its conservation by providing the motivation and means necessary for its preservation and development. Reciprocally, by regenerating a country's cultural heritage, tourism contributes to the cultural enrichment of its visitors by giving them access to traditional forms of artistic expression — and these, according to Sessa, have a special allure for the citizens of developed countries, whose own cultural traditions have been sapped by industrialization. In this perspective, international tourism leads to a double flow of exchange — of economic values toward the countries receiving tourists, and of cultural values toward the countries emitting tourists. Thus, Sessa writes:

> *Culture and the tourism economy, instead of remaining in opposition, derive a reciprocal advantage from each other.* (Sessa 1970: 117)

To conclude this short review, the thesis of the convergence of interests between culture and economy on the one hand and between developed and under-developed countries on the other — with international tourism as the wonder-working interface — indeed appears to be the keystone of the doctrine issuing from the Rome conference. This doctrine conceives international tourism as the adjusting of a supply to a demand. It makes the growth of international tourism dependent on a demand registered in developed countries, whose determinants are perceived as consequences of economic growth: industrialization and urbanization give rise to a demand for leisure and travel, which can be satisfied thanks to the lower transportation costs and the greater amount of leisure time permitted by technical progress and labor productivity (Lanfant 1972; Picard 1980). And if under-developed countries want to benefit from tourist expenditures, they must offer tourist products that correspond to the demands expressed on the market. Thus, the idea is that as long as the supply offered by the receiving countries responds to the demand of the emitting countries, the wealth of the rich nations will flow to the poorer ones through some system of communicating vessels that will gradually eliminate the initial difference in their standards of living (Lanfant 1980a, 1980b).

The question of the impacts of tourism

In the years following the Rome conference, a vast campaign was directed at the Third World countries, encouraging them to open their borders to tourists and to foreign investors, conceding to the latter tax breaks and financial guarantees. Many countries ventured into tourism enthusiastically, and large projects got under way with technical and financial assistance from the United Nations Development Program and the World Bank. The United Nations proclaimed 1967 the "Year of International Tourism"; the World Bank opened a Tourism Project Department in 1969; and UNCTAD published its recommendations on tourism policy aimed at the governments of developing countries (UNCTAD 1971).

Yet, although international tourism has seen spectacular growth since the 1960s, the unconditional exaltation of tourism as a factor of economic development was short-lived. Even before the world recession following the rise of oil prices in 1973–74, the hopes aroused by the Decade of Development proved unfounded. When the situation was reassessed, international tourism, far from being what a World Bank expert had previously called "the very engine of development", was, to the contrary, considered by some observers to be a transfer of the riches of countries receiving tourists toward those emitting them — a form of imperialism perpetuating the dependence of the Third World on the industrialized nations (Nash 1989). At the same time, the idea that tourism would help assure the conservation of cultural heritages by inscribing them into the economic circuit was vehemently challenged by a number of observers, who denounced the damage wrought by the commercialization of indigenous cultural traditions converted into tourist attractions (Turner & Ash 1975).

Over the course of the 1970s one thus sees a refutation of the theory of complementary interests — between developed and under-developed countries on the one hand, and between cultural and economic values on the other — that was the crux of the doctrine of development through tourism. By this time, most analysts agreed that the economic benefits imputed to tourism had been greatly over-estimated and that its sociocultural costs, as well as its repercussions on the environment, had been neglected. After reviewing the relevant literature, the authors of a study on the impacts of tourism published in the early 1980s came to this conclusion:

From the evidence which has been presented it is clear that the economic impacts of tourism are largely beneficial, the social impacts are mainly undesirable, and the environmental impacts are mixed. (Mathieson & Wall 1982: 185)

Why this long overdue attention to the costs of tourism? Although there is some genuine concern about the benefits of international tourism to the host societies, the main issue is the interests of the tourism industry — for after a promising take-off, the growing competition between destinations, the rise of marginal costs, the overloading of tourist infrastructures and the degradation of the resort areas' environment began to worry the professionals. As a well-known expert writes:

The overwhelming focus on the economic aspects of tourism may have sufficed, until tourism became increasingly competitive during the world economic recession, and the realization dawned that unless one could maintain the quality of the tourist experience, and of the tourism destination environment, *the industry would be placed at risk in terms of its long-life dimensions.* (Travis 1984: 22 [emphasized in the text])

Thus a cry of alarm rings out:

Tourism can destroy tourism. Tourism as a user of resources, can be a resource destroyer, and through destroying the resources, which give rise to it, make the resource-based tourism shortlived. Impacts, benefits and costs can and should therefore be evaluated in advance of tourism development. (Travis 1982: 257)

It is clear, then, that the question of the impacts of tourism arose when the tourism industry found itself confronted with the problem of sustainable development: how to develop tourism without exhausting the resources it exploits, whether they be natural or cultural?

2. The problematic of the sociocultural impact of tourism

Concern about the impacts of tourism did not arise only within the tourism industry. As of the early 1960s, a few anthropologists and sociologists were interested in the sociocultural changes brought about by tourism (Nuñez 1963; Forster 1964). It was only in 1974, however, that the American Anthropological Association devoted its annual meeting to the theme of "Tourism and Culture Change", with the declared intention of having tourism recognized as a legitimate object of anthropological study by stimulating research on its impacts in host societies (Smith 1989). Around the same time, two particularly sensitive island regions — the Pacific and the Caribbean — were the object of a series of conferences concerning the impacts of international tourism. But it is primarily the joint UNESCO/IBRD "Seminar on the Social and Cultural Impacts of Tourism", held in 1976 in Washington, that concerns us here — not because of the particular interest of its results (which are hardly different from those of the conferences that preceded it), but because of the breadth of its perspectives and the repercussions caused by its institutional setting, which henceforth form a point of reference for the problematic of the sociocultural impact of tourism (de Kadt 1979).

The task put to the participants invited to the Washington seminar — experts and academics (for the most part, anthropologists, sociologists and economists) from countries emitting tourists as well as those receiving tourists — was formulated as follows:

- to identify the different impacts of tourism on the receiving regions;
- to distinguish the beneficial impacts from the harmful impacts for those regions;
- and finally, to maximize the positive impacts while minimizing the negative impacts.

The cost-benefit analysis

The terms of reference elaborated by the World Bank and UNESCO reveal an implicit representation, not only of the results produced from installing tourism infrastructures in a region, but even more so of the way societies are thought to be affected by their opening to international tourism. It would seem that according to the organizers of the seminar, tourism is an enterprise that is potentially beneficial in regard to its economic returns, but whose extra-economic repercussions on the receiving milieu must be treated as costs that must be accounted for in an overall evaluation of its consequences. Hence the problem that the experts were called upon to resolve: *how to maximize the economic benefits of tourism for the receiving country while minimizing the sociocultural costs for the local population?*

Now, if we concede that policy-makers for a tourism development project are inclined to treat its social and cultural implications as costs, we must be aware that this approach bears heavy consequences for analysts, in that it implies reducing qualitative matters to quantitative elements, for it means that the effects not yet taken into account in the economic calculation — that which the economist calls "externalities" — be "internalized" in such a manner as to permit allocating a monetary value to the extra-economic damages imputed to touristic activity. This internalization procedure necessarily presupposes that any damage caused by an economic activity can, by definition, be compensated for by an equivalent gain in monetary value, the only condition being that one can pay the price. Such an approach is appealing because of the implicit fairness of the idea, and it offers the considerable advantage of soothing the conscience of the economist who employs it, while permitting the authorities responsible for the project to justify their decisions by the scientific rigor of the information on which they are based.

But this enlargement of the jurisdiction of economic analysis is based on the idea that rates of equivalence between heterogeneous "goods" actually exist, even before they are taken into account by the market and transformed into exchangeable commodities. In other words, the premise governing this operation is that of the commensurability of goods, which authorizes the reduction of qualitatively different values to a single monetary value. The result is that the integration of the sociocultural impact of tourism and of its economic impact in a reckoning of general optimization — willingly presented by its promoters as a subordination of economic criteria to policy choices — in fact indicates a growing encroachment of economic rationalization, not only in policy-making but even in scientific research.

This encroachment is empirically detectable by means of a discourse analysis. If one applies this analysis to the proceedings of the seminar, one discovers that there is a "conceptual scheme" operating behind all the papers presented — despite the great variety of questions posed and positions defended by different contributors, whether from countries emitting tourists or receiving them — and this conceptual scheme shapes the signifying structure of their discourses. In other words, all the discourses analyzed are structured by the same system of oppositions:

- the opposition between under-developed countries receiving tourists and developed countries emitting tourists (and, associated with the latter, the international tourism industry, its agents and apparatus) — that is, an *opposition between local societies and international tourism expressed in terms of "inside" and "outside"*;
- the opposition between sociocultural costs and economic benefits, which is in effect reduced to an *opposition between cultural values and economic values.*

Finally, and most significantly, the treatment of these oppositions proceeds uniformly along the same strategy, which consists in reducing the resolution of the conflicts engendered by the touristification of a society to the problem of maximizing certain fixed objectives. And this, in the end, rests on *the capacity of touristic exchanges to open the "inside" toward the "outside" by permitting the transmutation of cultural values into economic values* (1).

A market approach to international tourism

If one compares this analysis of the Washington seminar to the doctrine that emerged from the Rome conference, one can see that the problematic of the sociocultural impact of tourism has actually challenged the theory of tourism as a factor of economic development. The premise of a convergence of interests between underdeveloped and developed countries, ensured by the conversion of cultural values into economic ones, has in fact disappeared: where there reigned a pre-established harmony between two poles, there is now opposition. But the reassessment of tourism goes no further than this, since the poles remain the same and the frame of reference has not changed. The resolution of oppositions by the problematic of impact shows that we are still dealing with the same conceptual scheme, framing a market approach to international tourism, in which the two sides of the tourist exchange are treated as a supply and a demand.

This approach has two defects. First, the very fact of speaking of the "impact" of tourism infers a ballistic vision that leads to perceiving the so-called "host" society as a target struck by a projectile, as a "receiving milieu", inert and undifferentiated,

---

(1) The reader interested in the questions raised here may refer to the analysis of the proceedings of the Washington seminar that URESTI undertook for UNESCO's Human Settlements and Socio-Cultural Environment Division (Picard 1979).

passively subjected to external factors of change that can be financially accounted for. In this perspective, the receiving society is treated as a blank space where a demand is projected onto a supply — that is, as a space to be developed according to a foreign logic, thus stripping it of its distinctiveness by denying it any capacity for initiative.

Second, the problematic of impact assigns to "sociocultural" matters a residual status, with this peculiarity: that, instead of the sociocultural encompassing the cultural, here the cultural actually subsumes the sociocultural. When framing the problem this way, that which is "cultural" is first of all "non-economic" — simultaneously, that which must be quantified so that it may be accounted for in the cost-benefit analysis as a cost to be compensated for by a superior economic benefit, and that which must be monetarized by incorporating it into the tourist product. Thus culture is transformed from "heritage" into "capital". The result is that as economic rationalization encroaches on the discourse, economic value seizes its referent: the internalizing of the sociocultural costs in calculating optimization signals the inscription of the receiving society's culture into the monetary circuit as a tourist product. And whether seen as a cost to be reduced or as a capital to be maximized, culture is never defined here as a reality in itself, but always in relation to the economic: as a potential factor awaiting its instrumentalization by tourism, a tourist resource, a raw material to be exploited with care if it is not to lose its exchange value.

Thus it emerges from the analysis of the Washington seminar that a double determination weighs on the study of the local implications of international tourism: one epistemological, the other of an institutional character. Not only is research subject to the imperatives of policy, in the sense that one expects the researcher to assume as his own an objective of social control that will allow the tourist product to be more finely tuned to the demands of the international market, but, more deeply, if this subjection can remain effective — and this is often without the researcher's knowledge — it is because it is embedded in a coercive conceptual scheme that at once frames the problematic and obscures the issues involved in the touristification of societies.

If it is indeed necessary to refute the problematic of impact, it is because it is part and parcel of the explanatory model propagated by international tourism and thus it participates in the very phenomenon it studies. The analysis of the Washington seminar has allowed us to demonstrate that international tourism — to the extent that it is invested with economic rationality and that it is sustained by a marketing objective — bears an explication of social facts that is skewed by a coercive logic. In these conditions, one may well ask what really happens when a society embarks on a career of international tourism — whether, in receiving tourists, a society is engaged not only in building hotels and setting up tourist services, but also, and more importantly, if it is not consequently drawn into borrowing the explanatory model which enables it to account for that which is happening to it.

From this perspective, we realize that it is no longer possible to consider the promotion of international tourism as a movement coming from outside, since the explanatory model which allows international tourism to justify itself is already inside the societies where its apparatus implants itself. And if this is indeed the case, one must question this conceptual borrowing, not only in terms of the perception local authorities have of tourism and its issues, but also, and above all, in terms of the representation they come to form of their own society once it has become a tourist product for sale on the international market.

Reformulating the problematic of the sociocultural impact of tourism

Since the beginning of the 1980s, there have been insistent calls to "reformulate the problematic of the sociocultural impact of tourism", to borrow the title of an article by the French sociologist Jean-Maurice Thurot (1981). In fact, many researchers presently reject both the conception of international tourism as an external factor of change and the assessment of its local implications in terms of costs and benefits (Allcock 1989; Barnier 1983; Bruner 1989; Cohen 1979; Crick 1989; Nash 1981; Wood 1980). Actively involved in these debates, the Unité de Recherche en Sociologie du Tourisme International organized an international seminar at Marly-le-Roi in 1986, bringing researchers together to take a fresh look at the issues ten years after the Washington seminar (2). Was the epistemological obstacle of the problematic of impact on the way to being resolved?

Attempts to overcome the obstacle took place mainly in two directions. In reaction to the problematic of impact, which reduced the receiving milieu to nothing more than a venue for outside forces, we first witnessed attempts to restore to this locale a certain capacity for initiative. For the researchers engaged in this direction, this meant promoting the observed milieu to the status of "local society" by paying attention to its voice — that is, by examining the perceptions, opinions and attitudes of the native population, as well as local initiatives to appropriate the tourism industry and its benefits, while insisting on the necessity of adapting the concepts and methods to the particularities of the society under scrutiny. But by emphasizing the specifics of the host milieu, the localized approach leads to apprehending the relations between tourism and society in terms of a dichotomy between "the inside" (local society) and "the outside" (international tourism) — the same terms that structure the problematic of impact. As a result, the proponents of this return to the "local" end up reversing the perspective, moving the point of view from the outside to the inside, without, however, breaking with the inside-outside frame of observation.

If, therefore, one admits that the common defect of the problematic of impact and of the localized approach resides in the bisecting of their object, one is led to look for a way out of this impasse by studying the relationship of tourism and society in terms of reciprocal interaction. In other words, one will look at not only what international tourism does to a society but also what this particular society makes of tourism. Thus an increasing number of researchers address the observable interactions between the visitors and their hosts. Promising as this may appear for the reciprocity

(2) The papers presented at the seminar at Marly were published in two special issues of the journal *Problems of Tourism*, under the title *L'"impact social et culturel du tourisme international" en question: réponses interdisciplinaires* (URESTI 1987).

of perspectives that it instates, this approach overlooks the fact that the implications of tourism do not necessarily occur in the actual encounter between the tourists and the local population. But more seriously, it remains locked in the conceptual scheme that structures the problematic of impact, in that it tends to treat the interaction in the fixed terms of an inside and an outside.

The proceedings of the Marly seminar thus confirm that the dichotomy between what is conceived as being inside and what is seen as coming from outside remains the major obstacle to understanding the processes and issues of the touristification of societies. And this means that we must push critical assessment further if we want to break out of the harness of the dominant frame of observation and the radiocentric model on which it is based. We will then be able to apprehend tourism and society in the same process. And in order to do this, rather than speak of tourism and its impacts on a receiving milieu, it would be preferable to speak henceforth of *touristification* to designate the process by which a society becomes a tourist product.

3. In search of a "good" tourism

At the same time as it was being criticized by researchers, the problematic of impact led to the quest for a tourism whose benefits would override its costs. This quest for a "good" tourism — that is, a formula of tourism development that would genuinely benefit not only the host society but tourists as well, without forgetting, of course, the interests of the international tourism industry — would become the pet project of the World Tourism Organization (WTO).

During the Rome conference, the United Nations had recognized the International Union of Official Travel Organizations (IUOTO) — a non-governmental organization of a technical character — as their principal instrument for the promotion of tourism. The rapid expansion of international tourism trade eventually made it necessary to create an organization vested with the authority to treat problems of tourism at a governmental level. This was done in 1975 with the transformation of the IUOTO into the World Tourism Organization, an inter-governmental organization with a global vocation. The reinforcement of the WTO's authority was accompanied by broader membership — host countries of the Third World were now in the majority — and was expressed in a radical doctrinal change, clearly manifested at the World Tourism Conference held in Manila in 1980. At the conclusion of this conference, an official declaration proclaimed that henceforth priority should be given to the social, cultural and educational aspects of tourism over its economic aspects:

> *Tourism acquired, beyond its well-known quantitative dimensions, a cultural and moral dimension that should be promoted and protected against the negative distortions due to economic factors.* (WTO 1980: art. 14)

Culture as a factor of tourism development

This change in priorities had been heralded by a rapprochement between the World Tourism Organization and UNESCO. Present at the Rome Conference, UNESCO was interested in tourism because of the economic rationale it provided for financing the preservation of cultural heritages. Sometime later, the WTO urged its member states to adhere to the "International Convention Concerning the Protection of the World Natural and Cultural Heritage", adopted at the initiative of UNESCO in 1972, and it co-signed the "Charter of Cultural Tourism" elaborated in 1976 by the International Council on Monuments and Sites (ICOMOS). Then an agreement was signed in 1978 between the Secretary General of the WTO and the Director General of UNESCO stating that they were to be consulted on questions concerning the promotion of cultural tourism, the protection of the cultural and natural world heritage, and the conducting of studies on the sociocultural repercussions of tourism. And when the "World Conference on Cultural Policies" met in Mexico in 1982, UNESCO urged its member states:

> *... to take measures to improve the conditions of international cultural tourism and to promote and protect the objects of cultural tourism.* (UNESCO 1982: 97)

What conception of the relation between tourism and culture ensued from the cooperation between the WTO and UNESCO? In this regard, one cannot help being struck by the insistence placed on the recognition and protection of "cultural heritages" and "cultural identities" at the Conferences of Manila and Mexico. We may read in the Mexico Declaration:

> All cultures are part of the common heritage of humanity... *One must recognize the equal dignity of all cultures and the right of every people and every cultural community to affirm, preserve, and command respect for their cultural identity.* (UNESCO 1982: art. 4 & 9 [emphasis added])

— while the Manila Declaration states that:

> All touristic resources belong to the heritage of humanity. *The national communities and the entire international community must make the necessary efforts for their preservation.* (WTO 1980: art. 18 [emphasis added])

Looking at these passages side by side allows us to understand why the identity and cultural heritage of the world's peoples arouse such solicitude. If cultures — all cultures — belong to the common heritage of humanity, it is in the sense that they constitute touristic resources, and it is in this capacity that humanity, and each national community in particular, must guarantee their preservation. Consequently, the WTO, after consultation with UNESCO, established governing principles for the elaboration of cultural and tourism policies for each country, insisting on the need to integrate cultural and touristic objectives in the national development policy. In 1985, in a report on the "Safeguarding and promotion of culture as a factor of tourism development", the Secretary General of the WTO emphasized:

... that the duty of tourism organizations is not limited to exploiting the natural and cultural heritage for touristic ends, to diffusing information about it and ensuring its promotion, but that it is incumbent upon them as well to actively participate in the protection and restoration of this heritage, as well as to take measures aimed at reducing to a minimum the negative effects that tend to accompany its promotion for touristic ends. (WTO 1985: 13)

To this end, the Secretary General's report proposed the implementation of a "well-conceived cultural tourism",

... based on a close co-operation between the cultural and touristic spheres, that can only engender positive effects and be a source of mutual advantage for both sectors. (WTO 1985: 26)

For a cultural tourism integrated into the host society

To know more precisely what a "well-conceived cultural tourism" might be, one must refer to the studies carried out by the WTO in consultation with UNESCO (WTO 1979, 1981), in which one may read in particular that:

... tourism contributes to saving all those cultural values that have a touristic value. (WTO 1979: 19)

Indeed, if we admit that tourism safeguards those cultural values that have a touristic value, it follows logically that the cultural values one wants to safeguard should acquire touristic value. Once these premises are admitted, cultural tourism appears then as the ideal solution in that it confers a touristic value to manifestations of the indigenous culture. But for cultural tourism to accomplish its mission, it needs the active participation of the tourists as well as that of the local population, and they must establish relationships that are appropriate between hosts and guests. Thus we see the simultaneous promotion by the World Tourism Organization:

- of a form of touristic practice: an active tourism, interested in the society visited, in its inhabitants and in their cultural traditions, as opposed to a passive tourism oriented toward consumption and leisure. This new tourism practice corresponds to a new approach to cultural heritage, "marked by the transition from a passive conception of protection of the heritage to a dynamic conception of promoting it for multiple aims which may be educational, utilitarian, economic" (WTO 1981: 14);
- of a form of tourism planning: a tourism integrated into the host society and managed by the local population, as opposed to an enclave tourism "symbol of an ethnocentric and colonialist conception of tourism, omnipresent evidence for the local populations of another world arrogantly affirming its style, its power, its superiority" (WTO 1981: 42).

This is a flagrant reversal of opinion since the Rome conference. The recommendations of the conference proposed that tourism facilities be concentrated rather than dispersed, and this was the strategy followed by the World Bank — as may be seen, for example, in the directives of the Bali Tourism Development Master Plan. This initially dominant choice of a tourist complex "enclaved" in the host society was in keeping with the conception of international tourism prevalent at the time that saw the tourism sector of under-developed countries as a foreign body encysted onto the national territory, as if the local society could not really be affected by an activity taking place on its edges. This formula was progressively challenged in favor of a conception of tourism development "integrated" into the host society as the vision of international tourism grew larger and its impacts on the host society attracted more attention. The significance of this opposition, which was essentially spatial in the beginning, became considerably greater by acquiring a strong ideological charge (Cazes 1982).

In short, a *bad tourism*, introverted and indifferent to its environment, had now to be replaced with a *good tourism*, interested in the particularities of the place and able to fuse harmoniously with the host society. This amounts to trying to purge tourism of all possible ills — specifically, those revealed by a computation of the sociocultural costs. By projecting all the evil onto a "bad object" and doing away with it, that leaves only what is "good", and tourism is thereby absolved. In effect, by integrating tourism development into the host society — thereby denying the opposition between international tourism and local societies demonstrated in Washington — the convergence of interests proclaimed in Rome is restored.

This good tourism, therefore, is *cultural tourism*, which is presented by the experts of the World Tourism Organization as conducive to a *cultural renaissance* in the host societies in that it stimulates in local populations a pride and interest in their traditions, threatened with obsolescence by modernization. To prevent the lowering of quality and loss of authenticity caused by the commercialization of local cultural traditions, they recommend encouraging indigenous artists to create for their own society rather than for tourist consumption. The tourists should be invited to share the experience of these local artistic creations but should not constitute the reason for their existence. In other words, host societies should offer visitors authentic cultural performances, rather than fabricate artificial tourist attractions for them.

In this way, the participation of tourists in these cultural performances, while being an occasion for a culturally enriching experience for them, should also be a chance for the local population to affirm their cultural identity by presenting it to foreign visitors, whose financial contribution can be used for the upkeep of their traditions. Thus, by reinforcing the relations between touristic practice and local cultural manifestations, tourism — far from degrading the culture — contributes to safeguarding the culture precisely to the extent that it benefits from it.

4. Can the Balinese profit from tourism without losing their culture?

As it turns out, Bali occupies a prominent place in this argument. Looking over the literature on the sociocultural impact of tourism, one finds that for most observers, the island of Bali is a model example of this "well-conceived cultural tourism" that the World Tourism Organization dreams of — a destination where tourism has contributed to the preservation and regeneration of the indigenous cultural heritage to the extent that one could speak of a cultural renaissance (3). Nonetheless, in spite of this large convergence of favorable opinions, there is no lack of authors who cite Bali among the destinations where tourism has corrupted the indigenous culture (4).

These disagreements should suffice to sow some doubt, not only about the pertinence of the criteria of analysis employed by these different authors, but also about the soundness of the ethnographic or sociological foundations of the works to which they refer. A careful reading of these papers reveals that most of the opinions that find tourism beneficial for Balinese society and its culture are based on two references, whose authors, however old their works, continue to be cited as authorities in the literature on "the sociocultural impact of tourism". These references are the paper presented in 1974 by Philip McKean at the meeting of the American Anthropological Association (McKean 1989) and that presented in 1976 by Raymond Noronha at the Washington seminar (Noronha 1979).

Cultural commoditization

The first reaction to the Indonesian government's decision to develop international tourism in Bali came from an American observer familiar with Southeast Asia, Willard Hanna, who in 1972 published a fiery article on the ravages of tourism on the island (Hanna 1972). He posed the problem in the same terms as the authors of the Master Plan: can the Balinese profit from tourism without losing their culture?

> *How to exploit the tourist potential of the Island of Bali for the benefit of the culturally rich but economically poor Balinese, without at the same time inducing vulgarity or commercialization... In other words, the intent is to maximize the benefits (profits) and minimize the detriments ("social and cultural pollution") and thus preserve Balinese values by the acquisition of desperately needed foreign valuta.*
> (Hanna 1972: 1)

His response states clearly that, to him, the problem is nowhere near being resolved, and that if tourism in Bali might be seen as a "commercial triumph", it is, on the other hand, a "cultural tragedy". He sees proof of this in the already noticeable transformations in Balinese art forms, be they painting and sculpture converted into commodities and vulgar souvenirs, or the performing arts shortened and simplified

(3) This is what emerges especially from the Washington seminar, where no less than three of the 22 papers presented were about Bali, the only region treated by several participants, of which one was a Balinese. Among the numerous laudatory references to Bali we may mention Cohen 1988: 382; Dogan 1989: 223–224; Macnaught 1982: 373–374; Travis 1984: 24; Turner & Ash 1975: 155–160.

(4) Among the critical references to Bali we note Crandall 1987: 376; van Doorn 1989: 82; Greenwood 1989: 173; O'Grady 1981: 25–34; Pizam & Milman 1984: 12.

for foreign audiences. But above all, he evokes the near future when the Balinese will no longer be able to tell the difference between the authentic manifestations of their artistic traditions and their commercial by-products intended for the tourist market. And he predicts that the day will soon come when even the tourists notice the cultural degradation of Bali and will stop going there.

Contrary to this prediction, tourists continue to flock to Bali in ever greater numbers. This reinforces the alarmist argument; but this argument today is advanced less by researchers than by journalists and travel writers — not to mention tourists or long-term residents, always ready to lament that things are not what they used to be. In fact, there are barely two ethnographers who have taken up the analysis exposed by Willard Hanna on their own account (Francillon 1990; Turnbull 1982). Be that as it may, the accusations against "cultural commoditization" (Greenwood 1989) generally revolve around the following issues:

- the dispossession of the Balinese, whose cultural heritage has become a commodity intended for foreign visitors;
- the falsification of authentic Balinese traditions, which are manipulated to make them conform to the expectations of tourists;
- the profanation of religious ceremonies, by their conversion into commercial performances;
- and finally, a loss of meaning that could sow widespread anomie in the heart of Balinese society.

Cultural involution

While Willard Hanna was giving free rein to his furious disapprobation, Philip McKean, an American anthropologist who studied the development of tourism in Bali in 1970–71, was fine-tuning his arguments in support of a thesis that took the opposite stance: far from destroying Balinese culture, the arrival of a growing number of tourists would have, according to him, the consequence of strengthening the attachment of the Balinese to their cultural traditions (McKean 1973).

McKean begins by challenging the approach adopted by the few anthropologists and sociologists who preceded him in the study of the impacts of tourism on host societies, not without tossing several well-honed barbs along the way at foreign intellectuals — such as Hanna — who panic over the arrival of tourists in Bali. He reproaches his predecessors collectively for a common preconception: the idea that the cultural changes arising from tourism are produced by the intrusion of a superior sociocultural system in a supposedly weaker receiving milieu; that the changes bring about the destruction of the indigenous traditions; and that they lead to cultural uniformity and the disappearance of the inhabitants' ethnic identity.

In pursuit of his argument, McKean examines the capacity of the Balinese to preserve their cultural heritage and to affirm their cultural identity in the face of the tourist invasion of their island. According to him, the tourists' money would revive the interest of the Balinese in a number of their traditions that were in danger of becoming obsolete, while at the same time stimulating their artistic creativity. And above all, the Balinese' sense of identity and pride in their culture would be reinforced by the visitors' admiration. Thus, by becoming the patron of Balinese culture, tourism would contribute to its preservation and even to its renaissance, insofar as it is a source of both profit and prestige for the Balinese (5).

McKean theorized this conclusion with the concept of "cultural involution", freely borrowed from Clifford Geertz (1963), which expresses the following paradox: the Balinese, he tells us, aspire to become modern while at the same time seeking to maintain their cultural traditions, and to do so, they need money; the tourists, who are bearers of modernization, are drawn to Bali essentially by the wealth of its traditions; consequently, for reasons of both cultural conservation and economic necessity, the Balinese cultivate their traditions with a view to procuring the necessary means for their modernization.

Thanks to this process of cultural involution, the modernization of Balinese society may be based not on industrial productions, whose destructive effects on traditional social structures are well known, but on cultural productions, thus permitting the establishment of a post-industrial society based on tourism services. This would have the merit, according to McKean, of consolidating the traditional social ties that ensure the stability of Balinese society. In this perspective:

> *The entertainment, education, and care of international visitors would then pay the Balinese to do what they have learned to do so well for their own satisfaction — perform their arts and religion, their crafts and ceremonials.* (McKean 1973: 35)

If such a result is possible, it is because tourism in Bali is a "cultural tourism", which McKean defines in opposition to "environmental tourism". In environmental tourism, tourists are motivated by the landscape, and the local population remains foreign to the touristic exploitation of their territory, when indeed they are not an obstacle to its development. In cultural tourism, on the other hand, tourists are drawn by the manifestations of the indigenous culture, and the population is the raison d'être of the tourism industry, which could not prosper without its collaboration. Thus, the interaction between tourists and Balinese would consist for the latter in presenting their cultural productions to foreign visitors in anticipation of monetary gain in return. And the transaction can take place only on the condition that both parties find satisfaction — the tourists, who derive a valuable aesthetic experience, and the Balinese, who find the opportunity for a supplementary income.

This interaction is conceptualized by McKean in terms of relations between the "inside" and the "outside". The artistic and religious traditions of the Balinese (the "inside") are judged worthy of interest by the tourists (the "outside"). And it is precisely this interest shown by the tourists for their traditions — by the continuous process of adjustment of the inside to the demands and expectations of the outside

(5) Several authors have taken up McKean's analysis on their own account, particularly Lansing (1974) and McTaggart (1980).

that it created in the first place — that will reassure the Balinese in their self-confidence and sense of identity, while sharpening their artistic talents:

> *The "outside" evaluation provides reinforcement to the "inside", both economic and aesthetic.* (McKean 1973: 277)

To support his demonstration, McKean takes up the conception of culture as "performance", elaborated by Milton Singer (1972) in the wake of Robert Redfield. He considers the various manifestations of Balinese culture as "cultural performances", which may be distinguished in terms of the different audiences for which they are intended, respectively the gods, the Balinese and the tourists. According to McKean, belief in the presence of divine spectators at performances intended for the Balinese is a guarantee of the preservation of their traditional values, while those presented for tourists have only a commercial intention and are devoid of any religious significance. In these conditions, the presence of a foreign audience — instead of diminishing the importance or the quality of performances destined for divine and Balinese audiences — to the contrary, encourages more care and refinement, thanks to the profits from commercial performances. Thus the traditional performances confer an authentic character to tourist performances, while the latter procure for the former a material contribution in return.

And if this is so, it is because, far from being tempted to replace their gods with tourists, the Balinese have only added another audience to their traditional cultural performances. The result is that today the tourists' money pays the Balinese to do what they have always done — to express their culture — and it permits them to devote themselves to it entirely. McKean concludes from this that the Balinese' presentation of their culture to tourists, by reflecting a magnified image of themselves, helps to sharpen their awareness of their cultural identity, and thereby also to consolidate their position in the Indonesian nation:

> *The maintenance of self-respect through "presentation of culture" may be one of the primary factors in continued Balinese existence as a unique cultural entity.* (McKean 1989: 128) (6)

Boundary maintenance

McKean's argument had considerable repercussions, both in Bali and beyond. In the realm of academic literature on the "sociocultural impact of tourism", it contributed largely, as we have seen, to making Bali an exemplary model of successful cultural tourism. Perhaps of even greater consequence is the fact that, as we shall see, McKean's conclusions appeared just in time to support the tourism doctrine elaborated by the Balinese authorities.

Beyond its repercussions, the theory of cultural involution presents the significant

(6) In the epilogue added to the 1989 edition of *Hosts and Guests*, McKean forcefully reasserts the accuracy of his earlier predictions.

advantage of freeing us of the speculative pitfall of cultural "pollution" versus "renaissance", and points us toward an analysis that can be tested empirically. McKean's demonstration stakes its validity on the capacity of the Balinese to maintain an explicit distinction between the cultural performances intended for their own use and those created specially for their foreign visitors. This is what he acknowledges in the conclusion of his thesis, when he affirms that tourism would finally reassure the Balinese in their sense of "boundary maintenance" (7) between what they produce for themselves and what they produce for their visitors:

> *Acknowledging that there is "leakage" across the boundaries between the realms, I nevertheless have argued that for a number of social, religious, and economic reasons the Balinese are likely to keep the realms distinct in terms of content, though interrelated in terms of structure»* (McKean 1973: 287) (8)

It is here that McKean's demonstration is opposed to Hanna's argument. For Hanna, Balinese culture became a tourist commodity to the extent that the Balinese have come to confuse the attractions they sell to tourists with their authentic cultural traditions — that is, they are no longer able to differentiate between what belongs to culture and what pertains to tourism.

Whatever the case may be, we may note that however much their conclusions differ, Hanna and McKean both see the relationship between tourism and culture as a transaction between the indigenous population and foreigners, bearers respectively of cultural and economic values. Their common frame of reference is structured by the relation between international tourism (whose attributes are "the outside" and "the economic") and the local society (whose attributes are "the inside" and "the cultural"). What puts them into opposition, making their diagnostics irreconcilable, are the consequences that they attribute to the transaction between tourists and Balinese:

- for Hanna, a *substitution* of economic values for cultural values, of a foreign public for an indigenous public, a substitution that he perceives as a fatal process;
- for McKean, an *adjunction* of economic values to cultural values, of a foreign public to the indigenous public, an adjunction conceived as a revitalizing process.

If Philip McKean established Bali's reputation as an exemplary model of successful cultural tourism, it was Raymond Noronha — the anthropologist,

---

(7) The expression "boundary maintenance" is taken from Fredrik Barth (1969). For this author, it is the ethnic boundary that defines the group, not the cultural stuff that it encloses:

> *When defined as an ascriptive and exclusive group, the nature of continuity of ethnic units is clear: it depends on the maintenance of a boundary.* (Barth 1969: 14)

(8) Another argument often voiced by foreign observers along similar lines concerns the "away-ness" of the Balinese, the apparent "indifference" they display toward foreigners intruding into their world, indeed their striking ability to go about their own business as if they were not aware of being the object of the tourist gaze.

consultant to the World Bank and, for a time, "cultural advisor" for the Bali Tourism Development Board — who made use of the lessons of McKean's thesis by extracting the gist of his argument in such a way as to make it a criterion that could be applied to the analysis of other tourist destinations.

Why, asks Noronha, "has tourism not destroyed Balinese culture?" It is, he tells us, because the Balinese have learned to distinguish their cultural performances in terms of the public for which they are intended, with the result that the meaning of a Balinese cultural performance is in no way affected by its presentation to tourists:

> *Although at times the dividing line between the two types is thin, the independence of meanings has permitted traditional arts to maintain both their quality and purpose without being radically affected by the advent of tourism. In fact, the income gained from a tourist performance and sale of crafts is channeled back to strengthen the religious and temporal bonds that are the sources of strength for the Balinese: the* banjar *and the village temples. Tourism has thus affirmed these most important ties which link the past with the present and the future and which form the* boundaries *through which no outsider can penetrate.* (Noronha 1979: 201-202 [emphasis added])

A number of observers have followed Noronha's example and evaluate the integrity of a culture faced with the challenge of tourism by this criterion: are the cultural performances still held, and held meaningful, without tourists? (Cohen 1988; 382; Goldberg 1983: 492; Graburn 1984: 399; Greenwood 1982: 28; Macnaught 1982: 373, 376; McTaggart 1980: 464) (9). For example, the Swiss sociologist Jean-Luc Maurer conceived four criteria for evaluating the sociocultural impact of tourism on a host society, among which figures predominantly what he calls its "degree of cultural functionality" — that is, its capacity to differentiate between the sacred and the profane. Applying this criterion to Balinese society, he sees the emergence of two distinct and juxtaposed spheres of cultural production — one intended specifically for internal consumption, the other essentially for external consumption. This leads him to conclude that:

(9) In an article judiciously entitled "Unbounded Ethnicity", Jafar Jafari characterizes tourists as an ethnic group with an unusual propensity for crossing boundaries. As a result, the expansion of international tourism tends to disrupt that which was traditionally contained and kept separate by these boundaries — in this case, the identity of ethnic groups, who define themselves in the contrast between "us" and "them". Now, insofar as the attraction of a destination is due to the cultural differences that the tourists perceive there, these differences must be conserved for the tourists, which implies maintaining the boundaries of the visited group. This is what Jafari calls the "touristic dilemma":

> *The touristic dilemma is clear: to freeze or not to freeze, to maintain boundaries or to remove, to assimilate or to segregate, or in short — the sword cuts with both edges.* (Jafari 1984: 14)

The Balinese know perfectly well where to draw a clear line between the sacred and the profane; between what can be sold and what must be protected at all costs. (Maurer 1979: 97)

It is significant that a decade later, at the conclusion of a re-evaluation of the sociocultural impact of tourism on Bali, Maurer considered that — according to his criteria of internal cohesion, cultural creativity and social solidarity — Balinese society was presently threatened with becoming dysfunctional. But he continues nonetheless to affirm that:

However, if there is one criterion that Balinese society appears to have maintained intact, it is the distinction between sacred and profane. (Maurer & Zeigler 1988: 81)

In short, although the responses differ, the question posed and the criteria held by those who ponder the impact of international tourism on Balinese society and its culture are remarkably constant: *Is there, or not, boundary maintenance? — or more specifically, are the Balinese able to distinguish clearly between that which they sell to tourists and that which they reserve for themselves, between their religious ceremonies and the commercial performances derived from them?*

Chapter Five

Cultural Tourism

So far, the Balinese have been those of whom one speaks, but who speak not. Obviously, it is hard to know what they thought during the colonial era about the arrival of tourists on the island, partly because of the dependent state of Balinese society and its traditional leaders, but also because this new phenomenon only slightly affected the general population. I have noted the position of the Balinese nationalists, however, who objected to certain aspects of the tourist image of their island propagated by the Official Tourist Bureau and the promotional services of the KPM — chiefly, the diffusion of photographs of bare-breasted Balinese women. This modernist intelligentsia also reproached the Dutch government for wanting to turn Bali into a museum for the selfish pleasure of tourists and others nostalgic for a bygone era. Above all, they objected to the appropriation of tourism profits by foreign firms.

Since the independence of Indonesia, the Balinese have had a right to speak out. They now have authorized spokesmen, official institutions and a press through which they can express their opinions and try to assert their views. But it was not until the central government announced its intention to make Bali the pilot project for tourism development in Indonesia that the Balinese authorities decided to take a position on tourism.

I will first describe how the Balinese responded to what they have called the "challenge" of tourism, after which I will present the main points of the Balinese tourism doctrine — "Cultural Tourism". We will then be in a position to see to what extent this doctrine has actually inspired the tourist policy implemented in Bali.

1. The Balinese response to the challenge of tourism

As we have seen, the Balinese were not involved in the elaboration of the Bali Tourism Development Master Plan; the Indonesian government's decision to cash in on the charms of their island to replenish the coffers of the State was simply presented to them for approval. The fact is that behind the façade of official consent in its ratification by the Provincial Assembly, the plan drawn up by SCETO provoked genuine reservations on the part of the Balinese authorities. These reservations concerned the directives set out by the Master Plan — not the decision itself to develop tourism on Bali, which to my knowledge has never been an issue of organized opposition on the island.

Bali's first "Tourism Week"

The publication of the Master Plan by SCETO in April 1971 coincided with the launching by the Director General of Tourism of the first "Tourism Week" (*Pekan Pariwisata*) in the country's main tourist regions. Coordination of this event in Bali was entrusted to the Regional Board for Tourist Development (Bapparda), a semi-public body created by the Governor in 1970, composed of members of the administration and the tourism industry, and responsible for advising and assisting the provincial government in matters relating to tourism. Tourism Week was opened with a ceremony welcoming the 250,000th visitor to arrive at Ngurah Rai airport since its inauguration, followed by a parade through Denpasar and a reception at the Governor's mansion. The parade was composed of students of the tourism academy and the hotel school, students of the Conservatory of Music and the Dance Academy, employees of the Bali Beach Hotel in uniform, tour guides wearing traditional Balinese dress, and many other figures of the Balinese establishment. The parade route was lined with banners bearing slogans such as "Tourism Develops Bali", "Tourism is an Incentive to Balinese Arts" and "Tourism in Bali is Cultural Tourism". In the reviewing stand were the island's dignitaries: the Governor; the directors of the provincial branches of the main ministries concerned in one way or another with tourism; delegates of the Provincial Assembly; heads of various faculties and academies; the director of the Garuda office and the manager of the Bali Beach Hotel, and so on. The Governor gave a speech on the importance of tourism for Bali and on perspectives for its future development.

Widely covered by the regional media, Tourism Week was an undeniable success for its promoters. Their task was a delicate one, however, for they had both to inform the Balinese of the government's decision to develop international tourism on their island and to calm the misapprehensions that this decision would surely arouse, while at the same time showing Jakarta that the Balinese were perfectly aware of the implications of tourism for their future and fully capable of taking on its development. It seems that the Balinese authorities were quick to understand the advantage of Bali's being chosen as Indonesia's touristic "show window" and decided to use tourism to strengthen their bargaining position in relation to the central government.

I must explain that what I call the "Balinese authorities" here is not limited to the personnel of the Indonesian State apparatus on the island — that is, the Governor and his advisors, the elected members of the Provincial Assembly and the high officials of the civil and military provincial administration — but includes also academics and journalists, bureaucrats and technocrats, as well as business people and the professional middle classes: in short, the different components of Balinese public opinion, those among the Balinese authorized to speak in the name of their society and who are thus in a position to monopolize legitimate discourse on Bali. Although it would be wrong to suggest that they share the same views or concerns, one finds nonetheless that the members of this group tend to close ranks when it comes to making the voice of the Balinese heard on the national scene and defending Bali's position in multi-ethnic Indonesia. These opinion leaders and opinion-makers, who live for the most part in Denpasar, are the actively culture-producing people who formulate, propagate and explain contemporary issues and emerging ideas to the rest of the population. Their role is that of mediators between two worlds, traditional and modern, rural and urban, Balinese and Indonesian. It is to them that I refer in the rest of this work when I speak of "the Balinese" without further qualification.

The members of this modernist Balinese elite thus form an *intelligentsia* — in the sense given this term by Robert Redfield (1953), in the perspective opened by Arnold Toynbee and Gordon Childe — distinguished from the *literati* who hold a traditional knowledge that is specifically Balinese. Whereas the literati remain entrenched in the village sphere, whose world-view and values they uphold, the intellectuals straddle two worlds — the ethnic group from which they originate and the national collectivity in which they participate. As such, they assure the connection between the village and the state by speaking on behalf of the Balinese to Jakarta and by conveying the instructions of the center to the province, which allows them to affirm their ethnic identity while furthering the integration of Bali within the Indonesian nation. In this regard, we may note that the holders of traditional authority, the aristocracy of *triwangsa* — whose field of action has always been supra-village — after enduring the ostracism of Sukarno for their "feudal" inclinations and the conspicuous sympathy that many of them showed for the colonial order, have on the whole succeeded remarkably well in effecting a reconversion in Suharto's Indonesia, taking advantage of their client networks and the very real prestige that they enjoy in order to gain positions of power in government and business.

The Discussion Club on the Development of Bali

One of the first responses to the Master Plan came from the Discussion Club on the Development of Bali (*Klub Diskusi Pembangunan Daerah Bali*), an association founded in 1970 in Denpasar by members of the Balinese intelligentsia with a view to creating a forum for the free exchange of ideas and to advising the government on the orientations of regional development. From the club's first meetings, tourism became the main subject of discussion; and when the projected plans of SCETO became known, its members took an openly critical position. According to its detractors, manifestly frustrated at not having been consulted by the foreign experts, the plan did not take Balinese interests sufficiently into consideration, on three points in particular:

- first, it did not draw sufficient attention to the repercussions of tourism on Balinese society and culture;
- second, the concentration of resort areas in the south of the island — and the Nusa Dua project in particular — did not take into account the imperatives of a balanced regional development;
- finally, being imposed from the outside, the plan deprived the provincial government of prerogatives that it should enjoy regarding tourism policy.

In short, the Balinese condemned the Master Plan for being a plan to develop tourism in Bali, rather than a plan to develop Bali through tourism. Indeed, as we have seen, the Master Plan was conceived to redress the national balance of payments rather than to stimulate regional development — as demonstrated by the fact that it was based on a market study of tourist arrivals in Bali and not in consideration of the actual needs of the population. In response to the plan, the Balinese authorities turned the perspective around and formulated a tourism doctrine that would be truly beneficial for Bali and which is precisely expressed in the slogan: "Tourism for Bali, not Bali for Tourism" (*Pariwisata untuk Bali, bukan Bali untuk pariwisata*). The tenets of this doctrine are as follows:

- tourism in Bali should be "cultural", in the sense that it should emphasize Balinese culture, the main attraction of the island for tourists;
- tourist resort areas should be distributed around the island in such a manner as to permit the active participation of the Balinese in the tourism industry, while ensuring an equitable distribution of revenues among the population;
- the Balinese should take advantage of their island's prestige abroad and of the economic importance of tourism for the national coffers, in order to gain recognition of their cultural identity by the central government and to consolidate their position within the Indonesian nation.

Of these three objectives, the first was affirmed with the greatest amount of fanfare; but it was undeniably in the third that the Balinese gained the most tangible results — even though, as we shall see presently, these results were somewhat ambiguous.

The Seminar on Cultural Tourism in Bali

The Balinese did not wait until the publication of the Master Plan in 1971 to address the central government's intention to make their island a pilot region for the development of international tourism in Indonesia. Not having been associated with the studies commissioned by Jakarta in 1967-68, it was on their own initiative that the Balinese authorities made their position known as early as 1968. In January of that year — barely two years after the massacres that had bloodied the island — the provincial government convened a First Working Discussion on Tourism in Bali (*Musyawarah Kerja Pariwisata Daerah Bali I*) with the goal of "defining the identity and personality of Balinese tourism". The proceedings published at the conclusion of this meeting declared that "Bali must be developed on the basis of its culture, which is founded on the religious character of the Balinese community", while making an appeal "to preserve and promote Balinese culture in its most authentic form in order to attract tourists" (Mukerda 1968: 1).

These declarations had no immediate discernible effect on the tourism development plans for Bali, and it was only in October 1971, some months after the publication of the SCETO report, that the Governor convened a Seminar on Cultural Tourism in Bali (*Seminar Pariwisata Budaya Daerah Bali*), under the joint auspices of the touristic, religious, cultural and academic authorities of the island (Seminar 1971).

It is characteristic of the power relations between the center and the province — and also of the cultural repugnance shared by Balinese and Javanese alike for attacking problems head on — that the proceedings of the seminar say nothing of the orientations of the Master Plan, and in fact barely allude to the plan at all. Far from being a response to the decisions of Jakarta and the foreign experts, the recommendations formulated by the participants of the seminar allege to emanate exclusively from the idea that the Balinese authorities have established of what tourism in Bali should be — that is, a "Cultural Tourism" (*Pariwisata Budaya*) (1). Moreover, for a reader ignorant of the critical position of the Balinese in regard to the Master Plan, Cultural Tourism could easily pass for a simple re-phrasing in Balinese terms of the dispositions of the SCETO plan.

But what is most significant is the openly defensive character of the recommendations of the 1971 seminar, whose alarmist tone contrasts with the unconditional optimism that prevailed in the 1968 discussion. While it is understood that the development of tourism should generate considerable economic returns, it is also recognized that the intrusion of tourists is likely to have profound repercussions on Balinese society and culture, some of which could be damaging if they are not addressed. On the one hand, the participants acknowledge that the artistic and religious traditions that made Bali famous worldwide constitute the island's main attraction for tourists, making the culture the most precious "resource" (*sumber*) for Bali's economic development; on the other hand, they cannot help seeing the invasion of their island by hordes of foreigners from the most diverse horizons as a threat of "cultural pollution" (*polusi kebudayaan*).

Thus, tourism appears to the Balinese as a "challenge" (*tantangan*): "How to develop tourism without bringing about the ruin of the Balinese culture?" Such is the delicate mission incumbent upon Cultural Tourism — to take advantage of the Balinese culture to attract tourists, while utilizing the revenues generated by tourism to preserve and promote the culture. Here is how the Governor defined Cultural Tourism in his inaugural address at the seminar:

> *Tourism as a genus proximum and Culture as differentia specifica bring about a capital consequence. The predicate, Culture, restricts the acceptation of Tourism. All that runs counter to Balinese cultural values must be prohibited. Our tourism industry must be an industry of Cultural Tourism, that is, an industry in which the raw material and that which is "sold" is Culture, with this restriction — that the development of Tourism will not undermine the values of our Culture, which is the principal attraction of Bali for tourists.* (Seminar 1971: 1)

Before examining in detail how the Balinese have risen to the "challenge of tourism", it is useful to stop and consider this fact: from the 1930s to the 1970s, the problem to be resolved by those charged with developing a tourism policy in

(1) The Indonesian syntagma *Pariwisata Budaya* is formed from two neologisms of Sanskrit origin. The term *pariwisata* ("tourism") — which officially replaced the word *tourisme* at the conclusion of the Second National Conference on Tourism, held in 1958 — expresses the idea of leisurely travel. *Budaya* ("culture") — which began to be used in the 1930s, replacing the Dutch *cultuur* — relays the idea of the development of reason and of the character of an individual.

Bali — namely, the Dutch colonial administration, the SCETO consultants, the experts from the World Bank and the Balinese authorities — was formulated in the terms of a dilemma: tourism needs Balinese culture, but tourism is a threat to Balinese culture.

2. The doctrine of Cultural Tourism

As it is defined in the proceedings of the 1971 seminar, Cultural Tourism appears as a tourism that nurtures the resources it exploits, a tourism, in short, that develops culture at the same pace as its own development. The provincial government thoroughly embraced the formula of Cultural Tourism. Its incantation wove a spell over the Balinese establishment, appearing in every declaration and every decision concerning tourism on the island, and it gave rise to a veritable body of doctrine, refined and popularized throughout the 1970s in a series of surveys and seminars on the development of tourism and its impact on Balinese society.

The sociocultural impact of tourism

In 1972, a program of interdisciplinary research was launched by the University of Bali, Universitas Udayana (UNUD), with a view to evaluating the "sociocultural impact" (*dampak sosial budaya*) of tourism. The following year, UNESCO, which had just voted to finance a Pilot Study on the Effects of Tourism on Social, Economic and Cultural Life — and had previously published a report on The Development of Cultural Tourism in Central Java and Bali (Tunnard & Pollaco 1970) — decided to carry out this study in Bali because of the threat posed to the cultural heritage of the island by a rapid development of tourism. To this end, UNESCO lent financial assistance to the research program of Udayana University, which issued a series of six reports between 1973 and 1978 (UNUD 1973a, 1973b, 1974, 1975, 1976; Proyek Sasana Budaya Bali, 1978) (2). Their conclusions are revealing — not so much of the actual implications of tourism for Balinese society but of the perception generally shared among the intelligentsia.

This intelligentsia appears torn and in moral anguish. As academics, they rationalize the exploitation of Bali's abundant cultural "resources" for the development of international tourism because this serves the ultimate interests of Indonesia. But as Balinese, they are shocked by the thought that the most intimate expressions of their culture are listed in travel brochures along with hotel amenities and sports facilities. And indeed, what the foreign consultants see as merely a matter of the prudent management of resources is for the Balinese a veritable subversion of their values.

The distress of the Balinese intellectuals is revealed in the metaphors they use to describe tourism and its implications. The intrusion of tourists appears in their eyes as an inexorable vision of *physical violence*, like a tempest battering the coasts of the

(2) The two studies whose reports were published in English (UNUD 1974, 1975) received financial support from UNESCO, as part of a program on the Quality of the Environment executed by the Division of Applied Social Sciences. For a critical evaluation of the first four reports, see Francillon 1975.

island, whose tidal waves inundate the very heart of the villages and wash away their foundations (*arus deras yang melanda Bali*).

This foreign penetration is frequently likened to a *sexual aggression.* The Balinese readily depict their island as a pretty girl whose charms draw the attention of visitors who vie for her favors (*gadis cantik setiap orang asing ingin menjamahnya*). But who knows what will become of this young girl subjected to such avid pursuit: will she become a beloved wife, respected till the end of her days, or will she end up as a discarded whore?

Finally, as for the perils that tourism inflicts on the social organism, it is the reference to an *infectious disease* that predominates, in the guise of a pernicious fever spreading through the villages, breeding "discord" (*sengketa*) and "defilement" (*kecemaran*) in its wake (3). If the Balinese social organism proves to be insufficiently resistant, the fever propagated by the tourists may be mortal. On the other hand, if the necessary preventive measures are taken, the Balinese community will pull through strengthened and immunized against all ills. It could hardly be put more clearly that for the Balinese tourism is a matter of life and death (*pariwisata merupakan hidup-mati masyarakat Bali*).

It is not surprising, then, that they regard it with ambivalence: tourism appears simultaneously as an ill and as a cure, at once necessary and unavoidable, the principal engine of development and the accelerator of a modernization as ardently desired as it is feared. In this respect, a scrutiny of the statements of this period is rewarding for what it reveals about the impacts imputed to tourism. Classed in categories — economy, religion, society, attitudes, arts — these impacts systematically appear to be contradictory in their effects. For example, in regard to the impact of tourism on the arts, the Balinese seem to take on both the analysis of Hanna and that of McKean, accusing tourism of commercializing their artistic productions and at the same time seeing it as a stimulus for artistic creativity. The position of the Balinese authorities could be summed up this way: on the one hand, they are in favor of tourism because it helps Bali become modern by expanding the monetary economy and giving more people jobs, and that will naturally speed up the process of social differentiation necessary for modernization; on the other hand, they deplore the monetarization of social relations that comes with it and the mercantilism that it inspires in individuals' attitudes.

This discourse of disapproval is never so vehement as when it concerns matters of religion. Hence the never-ending denunciations of the desecration of temples besmirched by impure beings (notably by menstruating women), the profanation of ceremonies (perturbed by photographers standing in front of people as they pray), the commercialization of sacred dances (performed for tourists outside their proper ritual context), the misuse of liturgical implements (appropriated as hotel decorations), the theft of religious antiquities and cult objects, and the dereliction in regard

(3) An alternative formulation of the same metaphor likens the development of tourism to the proliferation of cancerous cells that end up killing the organism from which they prosper.

to their religious duties of Balinese employed in the tourism industry. But one also reads in these statements that the interest of the tourists reinforces the importance that the Balinese give their religion and that the revenues of tourism help finance the maintenance of the temples.

It is striking that in these impact studies the system of values underlying these value judgments, imputing such and such an effect to tourism, is never made explicit. More striking still, these different effects are always dissociated from each other, as if they did not participate in the same process of social transformation of which tourism is effectively, but not exclusively, a part. It seems that the Balinese are unable to consider the two contradictory sides of the process together — that they cannot bring themselves to evaluate their culture by the yardstick of its economic value, and refuse to render commensurable things which are not.

The fact is that throughout the reports of the Balinese academics, tourism and culture appear to pursue conflicting interests. These conflicts, generally qualified in terms of "shock" (*benturan*), or "collision" (*bentrokan*), are expressed in a play of joint oppositions in which the values cherished by the Balinese — "us" (*kita*) — bear to the values brought by the tourists — "them" (*mereka*) — the same relation as "inside" (*dalam*) to "outside" (*luar*) and "cultural values" (*nilai budaya*) to "economic values" (*nilai ekonomi*):

$$\frac{\text{us}}{\text{them}} = \frac{\text{inside}}{\text{outside}} = \frac{\text{cultural values}}{\text{economic values}}$$

The tourists are described as foreigners — or more precisely, as Westerners — coming from countries where the sense of cultural values has depreciated, to the point where the (occidental) values propagated by the tourists are diametrically opposed to the (oriental) values honored by the Balinese. In short, "they are tourists and we are civilized" (*mereka adalah wisatawan dan kita adalah orang yang berbudaya*). If the Balinese, then, are people of culture, the tourists — those "walking dollars" (*dollar berjalan*) — are people of money. Cultural Tourism thus represents for Bali an exchange of cultural values for economic values.

This, indeed, is what comes out of the evaluation procedure applied by the Balinese academics to the impacts of tourism, a procedure based explicitly on the *opposition of the economic and the cultural.* These poles are generally expressed as follows:

- the economic impact is considered positive on the whole, in terms of the foreign exchange earnings, the increase in revenues and the creation of jobs generated by the tourism industry;

- whereas the sociocultural impact is generally perceived as negative, whether it implies the profanation of temples and religious ceremonies, a weakening of social ties, the liberalization of morals contaminating the youth, or the mass production and lowering of quality that accompanies the commercialization of artistic works.

Thus the price the Balinese must pay to raise their "standard of living" (*taraf hidup*) seems to be the violation of their "code of living" (*tata hidup*) — a challenging dilemma if ever there was one.

The fostering of culture and the development of tourism

How will the Balinese be able to acquire economic values without renouncing their cultural values? How will they be able to raise their standard of living without infringing on their code of living? In short, how can they maximize the economic benefits of tourism while minimizing its cultural costs?

Such were the questions debated over the course of five seminars organized between 1977 and 1979, some by the Directorate General of Tourism on its own, the others in collaboration with the Directorate General of Culture (Ditjen Pariwisata, 1977, 1978; Proyek Sasana Budaya Jakarta, 1978, 1979a; Proyek Sasana Budaya Bali, 1979). These seminars led to recommendations that are clearly divided between two objectives: those seeking to protect Balinese society and cultural values from the impact of tourist commercialization; and those aiming to develop tourism and make it profitable for the population.

By somewhat forcing the distinctions for the sake of the argument, one may consider that the first preoccupation emanated from the spokesmen for the Directorate General of Culture, anxious to preserve the integrity of the Balinese cultural values and led therefore to denounce the cultural costs of tourism; and that the second one emanated from the officials of the Directorate General of Tourism, wishing to expand their field of action and thus inclined to emphasize the economic benefits of the tourism industry. In this perspective, the seminars appear to be a venue of confrontation between defenders of the culture and promoters of tourism. But such an interpretation, however well-founded it may seem, runs the risk of side-stepping the issue, because the formula of Cultural Tourism is framed precisely to reconcile the proponents of the culture to the partisans of tourism by conciliating their respective interests.

This is what is expressed in the title of the seminars organized jointly by the Directorate General of Culture and the Directorate General of Tourism, "The Fostering of Culture and the Development of Tourism" (*Pembinaan Kebudayaan dan Pengembangan Kepariwisataan*) (4). This idea was spelled out in the opening talk of the seminar of 1978 by the Director General of Culture at the time, a well-known Balinese academic who would soon become Governor of Bali:

---

(4) The English translation conveys only imperfectly the idea transmitted by the Indonesian terminology. The term *pembinaan* implies an intentionality, a concerted effort to form, foster, cultivate, promote a quality that is not considered as established but which should be developed in a determined sense. Above all, the notion of *pembinaan* emphasizes the mobilization of society to serve the needs of the state. *Pengembangan*, on the other hand, expresses the idea of an unfolding, of an opening out, of a growth analogous to a natural evolution, to the image of blossoming.

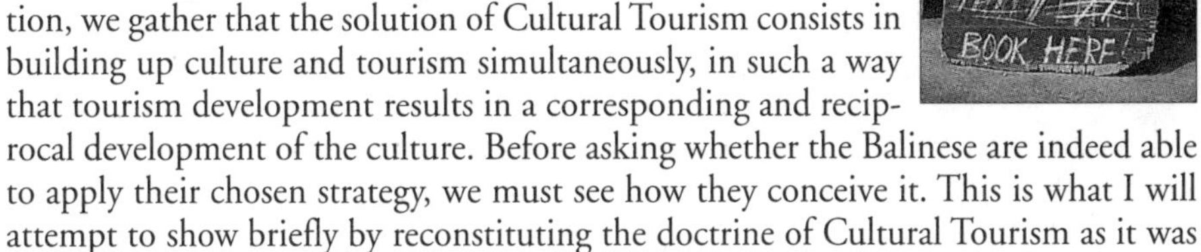

How can we assure the fostering of culture in the context of an accelerated development of tourism? How can the development of tourism be made to profit from the fostering of culture to contribute to the prosperity of the population? And how can the culture put tourism development to the service of its own fostering? (Proyek Sasana Budaya Jakarta, 1978: 13)

Following the meandering of this rather laborious formulation, we gather that the solution of Cultural Tourism consists in building up culture and tourism simultaneously, in such a way that tourism development results in a corresponding and reciprocal development of the culture. Before asking whether the Balinese are indeed able to apply their chosen strategy, we must see how they conceive it. This is what I will attempt to show briefly by reconstituting the doctrine of Cultural Tourism as it was elaborated in the course of the seminars.

Developing tourism

First of all the Balinese are reminded that they hardly have any choice: they have no other wealth to exploit than their culture, no other products to sell than the artistic and ceremonial productions that had won their island such esteem among foreign visitors in earlier times. Therefore Bali's economic development could come only from the development of tourism, and tourism in Bali could only be cultural tourism. In this regard, it is clear that the Balinese are genuinely flattered by the prestige accorded to their culture abroad, and they appear eager to offer tourists the best of their traditions. But attributing Bali's tourist success to the allure of its cultural manifestations leads them to link the fate of their culture to that of tourism. This contradicts the view of the foreign consultants who, as we have seen, predicted that tourism in Bali would thrive even after the cultural manifestations had died off, probably around the mid-1980s when the Master Plan had been fully implemented (5).

What is specific to Cultural Tourism in Bali is that the Balinese are not content with offering their visitors simulated attractions staged only for tourists. Unlike other

(5) If the truth be known, the idea that tourists are genuinely interested in discovering the cultural riches of their island seems rather more a pious wish on the part of the Balinese than an objective fact. Strictly speaking, "cultural" tourism concerns only a minority of tourists, essentially those who stay in Ubud or its environs, wishing to see the "authentic" face of Bali, as it is presented in their guidebook, and anxious to distinguish themselves from the tourists lolling about at the coastal resorts. Most tourists do not leave their beach — be it Nusa Dua, Sanur or Kuta — except to go shopping in Celuk, Mas or Ubud, to admire Lake Batur or the famous temple of Tanah Lot, to watch a "Barong and Kris Dance" at Batubulan, or, for the lucky ones, to see a cremation. As confirmed by the market study on which the Master Plan is based, Bali is for most tourists just a tropical paradise, whose cultural image confers an added value to their trip, compared to a vacation in Hawaii or the Maldives, for example.

destinations — such as Hawaii, where the indigenous culture is dying off and which can present only artificial shows specially fabricated for the consumption of tourists — in Bali, visitors are allowed to attend cultural events that are "authentically Balinese" (*asli Bali*) (6). These events are festivities and celebrations of all sorts, such as temple festivals, rites of passage, processions and cremations that provide the occasion for those sumptuous ritual pageants of which the Balinese are so fond.

But if one wants tourists to have access to the events that they are invited to attend, they must be given the chance to move about the island on their own, and in particular to go into the villages, the very centers of traditional Balinese culture. In this regard, we note that the participants of the 1968 discussion wanted to make every village a "tourist object" (*obyek pariwisata*). And with this in view, they proposed a program aimed at making the villages clean and trim (7), their inhabitants smiling and hospitable, and their cultural manifestations attractive. In drawing the tourists into the villages of the interior, rather than confining them to the coast, the Balinese hoped that they would go there to spend their money, allowing tourism to contribute to a balanced development of the island. This is why, contrary to the option proposed by the Master Plan, the Balinese authorities declared themselves in favor of an integrated, cultural tourism, whereas the foreign experts preached an enclaved, seaside tourism. Instead of trying to keep the tourists at a distance, the Balinese wanted to take them into their midst.

For this strategy to bear fruit, the Balinese population must be able to reap the profits of tourism; and to do this, they must be made aware of the importance of the tourism industry for Bali's future and encouraged to participate in its development. To this end, information and public awareness campaigns exhorted the Balinese to behave as courteous and respectful hosts and to promote a pleasant atmosphere that would encourage the tourists to stay longer on their island or, even better, to come back again (8). They must also show concern for their island's good reputation, and were urged to rid themselves of certain unsuitable practices that might be harmful to Bali's tourist image (9). But for the population to feel genuinely concerned with

---

(6) For the Balinese authorities, the tourists appear as they are described by Dean MacCannell — they are in search of authenticity (MacCannell 1976). But the difference would be that in coming to Bali, they are assured of finding that which they seek, in the sense that what one shows them is, in fact, authentic and not the product of a staged performance meant to gull them.

(7) In their eagerness to present a pleasing image of Balinese village life, the participants in the discussion went so far as to recommend that owners of dogs take better care of them, no doubt thinking that the sight of these roving gangs of emaciated, maimed and surly animals might discourage visitors from venturing into the villages. For anyone who knows Bali even a little, such a recommendation is striking for being utterly unrealistic.

tourism, they must reap real rewards from its development; and the Balinese authorities point out that if one wants the population to participate in the tourist enterprise, it is not enough to merely exhort them to do so; they must be given the necessary means through appropriate financial, legal and technical assistance.

Fostering the culture

And yet, although the Balinese population are called upon to participate in tourism — and are even obliged to lend their support, since its development is the matter of a Presidential Decree — there will be no question of their selling their pride and lowering themselves to become a nation of flunkies and beggars. The Balinese authorities insist that in no case will the local population sacrifice their cultural values to the whims of the tourists, nor to the interests of the tourism industry. To the contrary, it is firmly declared that any practice that might damage Balinese cultural integrity should be outlawed.

In this sense, Cultural Tourism is not only a way of responding to the expectations of tourists in quest of authentic cultural manifestations, it is also, and above all, a means of protection, a "barrier" (*bendungan*), a "rampart" (*benteng*), erected to put Balinese culture beyond striking range of commoditization (*komersialisasi kebudayaan*). Given that contact with tourists is perceived as subversive and polluting, it is necessary to circumscribe and channel it and to do whatever one can to preserve Bali's cultural integrity. That being the case, one must also ensure that the tourists do not perceive any obstacles to their freedom of movement, lest they should come to doubt Bali's famous hospitality. Clearly, what worries the authorities is the thought of the cultural mingling that might come about if the Balinese are exposed for too long, or too intensely, to the influence of the tourists — for in this mingling is contained the germ of corruption and defilement, with, as corollary, the dreaded loss of identity.

---

(8) If the desire to please tourists and meet their expectations is manifest — on the part of the provincial government as well as of individuals hoping to reap the dividends of tourism — the incomprehension of the Balinese for the tastes and motivations of their visitors is certainly no less great than that for which one often reproaches the tourists vis-à-vis their hosts. It seems that especially in regard to aesthetics and the aggressive furnishing of tourist sites with "amenities", the efforts of the Balinese to comply with what they imagine to be pleasing to tourists are a frequent source of astonishment, disappointment and discomfort for the latter. This makes all the more praiseworthy the undeniable willingness of the Balinese to adapt themselves to the tourist market and its exigencies.

(9) Most of the references to these troublesome habits arise in the domain of "good manners". Thus the Balinese are asked to no longer bathe in the irrigation ditches alongside the roads in full view of everyone, and women (that is, only older ones nowadays) are again asked not to go bare-breasted in public. More serious, however, are the injunctions concerning certain practices that are judged unpalatable because they may shock the sensibilities of tourists, especially in regard to funerary rites. Among those practices so indicted are the use of gas blowers and the cutting up of the corpse to accelerate incineration, as well as certain demonstrations of ostracism on the part of *banjar* members toward the deceased, which can lead to explosions of violence, sometimes going as far as the deliberate abuse of the corpse (Connor 1979).

To safeguard themselves against the menace of cultural pollution, the Balinese population are admonished to strengthen their customary institutions and their moral defenses, it being assumed that they will be less vulnerable to the temptations offered by tourist money if they have an unshakable base of support — that is, the religious foundations of their cultural identity. Concretely, this entails first a tightening of the social control exerted by the *desa* and the *banjar* on the population, to stem the rise of individualism and mercantilism spread in the wake of the tourists. This alludes particularly to the youth, all too often eager to break out of the grip of communal laws and ties and to adopt the undesirable behavior introduced by tourists, and who tend to find every new idea coming from the West "modern" (*moderen*) and therefore attractive.

Moreover, the Balinese population must be made aware of the value of their cultural heritage so that they will feel responsible for its preservation. Religious instruction must be intensified to inculcate in them an understanding of the philosophical and ethical principles underlying their ceremonies. They must also be reminded that their art forms originate in their religion, so that when their celebrated creativity gallops away with modern forms they do not snap the vital ties to their roots — for that would ultimately lead to a denial of their identity. For the Balinese authorities, it seems, the local population must be armed with a fresh religious awareness of who they are so that they will not be seduced by the aesthetic and materialistic gaze that the tourists cast on their temples, their ceremonies and their artistic performances.

In other words, as long as the Balinese adhere to the religious core of their cultural values, the foreign influences to which they are exposed will affect them only superficially. In this regard, the authorities often allude to the capacity for selective adaptation for which the Balinese are famous and which has until now enabled them to filter foreign influences, adopting those which suit them and rejecting those which they consider incompatible with their values. For added security, however, it is recommended that they be instructed in the distinctions between artistic forms whose presentation must be maintained in keeping with tradition and those which may be adapted to suit the tourists. Here arises the necessity of issuing precise and explicit directives permitting artists to know what they are authorized to sell to tourists and what must not under any circumstances be commercialized. In short, the issue is to make the Balinese population understand to what extent their culture may be put to the service of tourism.

This concern for discriminating between what belongs to the culture and what belongs to tourism surfaces time and again, especially when one evokes the danger of "corruption" (*korupsi*), of "pollution" (*polusi*), of "defilement" (*kecemaran*), or of "profanation" (*provanasi*). And the passionate reaction of the Balinese authorities in this regard reveals a determination to maintain that which must remain the property of the Balinese — that which constitutes the "essence" (*intisari*) of their culture — at a remove from that which may be offered to tourists — that which is merely accessory because it is situated on the "surface" (*kulit*) of things. This dichotomy appears in various guises depending on the context, such as, for example, "the authentic and the commercial" (*mana yang asli, mana yang komersial*), "the pure and the polluted" (*mana yang suci, mana yang leteh*), or "the sacred and the profane" (*mana yang sakral, mana yang provan*).

Thus, the problem that poses itself to the Balinese is really to decide to what extent their cultural values can be assessed with regard to their economic value. If they are unable to distinguish between that which pertains to tourism and that which pertains to culture, the Balinese population run the risk of no longer being able to distinguish between their own values and those propagated by their visitors. And if this were the case, the Balinese culture would become a "touristic culture" (*kebudayaan pariwisata*) — defined as a state of confusion between the values of the culture and those of tourism.

To prevent the Balinese culture from degenerating into a touristic culture, it is required that a portion of the profits from the tourism industry be utilized for the preservation and promotion of Balinese culture — that is, the tourism firms must understand that it is in their interests to invest in the cultural sector and help cultivate the resources from which they live and prosper. Thanks to this new source of financing, the religious ceremonies and the artistic performances that embellish them will be able to be organized with ever greater brilliance, and tourists will come to Bali in ever greater numbers to admire them.

This is how the Balinese authorities attempt to turn to their advantage Jakarta's decision to develop international tourism in Bali in order to redress the national balance of payments. As soon as tourism makes Balinese culture the island's principal economic resource, it also makes it a decisive means of pressure in the hands of the Balinese, who declare to the central government,

> *If you want to gather golden eggs, don't kill the goose who lays them.* (Seminar 1971: 11)

If the touristic exploitation of Bali's cultural resources should, by misfortune, lead to their depletion, Bali's image as a tourist paradise would suffer. And if this should happen, the tourism industry not only would have caused the ruin of the Balinese culture, it would thereby have brought about its own loss as well. Thus, declare the Balinese, from the moment the government chose Bali as the principal tourist destination of Indonesia, it is in the government's interests — as in that of the tourism industry — to protect, foster and promote the Balinese culture.

3. The Balinese tourism policy

It would seem that the Indonesian government got the message. One of the results that can be ascribed to these various seminars is to have popularized the formula of Cultural Tourism beyond Bali. Initially elaborated by the Balinese according to their own experience and for their own use, the doctrine of Cultural Tourism was adopted as the official Indonesian tourism policy in 1977. And to ensure that the interests of tourism would coincide with those of culture, it was decided that the Indonesian tourism and cultural policies would be coordinated within a single organization. In 1979, at the conclusion of the second seminar on "The Fostering of Culture and the Development of Tourism", an agreement of cooperation was signed between the Director General of Culture and the Director General of Tourism, leading soon thereafter to the creation of a Commission of Cooperation for Fostering and Developing Cultural Tourism (*Komisi Kerjasama Pembinaan dan Pengembangan Wisata Budaya*), financed equally by the two Directorates and responsible to their respective Directors. The objectives assigned to this commission are defined as follows:

> *To take advantage of cultural objects to develop tourism, and to use the revenues furnished by the development of tourism for fostering and developing the culture.* (Proyek Sasana Budaya Jakarta, 1979b: 11)

For all that, can one speak of a Balinese policy of Cultural Tourism? One would think so, since the 1971 seminar explicitly referred to a "Policy of Cultural Tourism" (*Kebijaksanaan Pariwisata Budaya*). But in reality, the tourism development policy in Bali is governed by the Master Plan, which, as we have seen, was devised by foreign experts, set in motion by the Indonesian government and, moreover, the subject of a Presidential Decree. Given the institutional impotence of the provincial governments in Indonesia, there was never any question of reversing this decision. The problem facing the Balinese was how to accommodate it. Thus, Cultural Tourism is not so much an initiative as a response to a fait accompli — not a tourism policy but a concept that the Balinese authorities devised of the sort of tourism they thought they could live with and could hope to turn to their advantage.

The regulation of tourism

In his closing speech at the Seminar on Cultural Tourism, the Governor announced that the conclusions of the seminar would lead to a set of regulations giving the provincial government a legal apparatus enabling it to control and direct tourism development. But in fact, between 1971 and 1974, only three decrees were promulgated by the Governor, and of these only two deal at all directly with the problems under discussion. The three decrees are as follows:

- The *Decree forbidding the performance of sacred dances for tourists.* Although sacred dances are not to be staged outside their ritual context, tourists are permitted to watch these dances in the course of the ceremonies in which their execution is required.

- The *Decree on the activity of guides in the Province of Bali.* With a view to regulating the activity of tour guides, it is required that they carry a license and professional card issued by the Bali Government Tourism Office; that they wear traditional Balinese dress on the job; and that they belong to a professional association supervised by the provincial government.

- The *Decree on access to temples and other sacred Hindu sites on Bali.* To preserve the sacredness of the temples, it is stipulated that during the course of ceremonies, access is forbidden to all persons not belonging to the Hindu-Balinese community. Outside the periods of ceremonial activity, entry to the temples is permitted to tourists, with the condition that they are properly dressed and behave respectfully. Also, in order to avoid the commercialization of the temples, entry should not be made subject to an entrance fee, but provision may be made for voluntary contributions.

Following this, Cultural Tourism became the object of a regional regulation, a more important measure than a decree in that it must be ratified by the Provincial Assembly. The *Regional Regulation on Cultural Tourism*, which appeared in 1974, constituted until recently the only Balinese legislative text on tourism as a whole. Its stated objectives were the preservation and controlled exploitation of the island's natural and cultural resources, with the aim of making tourism an instrument of prosperity for the Balinese. But instead of the enforceable measures one would rightly expect, one finds here only exhortations and considerations of a general nature. This regulation was replaced in 1991 with another one of the same name, hardly more specific. One nonetheless finds confirmation that the temples are not "tourist objects", even if tourists are invited to visit them, on the condition, of course, that they show the respect required at sacred places. It also reiterates that the architecture of hotels, restaurants and souvenir shops must be in Balinese style — or at the very least, that buildings intended for tourism must be decorated with Balinese motifs, although in no case are they to borrow elements of religious architecture.

The jurisdiction of the provincial government

In spite of their limited scope, however, neither the decrees nor the regional regulation on Cultural Tourism were implemented — as even the Governor's spokesmen admitted, deploring their incapacity to enforce the decrees and penalize infractions, and denouncing the lack of support on the part of the population with regard to these measures. The fact is that the legal impotence of the Balinese government is patent. This is not particular to Bali but is generally the lot of the provinces, whose capacity for initiative is kept on a very short rein. This, indeed, is what one may conclude from the *Government Regulation on the delegation of parts of government administration related to tourism to the provinces*, published in 1979. This regulation attributes to the provincial governments an extremely restricted sphere of jurisdiction, basically limited to "tourist areas" and "tourist objects", to non-classsified hotels and restaurants, to guides and regional promotion. The central government reserves for itself research and planning, the development of "tourist destinations", "tourist products" and their marketing, the participation of the population, regulation and control measures, infrastructure and labor, classified hotels and restaurants, and travel agencies. Consequently, it is clear that the provincial government does not have the legal authority to conduct the tourism policy of its choice.

In Bali, one may discern this division of jurisdiction between the center and the provinces in the duplication of the tourism apparatus between the Provincial Office of the Department of Tourism, Post and Telecommunications (Kanwil Depparpostel) and the Bali Government Tourism Office (Diparda). Diparda was created by the

Governor in 1970, and it is the executive organ of the provincial government for matters of tourism. Its director is appointed by the Governor and answers to him. It is financed by the provincial government and is notoriously lacking in staff and the necessary means to carry out its functions, limited as they are. Initially responsible for the regulation and development of tourism in the province, Diparda was forced in 1979 to transfer a portion of its responsibilities to Kanwil Depparpostel, instituted the previous year. This bureau, which is financed by the Department of Tourism, was henceforth charged with carrying out the national tourism policy in the province, and its director is responsible to the Minister of Tourism (10).

Numerous Balinese officials and academics demand that more authority should be given to Diparda to manage all matters related to tourism development under the Governor's overall supervision and responsibility. They argue that the respective mandates for Diparda and Kanwil Depparpostel are not clearly defined, with undesirable overlaps and gaps existing between these two institutions as a result. In particular, they would like to give Diparda jurisdiction over the classified hotels and restaurants, protesting the arbitrary nature of the classification criteria applied in the hotel and restaurant industry. In their opinion, only matters requiring coordination or needing to be tackled at the national level because of implications for national issues, should be administered by the central government (Manuaba 1995).

Be that as it may, the legal impotence of the provincial government does not account for all its difficulties, nor can one blame the ineffectiveness of adopted measures entirely on bureaucratic laxity or the indifference of the population. A closer examination reveals that some of these measures — especially those concerning sacred dances and access to temples — raise delicate problems of arbitrage between considerations of tourism promotion and concerns about cultural protection. I will return to the question of sacred dances in detail in the next chapter, and for the moment simply observe that the prohibition against foreigners entering temples during ceremonies goes against the very idea of Cultural Tourism, that is, to make tourists welcome at Balinese cultural events, which most often take place in a temple. And if one takes the examination a bit further, one sees that this contradiction expresses the disagreements that divide the Balinese authorities over what should be done to attract tourists. Behind the formal agreement that unites the Balinese around the consensual formula of Cultural Tourism, there are divergent interpretations on the order of priorities to be respected and on the necessary compromises. But one must beware of too quickly drawing the conclusion that these divergences represent a conflict between the agents of the tourism industry — irritated by restrictions on their freedom of action — and the religious authorities, anxious about assaults on their traditional

(10) One must once again mention the Bali Tourism Development Board (BTDB), instituted in 1972 by Presidential Decree to supervise and coordinate the implementation of the Master Plan, but which, in fact, never had more than a consultative role and was finally closed in 1979, after the departure of the last foreign advisor.

prerogatives. In reality, they express the perplexity of the Balinese themselves, prisoners of the dilemma posed by the "challenge" of tourism. And in this sense, each one among them finds himself intimately divided in the identity crisis confronting him.

Chapter Six

Balinese Dance as a Tourist Attraction

To prevent Cultural Tourism from becoming what is seen as its opposite — a "touristic culture" — the Balinese authorities are continuously on guard to keep that which belongs to the culture separate from that which pertains to tourism, and they have issued numerous warnings to the population against the improper use of religious symbols in a purely touristic context. Among the debated practices are the use of statues, cult objects and temple ornaments to decorate hotels, restaurants and boutiques, the excessive commercial exploitation of cremations as tourist attractions, and the current fashion for foreigners to get married in a Balinese wedding ceremony — a vogue that made headlines in the regional press a few years ago with the wedding in Ubud, consecrated by a Balinese priest, of Mick Jagger and Jerry Hall. But the subject most bitterly debated, which has caused the greatest confusion and raised the thorniest problems, is the performance of sacred dances for tourists.

Contrary to what the doctrine of Cultural Tourism would have us believe, the great majority of tourists have no access to the cultural events organized by the Balinese for their own purposes. What glimpses of Balinese culture they see — aside from the made-in-Bali "art objects" that they buy as souvenirs — are limited for the most part to dance performances staged especially for them. Unlike handicrafts, however, the performances involve an interaction between the foreign consumers and the Balinese producers. Moreover, these celebrated dances that have done so much for Bali's fame not only constitute a theatrical event appreciated by tourists and Balinese alike, they are also the venue in which Balinese society stages itself for the Balinese, where its history is interpreted and its values affirmed — the crucible in which its members celebrate their belonging to the same community. For the Balinese, the question that arises with particular acuteness is how to discriminate between what they sell to tourists and what they reserve for themselves, between the performances that are part of their own customs and the attractions expressly conceived for the entertainment of their visitors.

It is this question that I will examine now, trying to determine whether the Balinese are in fact able — as McKean, Noronha and Maurer say — to differentiate their cultural performances in regard to the public for which they are intended. Before exposing the problems raised by the conversion of Balinese dance into a tourist attraction, I will briefly describe the most common tourist performances and indicate how they differ from the performances of the Balinese in their original customary context.

1. Is Balinese dance an art?

We know that the Balinese do not have a word to designate "art" or an "artist". What is perhaps less known is that, despite the omnipresence of dance in Bali, there are no terms in Balinese that convey the exact generic sense of "dance" or "dancer". In keeping with their marked preference for concrete verbal forms, the Balinese always refer to specific activities, inseparable from their context, which are thus not perceived as part of an abstract category, such as "art" or "dance", for example. And just as one always speaks of such and such a dance, the dancers are referred to by the dance they perform. Thus in Balinese the same word refers at once to the dance and the dancer, to the subject and the object of a particular dance. It is quite otherwise with the Indonesian language, which makes dance a form of "art" (*seni*) among others, taught in the conservatories and academies created by the Department of Education and Culture. Moreover, Indonesian terminology differentiates "dance" (*seni tari*) from "theater" (*seni drama*), whereas Balinese terminology encompasses both the choreographic and dramatic aspects of performances, and these are not clearly distinguished by the Balinese. In this sense, when one speaks of dance in Bali, one is dealing with music, theater and ritual, and they are virtually indissociable.

In order for their celebrated dances to be recognized by the Balinese as an art, the dances first had to be detached from the context of their performance. And to do this, this detachment, initiated by the Balinese for their own purposes, required the intercession of an external gaze, that of the tourists first, and then that of the Indonesians.

Unlike Javanese dances, appreciated by European connoisseurs since the end of the last century, Balinese dances acquired the prestige that they have today only after becoming tourist attractions. And it was not until the 1930s that these dances — celebrated today as Bali's most brilliant art form — were considered worthy of mention in the guidebooks and travel literature that had begun to proliferate in the previous decade. Meanwhile, the management of the Bali Hotel in Denpasar had taken the initiative of organizing dance performances conceived specially for its clientele. After independence, and especially after the establishment of the New Order, the arts of Bali — and above all its dances — were used to promote both the development of international tourism in Indonesia and the building of a national Indonesian culture. That is, as dance had become the brand image of Bali as a tourist destination, now it would incarnate the cultural identity of the Balinese on the national scene of Indonesia (Picard 1996).

Between offering and entertainment

The traditional context of theatrical performances in Bali is furnished by the many religious ceremonies (*yadnya*) that punctuate everyday life: temple festivals, rites of passage, funerals, exorcisms, etc. (Bandem & deBoer 1981; Basset 1990; Ramstedt 1993; de Zoete & Spies 1938). The dances performed in the course of a ceremony are at once an act of personal devotion for the dancers and a communal obligation for the members of the congregation responsible for organizing it. In this sense, it is not only a spectacle to be watched, but also — and in a way difficult to dissociate — a ritual to be enacted. The difficulty of separating ritual from spectacle was neatly expressed by Jane Belo, who observed that the Balinese conceive of their dances as an offering, while they present their offerings as a display:

> *... in Balinese culture no very sharp line was drawn between the performance of ritual and dramatics; any dramatic performance was in itself an offering to the gods, and the presumption was that the better the performance, the better the gods would be pleased.* (Belo 1960: 115)

That is, in Bali, theatrical performances are not destined only for humans, for the visible world (*sekala*). Among the tight crowd of spectators may be felt the presence, no less attentive and exacting, of the beings of the invisible world (*niskala*), who share with the Balinese a passion for good theater. Dance is thus simultaneously an offering to the gods and an entertainment for human beings. Or, as Tyra de Kleen wrote as early as 1921 in the first article on Balinese dance:

> *... at their temple feasts they combine two good purposes, namely to please their gods and amuse themselves. I would even say that these two things are identical with the Balinese.* (de Kleen 1921: 129)

Nonetheless, if most dances are organically related to a religious ceremony, they do not all figure in a ceremony in the same way; and here arises a problem of taxonomy, the more delicate in that the available criteria for distinguishing dances do not form a coherent system, and they intersect in several ways. Studies of Balinese dance and drama tend to approach this question by way of categories of sacred and profane, even though the first writers to resort to these terms were careful to warn their readers of the fundamental inadequacy of using categories radically foreign to Balinese reality (Spies & Goris 1937: 205; de Zoete & Spies 1938: 46) (1).

From gods to tourists

Rather than attempt here to present the different genres of dance common in Bali, it will suffice to quickly review the evolution of their sources of patronage, traditionally the temples (*pura*) and the courts (*puri*).

The temples are animated periodically in the course of ceremonies (*odalan*) whose purpose is to establish contact with the divinities associated with them. These deities

---

(1) Bandem & deBoer constructed their discussion of Balinese dances on the indigenous classification scheme of *kaja* / *kelod* ("toward the mountains / toward the sea"). But the fact that they associated the terms with, respectively, the sacred, the divine and the good on the one hand, and the demonic, the chthonic and evil on the other, does not really resolve the confusion (Bandem & deBoer 1981: VIII). Indeed, what we call, for lack of more appropriate terms, "divine" and "demonic" are in Bali ambivalent entities, capable of harming human beings as much as of protecting them. On this point, one may refer to my review of their book (Picard 1986).

are invited to descend into the human realm and occupy the shrines dedicated to them, after which they are bid to participate in the rituals and watch the performances presented in their honor (Belo 1953).

Before the colonial occupation, the courts constituted the exemplary centers of Balinese society, where the most elaborate ritual and artistic manifestations were staged. The kings and princes were in effect obliged to hold ceremonies attesting their ties to their deified ancestors and propitiating the supernatural forces on which the harmony of the kingdom and the well-being of their subjects depended. These ceremonies provided those who organized them with the pretext for a competition by which they could demonstrate their capacity to mobilize men and wealth to the service of their glory. To this end, the princes kept troupes of dancers and musicians, either at court or in the neighboring villages. Moreover, they were often accomplished dancers themselves, and it was not unusual for them to take part in the performances they organized.

The curbing of the power of the courts and their relative impoverishment following the colonial occupation reduced their means for holding spectacular ceremonies. Many princes eventually put their orchestras and dance costumes at the disposal of the villagers — to a *banjar* in the neighborhood or to a specially created troupe (*seka*) of musicians and dancers. This decline in the role of patronage traditionally exercised by the princely houses no doubt dealt a fatal blow to court theater — but at the same time it stimulated a renewal of artistic activity in the villages, where new musical and choreographic styles were invented (2).

After the traumas of the Japanese occupation and the struggle for independence, the degradation of the political and economic situation led to a dwindling of ceremonies and performances, and the number of troupes of dancers and musicians dropped sharply. As one Balinese observer at the time noted with resignation,

> *For the average Balinese, art is becoming too expensive and too alien to modern religious practice.* (Bhadra 1956: 71)

In this context of financial and artistic depression, the launching of tourism by the New Order undeniably stimulated music and dance by providing an audience that was willing to pay a good price to watch these performances that had made Bali famous. While this new public is indeed partly responsible for the proliferation of dance performances starting in the 1970s, one must emphasize that the return of the tourists coincided with a new interest on the part of the Indonesian government for the Balinese arts, which were being enlisted in the

---

(2) This evolution certainly did not escape the notice of observers at the time; but they held very different views. Some, such as Roelof Goris (nd.: 63) and Geoffrey Gorer (1936: 46), were distressed by the decadence of court theater; others, like Miguel Covarrubias (1937: 223-224) and Colin McPhee (1966: 4-5, 13-14), to the contrary, saw in the transmission of patronage from the court to the village a sign of new-found vitality in Balinese dance.

building of the national culture (Ramstedt 1992). Thus the present situation of Balinese theater expresses the joint influences of this double patronage that are sometimes difficult to distinguish clearly (3).

As long as their dances were being performed in their traditional contexts, the Balinese had no need to ask themselves where ritual ended and where spectacle began. But the arrival of the tourists confronted them with an unprecedented situation in having to interpret their culture before a foreign public. Of course, they had previously danced before guests — whether Javanese dignitaries or Dutch officials — but now they would have to adapt themselves to the presence of a constantly renewed and ever-anonymous audience, installed permanently on their island.

2. Tourist performances

The tourist performances take place either in the village where the troupes originate, where the spectators are brought by bus (Batubulan, Bona, Peliatan), or in the large hotels where they are generally presented as an accompaniment to a dinner (Nusa Dua, Sanur, Kuta). An intermediate case is that of troupes originating in Kuta, Sanur and above all Ubud, who regularly present dance performances to the tourists staying in their village. The tourist market supports a good hundred or more troupes — two to three thousand musicians and dancers — among the 5,000 troupes listed by the provincial cultural services. These are either troupes organized according to traditional criteria — that is, *seka* playing regularly for a Balinese public in a ceremonial context — or groups that are assembled for certain occasions with dancers and musicians engaged for the particular event. Most of these are concentrated in the districts of Gianyar and Badung, the principal tourist regions of the island. Before being authorized to perform for tourists, a troupe should in principle have a Certificate of Artistic Excellence (*Pramana Patram Budaya*) — conferred by the official arts council Listibiya — attesting to the quality of its performance. This condition prevails as well for troupes touring outside Bali.

The main problem facing a troupe that would like to perform for tourists —

(3) A number of institutions were founded by the government to teach, preserve and promote Balinese art traditions, and most especially the performing arts:
- The Conservatory of Traditional Music (*Konservatori Karawitan*, KOKAR), created in 1960 at the initiative of several Balinese artists. In 1979, it became the High School of Traditional Indonesian Music (*Sekolah Menengah Karawitan Indonesia*, SMKI), to be placed under the jurisdiction of the Department of Education and Culture.
- The Academy of Indonesian Dance (*Akademi Seni Tari Indonesia*, ASTI) founded in 1967 and placed under the jurisdiction of the Department of Education and Culture in 1969. In 1988, it became the College of Indonesian Arts (*Sekolah Tinggi Seni Indonesia*, STSI).
- The Consultative and Promotional Council for Balinese Culture (*Majelis Pertimbangan dan Pembinaan Kebudayaan Daerah Propinsi Bali*, Listibiya), instituted in 1966 at the initiative of a group of high officials, artists and academics, with the aim of preserving and promoting Balinese artistic traditions.
- The Art Center (*Werdi Budaya*), inaugurated in 1976 by the Department of Education and Culture with the aim of promoting the Balinese arts.

except for those originating in resort areas — is the difficulty of having direct access to the market. Dance troupes are heavily dependent on commercial intermediaries (hotels, travel agents, guides, drivers, etc.) who are in a position to put the troupes in competition with each other and to impose conditions on them — conditions of a financial nature, of course, but which may also concern the presentation of the performance or details of its contents. In 1986, with the aim of strengthening the negotiating power of the troupes vis-à-vis the intermediaries, the director of the Tourism Office grouped them together in an Association of Organizers of Tourist Performances (*Asosiasi Penyelenggara Tontonan Wisata,* Asprananta) — but it seems that up to the present time, this association has not been able to redress the power relations in its favor.

The price of tickets varies considerably depending on whether they are bought at the performance venue or through an intermediary. In 1994, they were sold at the location for between 5,000 and 6,000 rupiah (around US$2.30–$2.80). Most of the revenue is pocketed by the intermediaries, and the rest is divided variously among the performers, one part remaining in the troupe's coffers, the other distributed among its members, each of whom receives an inclusive sum between 1,000 and 10,000 rupiah per performance (4). The collective earnings of a troupe are used primarily to maintain its equipment, to finance the ceremonies in which its members participate, to honor community obligations and to pay the entertainment tax levied by the district.

The performances presented to tourists generally last an hour to an hour-and-a-half — which is short compared to those for the Balinese, which may last five hours or more. Their frequency varies; they may be daily or weekly or several times a week, and they take place either in the morning around nine or ten o'clock, or in the evening between six and eight. The performance takes place on a stage facing the audience seated in rows of chairs, or in an amphitheater. The scenery is inevitably a temple gate, thereby authenticating the cultural event which the tourists have been enjoined to attend. Generally, when they are presented in a village, tourist performances draw Balinese spectators, who may watch for free and stand behind the tourists. And, as with every gathering of tourists, these performances are assiduously attended by peddlers hoping to sell some souvenir there.

When one knows something of the extraordinary variety of art forms practiced in Bali, one cannot help being struck by the uniformity of the tourist performances. The great majority of these performances can be grouped under four main genres; and these, considered further, may be seen as belonging to two clearly distinct categories: dances that the Balinese themselves consider entertainment; and those that are fed by the fascination exerted by trance possession, where the spectacular character of ancient rites of exorcism is deliberately exploited (5, overleaf).

---

(4) In 1991, a circular emanating from the Governor fixed the minimum hourly wage to be paid by organizers of tourist performances at 10,000 rupiah for dancers and 7,500 rupiah for musicians; but it seems that this circular was never really enforced.

Legong Dance

It is significant that the arrival of the first tourists in Bali in the 1920s followed soon after the artistic revolution of *Kebyar*, a new musical style whose main consequence was to allow dance to be detached from its theatrical content as well as from its ritual context in order to be turned into an art form in its own right (6). Indeed, dance had to become autonomous before it could be treated as a product to be exploited at will for commercial ends. Once freed of the constraints which hindered its autonomous development, Balinese dance could be made accessible to spectators unfamiliar with the linguistic codes, dramaturgic conventions and literary references of the traditional dance dramas. Besides, with *Kebyar* a dance performance became a much more expressive and narrative event, dynamic and linear instead of static and cyclical, hence much more likely to be appreciated by Westerners than the old-fashioned styles of music and dance.

In the 1920s, the management of the *pasanggrahan* of Denpasar had the novel idea of entertaining its guests by organizing dance performances created especially for them and staged on request. After the opening of the Bali Hotel by the KPM in 1928, these performances became a regular attraction, presented every Friday evening to the tourists freshly disembarked from Buleleng, and a pavilion was built for this purpose on the terrace of the hotel. The orchestra and most of the dancers came from the neighboring *banjar* of Belaluan. Soon afterwards, other performances were organized for the tourists on Saturday mornings at Kedaton on the outskirts of Denpasar.

---

(5) One may note that the two categories of tourist performance — dance and trance, the gracious princess and the horrible witch — correspond to the two complementary aspects of the Balinese ethos — the Apollonian and the Dionysian — as it was characterized in the 1930s by Gregory Bateson and Margaret Mead, and as it has figured since then in the island's tourist image (Bateson & Mead 1942).

(6) The circumstances surrounding the birth of *Kebyar* around 1915 in North Bali remain obscure, and the relationship of this event to the social situation brought about by colonization has yet to be investigated. For all we know, it was initially a purely instrumental composition, displaying the virtuosity of the musicians with extremely fast and complex rhythms, full of sudden stops and starts, in a profusion of contrapuntal ornamentation. In line with this stylistic innovation, musical compositions took on a life of their own, independent of any ritual celebration, literary recitation or dramatic performance. This newly conceived "concert" music combined a pot-pourri of elements borrowed from various repertoires into a single composition. In order to accommodate the new music, certain instruments were transformed and a brand new orchestra was created, the *gamelan gong kebyar;* new dances were devised to interpret its rhythms choreographically. In these new creations, instead of the musicians having to follow the cues of the dancer (who was strictly bound by the conventions of the particular character, as in most dramatic dances), now it tended to be the other way around, with the dancer expected to embody the tempo and mood of the music and thereby acquiring a wider range of personal expression. Furthermore, while each dance genre previously required a specific type of orchestra, the success of the *Kebyar* style has tended since then to impose the use of *gamelan gong kebyar* for most occasions, and the specialized orchestras have fallen into disuse, either neglected or deliberately recast as *gamelan gong kebyar.* On these matters, one may consult Seebass (1996) as well as McPhee (1966) and Tenzer (1991).

The troupes formed for the KPM soon became famous among visitors: thus the orchestra of Belaluan was proclaimed "the finest gamelan of Bali" (Powell 1930: 189), while Kedaton was described as "the home of the best dancers of the island" (Yates nd.: 16) (7). And the reputation acquired by these troupes among the foreigners soon gave them considerable prestige among the Balinese themselves. Interestingly enough, the *Gong Belaluan* was the first orchestra to impose *Kebyar*-style music in the south, shortly before entering the limelight of tourist performances. And it was the virtuoso dancer known as Mario who popularized the *Kebyar*-style dance by creating the *Kebyar Duduk*, which would become one of the most famous attractions of the Bali Hotel (8).

When the Dutch government invited a troupe of Balinese dancers and musicians — most of them from the Ubud-Peliatan area — to perform at the Colonial Exposition in Paris in 1931, the performances destined for a foreign public were already well polished. The problem of duration was resolved in the same way as at the Bali Hotel — that is, by the juxtaposition of short dances and, in the case of dance theater, by the reduction of a dramatic genre to an accelerated series of the most spectacular episodes.

After independence, Balinese dancers once again were able to perform outside their island. Foreign impresarios organized international tours, the most famous of which is still certainly that headed by the Englishman John Coast, who in 1952 accompanied a troupe from Peliatan to Europe and the United States (Coast 1953). It was with this tour in mind that Coast fixed the program which henceforth became

(7) While most accounts of the time abound with praises for the performances organized by the KPM, a few more exacting connoisseurs manage to insinuate a much less flattering account, such as Philip Hanson Hiss, an American museum curator who visited Bali shortly before the war:

> *The KPM... has done much, perhaps too much, to make the dances and music both dramatic and interesting... When I first saw these performances, I was interested in the sheer virtuosity of some of the music and dances... Later, after I had seen dozens of performances in the different towns throughout Bali, I understood why these performances at the Bali Hotel, though by many of the same gamelans and dancers, appeared to lack something essential. The stage setting of the KPM is too over-powering and in some ways too artificial an atmosphere for Balinese dance and music. But most important of all, the people who form the natural background for all Balinese performances are missing... The KPM has also attempted to inject as much sex as possible into the dances, and sex is the one quality that is almost entirely absent from the Balinese dance, therefore its appearance strikes a false note. Furthermore, the KPM has, of necessity, employed the same dancers and orchestras over and over again because of the difficulty of bringing many people and instruments from great distances, and these particular musical clubs have received what, to them, is a considerable income. They have been playing to an uncritical audience, which has little notion whether the performance is good or bad; consequently there has been a steady slackening of effort.* (Hiss 1941: 64–65)

(8) The name given to Mario's famous creation was borrowed from Malay rather than Balinese. In fact, he first called this dance *Kebyar Jongkok* ("Crouching *Kebyar*" in Balinese, which more accurately describes its choreography). It was only after it became a tourist attraction that the dance was known — among the Balinese as well — by the name of *Kebyar Duduk* ("Seated *Kebyar*" in Malay).

the model par excellence for performances of Balinese dance.

This same program was taken up again in the late 1960s by the management of the Bali Beach Hotel in Sanur, where it was presented poolside at the dinner hour, and today it still constitutes the usual program of dances presented to tourists. It is comprised of a succession of short dances, deemed suitable to the tastes and attention span of foreign spectators. Some of these were extracted from their original contexts to become solo dances (*Baris, Topeng, Jauk*); some were conceived from the outset for a foreign audience (*Panyembrama, Oleg Tamulilingan*); others are abridged and simplified versions of court dances (*Legong*), or modern creations (*Kebyar Duduk, Taruna Jaya, Panji Semirang*). Rigorously standardized, these performances were collectively called "Legong Dance", even though they often conserved *Legong* only in name (9).

The advent of tourists thus greatly stimulated the rise of the so-called "free" dance performances (*tari lepas*) — free in the sense that they are detached from all ritual or dramatic ties. For anyone who is even a little familiar with dance and theater in Bali, it is obvious that such performances are far removed from the tastes of the Balinese public (10). And yet, the Legong Dance programs have met with clear success among the Balinese, and today they are frequently presented in the context of temple ceremonies.

In this regard, the history of the dance that opens presentations of Legong Dance — whether destined for tourists or the Balinese — is instructive. Originally this was a ritual dance, *Pendet*, performed in a temple by dancers carrying flowers, rice and incense in homage to the divinities seated in their shrines. In the 1950s, the practice spread to welcoming President Sukarno and his VIP guests at the airport with a *Pendet* dance on a grand scale. Later, the management of the Bali Beach Hotel decided to open every Legong Dance with a *Pendet*, as a way of welcoming the spectators. This brought objections from the island's religious authorities, concerned about the risk of desecrating a ritual dance — and they did not fail to denounce the impropriety of treating tourists like gods. At the beginning of the 1970s, a choreographer at the Conservatory of Music, I Wayan Beratha, was commissioned to compose a new dance

(9) Indisputably the best-known of all Balinese dances, the *Legong*, whose origin dates from the beginning of the 19th century, combines elements borrowed from a double tradition — partly from the *Sanghyang Dedari*, an ancient exorcistic dance executed by two very young girls in trance, and partly from *Gambuh*, the prototype of all forms of Balinese dance theater, probably originating in Java. From *Sanghyang* to *Legong* by way of *Gambuh*, one may see a movement toward the creation of a "pure" dance, detached from all ritual function and all dramatic content, and refined for the pleasure of the senses. Later on, *Legong* spread to the villages and was influenced by the *Kebyar*, which replaced the *gamelan pelegongan* with a *gamelan gong kebyar*, accelerated its rhythms and modernized its choreography. Its presentation to tourists reduced its duration from more than an hour to about ten minutes, and most of its eighteen or so known versions fell into disuse to the almost exclusive profit of the *Legong Lasem*. On the evolution of the *Legong*, one may refer to Bandem (1983)

(10) As attested by this remark by I Made Bandem, Head of the Academy of Indonesian Dance:

To the Balinese audience, this is akin to a meal consisting entirely of appetizers, (Bandem & deBoer 1981: 149)

A traditional Balinese statue in front of a temple (photograph by Rio Helmi).

A gigantic statue of the so-called Brahma Lelare *in Sakah (photograph by Rio Helmi).*

View of mount Agung from Ubud, Bali (photograph by Rio Helmi).

A royal cremation and mass cremation, Denpasar (photograph by Rio Helmi).

Panyembrama *(top) and* Kecak *(bottom) at the Art Center in Denpasar (photographs by Rio Helmi).*

The so-called "kris dance" (left) and the Barong Dance in Denjalan, Batubulan (below) (photographs by Rio Helmi).

Painting by I Made Budi used in 1991 as an advertisement by Garuda for the Visit Indonesia Year.

DK 1225 G

Artist's impression of the Garuda Wisnu Kencana (promotional leaflet 1994).

The Bali Nirwana Resort: "Naga dan Bali" . Cartoon by Jango Pramartha (1993) (photograph by Rio Helmi).

inspired by the *Pendet*, in the *Kebyar* style. This new creation, called *Panyembrama* (literally, "that which is offered to guests" in Balinese) or *Tari Selamat Datang* ("Welcome Dance" in Indonesian), has since replaced the ancient ritual dance at the opening of tourist performances. Eventually, this tourist version of a ritual dance returned to the temples, where it originated, after a number of dancers who had learned the *Panyembrama* at the Conservatory came to perform it instead of the *Pendet* in the course of temple ceremonies.

Ramayana Ballet

Inspired by the European ballet, the Ramayana Ballet was modeled on the performance of the same name created in Java in 1961 for the amphitheater built in front of the temple of Lara Jonggrang at Prambanan. The objective was to create a performance derived from Javanese court theater that would be accessible to a non-Javanese audience ignorant of its language and dramaturgical codes. Dubbed *Sendratari* — an Indonesian acronym composed on the bases *seni*, *drama*, *tari* (respectively "art", "theater, "dance") — this new genre was adapted the same year for a Balinese public by I Wayan Beratha, to celebrate the first anniversary of the Conservatory in Denpasar. The new dance, composed in *Kebyar* style and inspired by the Balinese legend *Jayaprana*, was an instant success. But it was not until 1965 that *Sendratari* became a recognized genre in Bali with the creation at the Conservatory of the *Sendratari Ramayana* by the same choreographer. In this new version of the *Ramayana*, the entire story of the epic poem was presented in a shortened form, keeping only the main episodes reduced to their simplest form to be compressed into a single performance (deBoer 1989).

To understand to what extent the *Sendratari* departed from the norms in force at the time, one must consider what theater was for the Balinese until then. In Balinese theater, the plot is secondary, to the point of being almost non-existent. A theatrical performance does not present a "play" — Balinese theater does not have "playwrights" and it does not recount the linear development of a narrative theme from beginning to end. To the contrary, for the Balinese, a theatrical performance is composed of a succession of separate scenes, a combination of independent elements that are juxtaposed one after the other. The theatrical conventions follow a precise code, but the progression of the performance is left to the free improvisation of a group of characters whom for lack of a generic term in Balinese we shall call *penasar* ("those who provide a foundation"), and who, if an analogy must be found, are something like the valet in the Western theatrical tradition.

The role these characters play arises from the particular nature of literature in Bali. The Balinese have a composite literary heritage at their disposal that provides a vast corpus from which they draw the inspiration that nourishes their dramatic art: the legendary kingdoms described by the Indian epics; the Javanese empire of Majapahit; and the Balinese principalities which succeeded it. The characters, circumstances and atmosphere respectively associated with each of these repertories are evoked by distinct literary genres. And each literary genre is characterized by its own linguistic and metrical codes which the Balinese these days tend to group under the generic term *kawi*, meaning "poetic language". The major consequence of this contemporary profusion of linguistic codes is to make translation and paraphrase necessary. For the Balinese, literature is not fixed in the circumstances of its writing but is a process that is constantly re-actualized, in the sense that a literary text is intended, not to be read, but to be heard in the course of a recitation — that is, to be sung (*pepaosan*) by a "reader" (*juru paos*) and then translated and paraphrased in vernacular language (*mabasan*) by an "interpreter" (*juru basa*) (Hooykaas 1979; Lansing 1983; Rubinstein 1988; Vickers 1986; Wallis 1979; Zurbuchen 1987).

Besides these sessions of poetry recitation, the actualization of the literary heritage in Bali takes place mainly in its theatrical performance. The choice of a narrative theme and dramatic genre is largely determined by its ceremonial context. But whatever genre may be considered, the particular structure of Balinese literature — indissociably comprising a text composed in an archaic idiom and its paraphrase improvised in the vernacular — requires the presence on stage of two distinct groups of characters. The first, who compose the world of kings and priests, of gods and demons, belong to the past evoked in the literature. They constitute a kind of structural equivalent of the reader in a recitation in that they speak in *kawi*. Their behavior is stereotyped and strictly obeys the linguistic and dramaturgical conventions that govern their literary source. The second group — the *penasar* — play the role of interpreters, in that they are charged with elucidating the teachings of the gods and ancestors in a language accessible to the spectators of today. As they go back and forth between the various characters of the classical past on the one hand, and between the world of literature and that of the daily life of the spectators on the other, the *penasar* act as mediators. And being simultaneously servants and advisors of the princes, in the guise of simple villagers or coarse buffoons, they enjoy considerable liberty of expression, interpreting the words and manners of their masters through parody and presenting a double grotesque of them, not hesitating to criticize them if they have a chance. But they are also charged with exposing the moral of the story, and they are enlisted as well in passing on various messages from the government to the spectators — messages that may deal with birth control or AIDS as well as the fostering of Balinese culture or the development of tourism.

The *penasar* generally come in pairs, usually representing an older and younger brother or a father and son. The elder is splendidly bombastic, infatuated with the importance of his duties, whereas the younger never misses an opportunity to mock his words or gestures. The more senior of the pair is imbued with the grandeur of his masters and remains tied to the values of the past; the second — slyly ingenuous — moves freely between the times and is a spokesman for the common man and problems of today (deBoer 1987; Hobart 1983; Emigh 1979; Kakul 1979).

As mediators, the *penasar* juxtapose contemporary problems and the exemplary situations of ancient times, thus establishing a continuity between the past and the present. By constantly placing the ancestral values in new contexts, they give them a pertinence that is always fresh, while by framing the changes that affect the daily life of the Balinese in the perspective of a well-established tradition, they are able to soften the shocks of what is new. In this way, the *penasar* help the Balinese to make sense of the modern world by integrating it into their cultural heritage and thereby contribute significantly to the famous capacity for selective adaptation that observers are prone to attribute to Balinese culture.

More precisely, by reminding the Balinese of their communal obligations, beliefs and values, the *penasar* show them what it is to be Balinese and how to behave as such. And on this well-established base of a shared vision of the world, they can thus project strange beings whose grotesque and inappropriate behavior belies their non-belonging to the Balinese world, whether they be demons of the past or tourists of today. By way of derision — by emphasizing the gross and ridiculous traits of that which is foreign, non-Balinese — the *penasar* disarm that which may be threatening or merely incomprehensible and allow the Balinese to make a place for them in the order of the world.

In any case, it should be clear by now that the distinctive character of Balinese theater, which permits it to endure by being enduringly entertaining, resides in the play of a dialectic between the stylized evocation of a literary theme and the parodic counterpoint offered by the *penasar*. We are now in a better position to evaluate the convulsion introduced to Balinese theater by *Sendratari*. Unlike traditional theater, which embroidered a literary theme perfectly well-known by the spectators and constantly renewed by the improvisation of the *penasar* and the response of the audience, *Sendratari* proceeds by fixing a complete narrative composed of a succession of episodes linked in a linear fashion through to the conclusion. Instead of literary characters expressing themselves in *kawi* with *penasar* to interpret their speech in Balinese, a narrator (*juru tandak*), seated among the musicians, comments on the progress of the storyline and speaks for the dancers who mime the action on the stage. The major consequence of this innovation is to render superfluous the traditional mediation assured by the *penasar*, reducing them to a subordinate position of attendants to the noble characters (11, overleaf).

Another prime innovation popularized by *Sendratari* is the adoption of a raised stage facing the audience (*panggung*). This innovation, which originated in the theater built on the campus of the Conservatory, is a radical departure from the traditional conception of a stage in Bali. The Balinese stage (*kalangan*) is a rectangular space on the ground, with rather vague boundaries, which the spectators surround on three sides, while the musicians are placed according to the type of orchestra they play. Always provisional, it is set up wherever the circumstances of a performance dictate. The spatial conception of the *kalangan* determines the traditional form of Balinese choreography, which is three-dimensional, whereas with *Sendratari* — as, by the way, with most *Kebyar*-style dances — the dancers facing the audience are limited to a two-dimensional space.

Since the 1960s, a number of literary themes have given rise to new *Sendratari*, and today this theatrical genre is — with *Drama Gong* — the most fashionable among the Balinese. As for the *Sendratari Ramayana*, it rapidly spread to the villages, where it enjoyed huge popularity during the 1970s. This success confirmed it as a genre in itself under the name "Ramayana Ballet". And it is under this name that it has become a standard tourist performance. In the course of this evolution of *Sendratari Ramayana* toward Ramayana Ballet, the narrator disappeared, taking *Sendratari* even further from Balinese theatrical conventions.

Barong and Kris Dance

This performance was born of the obvious interest of the early travelers for the masked figures of the *Barong* and *Rangda*. Most descriptions of these two mythical monsters make them the protagonists of a battle that always arises between a wicked "witch" and a friendly "dragon", between the practitioners of "black magic" and those of "white magic", consequently putting the accent on the conflict between a principle of destruction and a principle of protection. One may see in this interpretation the traces of a Western frame of reference — the conflict between good and evil — rather than the expression of the Balinese vision of the world for whom it might be:

(11) It is certainly no coincidence that, at the moment when the *penasar* were losing their *raison d'être* in *Sendratari*, their propensity for parody and buffoonery flourished in a new theatrical genre, *Drama Gong* (Listibiya 1970). Created in 1966, at the very time when the Balinese were killing each other, *Drama Gong* can be seen as the inverse replica of *Sendratari*. Initially inspired by the same themes, it treated them entirely differently, sacrificing choreography to verbal comedy and melodrama — so much so that in abandoning conventional stylization for a realistic style of playing, largely improvised, the contrast between the literary characters and the *penasar* becomes jumbled. The result is that even if the *penasar* recover in *Drama Gong* the pre-eminence they had lost in *Sendratari*, their primary function as interpreters has disappeared, since all the players speak in Balinese. It appears that the components of traditional theater ousted by *Sendratari* are exaggerated in *Drama Gong*, to the exclusion of all others. But what both genres have in common is the upheaval introduced by the disappearance of the role exercised until then by the *penasar*. Whether they are reduced to a minor role in *Sendratari* or take on a much greater presence in *Drama Gong*, the *penasar* no longer have the opportunity to assume their role as mediators because of the disappearance of the dialogical polyphony that until recently was still the distinctive feature of Balinese theater. To conclude, we may note that unlike *Sendratari*, where the predominant aspect is visual, the emphasis of *Drama Gong* on verbal comedy renders it inaccessible to a non-Balinese audience.

> *... not a question of good or evil, rather an issue of power, of like challenging like, a basic principle of Tantric magic, of establishing a rapport with the fearsome but ambiguous demonic.* (Lovric 1988: 42)

The life and well-being of the Balinese depend, in effect, on the intervention of supernatural forces, which can be invoked and propitiated by the execution of the appropriate rituals.

With *Rangda* and the *Barong*, we are dealing with fundamentally ambivalent powers that are at once destructive and protective, in the sense that the Balinese perceive these figures as being simultaneously responsible for epidemics or other catastrophes and for their prevention. The masks that represent them have been subjected to certain rites of consecration after which they have become the receptacle of a supernatural force. Once these masks are charged with "power" (*sakti*), they become magically dangerous to handle (*tenget*), and they can be manipulated only by those duly initiated (Belo 1949, 1960; Emigh 1984; Geertz 1994; Lovric 1987; Rickner 1972).

The mask of *Rangda* is a receptacle for the power of the deity Durga, who on the condition of receiving the veneration and offerings due her, is expected to protect the community against epidemics. This mask also has the power to control *leyak* — sorcerers who have acquired the ability to transform themselves and propagate illness.

The mask of the *Barong* may be found in various animal forms. The most common and most powerful, the *Barong Ket,* does not depict a particular animal but resembles the image of *Kala-Boma,* a protective symbol adorning gateways and other transitional spaces. The *Barong* is a fantastic beast animated by two men, and it is paraded through the village, dancing in front of each house courtyard, during the feast of *Galungan.* The aim of this protective rite is to control the *buta kala,* demons who transmit illness and are responsible for all sorts of calamities.

While they are not indissociable, the *Barong* and *Rangda* often confront each other in the context of "exorcistic" (12) rites, when it is considered necessary to restore a disturbed equilibrium. Toward the end of the last century, this ritual confrontation was embedded in a theatrical performance drawn from an ancient text of magic, *Calonarang.* For the Balinese, a performance of *Calonarang* is an exorcistic drama, a means of magically preventing and controlling epidemics. In order for the rite to be efficacious, it is necessary for the dancer wearing the mask of *Rangda* to become possessed by its inherent power, a sign that Durga is actually participating in the event and that she will consequently protect the community. The most spectacular part of this ritual drama, the final confrontation between *Rangda* and the *Barong,* involves a group of "followers" of the Barong possessed by *buta kala,* who hurl

(12) As Hildred Geertz remarks, the term "exorcistic", as with others drawn from Judeo-Christian theology, is misleading:

> *The ritual does not act to dispel evil beings from the vicinity, but rather to persuade them to transform themselves from malevolence to benevolence.* (Geertz 1994: 81)

themselves on *Rangda* with raised kris knives. At this moment, overcome by her power, they stop in their tracks, struck numb, and turn their knives against their chests in suicidal fury (*ngurek*).

It is easy to imagine that such a spectacle drew the attention of visitors in search of the sensational, and travelers' accounts made horrified allusions to it (13). In 1931 at the Colonial Exposition in Paris, an excerpt of *Calonarang* — which made a strong impression on Antonin Artaud (1931) — was presented by dancers from Singapadu (14). Some years later, Jane Belo undertook a study of trance in Bali, in association with Margaret Mead, Gregory Bateson, Katharane Mershon, and Walter Spies (Belo 1949, 1960). This informal group commissioned performances of the *Barong* and *Rangda* — including the *ngurek*, named the "kris dance" for the occasion (15) — by troupes from Denjalan, Pagutan and Tegaltamu in Batubulan, the village next to Singapadu. Unlike ritual performances, which generally take place at night, these were held during the day so that they might be photographed and filmed. In 1936, at the instigation of Walter Spies, the troupes from Denjalan and Pagutan began to compete with each other in presenting *Calonarang* performances for visitors. The same year, the dancers of Singapadu, seeing the success of their rivals, also decided to launch themselves into the business of producing commercial performances. In order to be more easily understood by a foreign audience, one of Singapadu's most famous dancers, I Made Kredek, devised a special hour-long story based on the exorcistic text *Kunti Sraya*, which emphasized the dramatic aspects and reduced the dialogue to a strict minimum. With this innovation, soon followed by the troupes from Batubulan, the Barong and Kris Dance was born, and it has been a success ever since (16).

This success was due in large part to its ambiguity. In fact, from the very moment that exorcistic rites began to be staged for them, foreign spectators began to wonder the ambiguity, such as Stella Benson who wrote after having watched a "kris dance":

> *I was prepared to be impressed either by a good show or by a storm of religious frenzy, but I wanted to know which I was witnessing.* (Benson 1935: 266)

---

(13) An example among many, taken from an account by Helen Eva Yates:
A barbaric Balinese dance is that called the Ranga [sic]... I had heard too much about it to care to see it... At the height of their fanatic contortions, they are said to whip out small krises, or long pins and other instruments of torture. They gouge their flesh, pull their hair, and prick their bodies until the blood runs. Then the onlookers rush up and drink the blood, — but this is too terrible even to tell. I only wish that I did not have to say it is true. Though strictly forbidden by Dutch authorities, these medieval customs are carried on to-day in Bali — behind closed doors, of course. (Yates 1933: 157)

(14) The presentation of *Calonarang* in Paris raised a problem never encountered before and that would soon cause the Balinese much concern: could one use ritually consecrated masks for a performance intended for non-Balinese, outside any ritual context? According to the participants that I was able to interview, the masks used in Paris had been made especially for that event and had not been consecrated. Thus they were devoid of any ritual power. Nonetheless, although on the whole my informants agreed that ritually consecrated objects should not leave Bali, there was one among them who thought that the masks used in Paris were to have been consecrated before leaving. If they were not, it was, according to him, only because there was not time.

The problem was precisely that in Bali the line between dramatic play and trance is extremely difficult to draw, as Jane Belo points out:

> *In Bali, not only would the entranced behave as if they were acting, but the actor would behave almost as if he were in trance.* (Belo 1960: 27)

And indeed it is this very ambiguity that would finally pose problems for the Balinese themselves when they were obliged to distinguish ritual from tourist performance, as we shall soon see.

In any case, after being interrupted by the war, performances of the Barong and Kris Dance were revived in the 1960s by the troupes of Batubulan and Singapadu (Sanger 1988; Suci 1977). And now, every morning, dozens of buses and taxis choke the road at Batubulan where three troupes perform simultaneously for an hour. After the performance, the tourists continue their excursion toward the artshops of Celuk, Mas and Ubud along the road to Lake Batur or the temple of Besakih.

Monkey Dance, Angel Dance, Fire Dance

Like the Barong and Kris Dance, these are derived from a rite of exorcism, the *Sanghyang*, traditionally executed during epidemics. There are numerous forms of *Sanghyang*, of which the two most prevalent are the *Sanghyang Dedari* and the *Sanghyang Jaran* (Belo 1960; Lovric 1987; O'Neill 1978; Suryani & Jensen 1993).

The *Sanghyang Jaran* belongs to the category of animal *Sanghyang*, in which a medium in trance is entered by the spirit of the animal invoked in the exorcism and imitates its behavior. In the *Sanghyang Jaran*, the dancer rides a bamboo hobby-horse

---

(15) De Zoete & Spies write in this respect:

The men who during the performance of the Barong play regularly become possessed are called by Europeans "kris-dancers", because in the frenzy of possession each man attacks himself with his kris, and leaps about in an extravagant way which to Europeans suggests dancing. But the Balinese would never dream of describing their violent contortions as dancing. (de Zoete & Spies 1938: 67–68).

They had certainly not anticipated that this term would become so popular among the Balinese that they themselves would talk about *penari kris* ("kris dancers" in Indonesian).

(16) The interest of foreign residents in the *Barong* and *Rangda* did not only give birth to a new performance intended for tourists; it seems that it also raised the importance of these figures in Balinese ceremonial life, to the point of conferring them with an emblematic status (Vickers 1989: 145). More recently, they have become highly prized advertising tools, permitting any sort of product to be associated with the glamor of Balinese magic.

barefoot through the coals of burning coconut husks. The *Sanghyang Jaran*, executed by one or more dancers, is accompanied by a male chorus called *cak*.

The *Sanghyang Dedari* is executed by two young pre-pubescent girls who, in a state of trance, are identified with celestial nymphs for whom they become the receptacle. Carried on litters or on the shoulders of men, they are conducted in procession to the four corners of the village. After the procession, they are taken back to the temple to which they belong where they dance, accompanied in turns by a chorus of women (*kidung*) and of men (*cak*). Their dance may be drawn from various repertories, generally *Legong* or *Calonarang*. At the conclusion of the ceremony, they produce a holy water which has the power to "dissolve impurities", and they prescribe ritual remedies required by the situation.

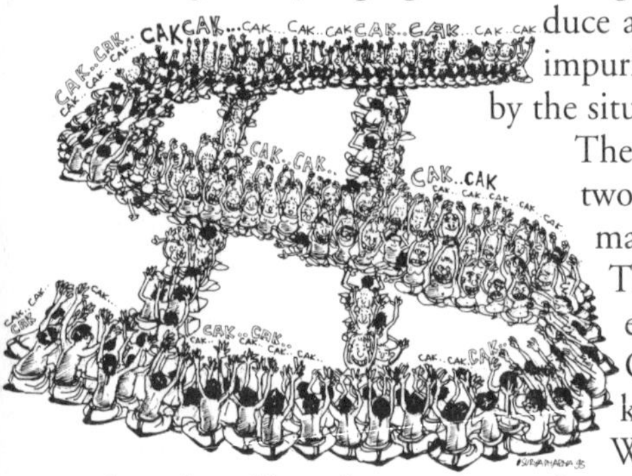

The touristic exploitation of *Sanghyang* occurred in two stages. First came the *Kecak*, inspired by the male chorus accompanying the *Sanghyang* trance. The initiative for using this chorus for theatrical ends is claimed by two villages in the region of Gianyar, Bedulu and Bona. Difficult as it is to know the origins with certainty, it seems that Walter Spies caught word of certain innovations introduced by a famous dancer from Bedulu, I Wayan Limbak, who happened to be his driver at the time. In response to his suggestions, a performance was composed using, instead of the usual musical accompaniment, a chorus of *cak* vocally reproducing the sounds and rhythms of the gamelan and illustrating an episode from the *Ramayana*. And when in 1931 Baron von Plessen asked Spies to be his advisor for the shooting of his film *Insel der Dämonen*, filmed in Bedulu, Spies modified the *Kecak* by enlarging the chorus to some 50 men seated in concentric circles for a more dramatic staging. Although this performance was an instant success among Spies's friends and passing visitors, the Balinese seem to have rapidly lost interest in it. In any case, it became popular among the tourists under the name of the "Monkey Dance", in reference to the male chorus playing the role of the army of monkeys sent by the prince Rama to rescue the beautiful Sita, his beloved wife who had been kidnapped by the demon Rawana.

Fallen somewhat out of fashion after the war, the *Kecak* came under the influence of the Ramayana Ballet toward the end of the 1960s, at the initiative of graduates of the Conservatory returning to their villages. The story, until then limited to one episode of the *Ramayana*, was extended to the entire epic, keeping only the principal motifs as in the *Sendratari*. The choreography, melodies and costumes were also modified in such a way as to adapt them to *Kebyar* style. These innovations were well received and had the effect of re-launching the vogue for *Kecak*, and it became one of the performances most admired by tourists. This new tourist product was so popular that — it is said — travel agents told the troupes they controlled that their *Kecak* must be in the *Sendratari* style or they would stop bringing clients.

During the 1930s, one of the most famous *Kecak* had been that of Bona; but when the tourists returned in the 1970s, the *Kecak* of Bona had lost its former reputation due to competition from other troupes and the standardization of tourist performances. To attract tourists again, some of the villagers decided to revive their *Sanghyang* which had become obsolete with the disappearance of the epidemics it was employed to combat. So they added a *Sanghyang Dedari* and a *Sanghyang Jaran* — renamed "Angel Dance" and "Fire Dance" — to their *Kecak* performances, and today this show is presented in Bona six times a week by three different troupes. The success of this initiative incited troupes in Kuta and Legian to offer similar performances to tourists staying in their village. But we note with interest that in Camenggaon and in Ketewel — two villages not far from Bona, where the *Sanghyang Dedari* is still carried out for exorcistic purposes — the priests there and, it seems, the village community unanimously declare themselves opposed to any attempt to turn this into a tourist performance.

Performances for the Balinese and performances for tourists

This short presentation of the main types of tourist performances should give clear evidence of the many kinds of interference that occur between performances intended for the Balinese and those that have been adapted for a foreign audience.

To summarize, the Legong Dance and the Ramayana Ballet are modern creations, directly conceived as mere entertainments. The performances of the Legong Dance were composed for the Bali Hotel, and the Ramayana Ballet was originally intended for an urbanized Balinese public, influenced by an Indonesian vision of the performing arts. Both being favorably received in the villages, they have both ended up occupying an important place in the Balinese repertory.

The performances derived from rites of exorcism — the Barong and Kris Dance on the one hand and the Monkey Dance, Angel Dance and Fire Dance on the other — each evolved in a particular way. Besides their appearance in tourist performances, the *Barong* and *Rangda* are used by the Balinese for ritual purposes — on their own, or in the context of a performance of *Calonarang*. The *Kecak*, already long detached from its ritual context, has become an entertainment used almost exclusively for tourists. As for the *Sanghyang Dedari* and the *Sanghyang Jaran*, which have never been regarded as entertainment by the Balinese, they are still performed today as exorcistic rituals in some villages; in others they have been converted into tourist attractions.

Finally, with the *Panyembrama* — the welcome dance that opens the Legong Dance program — the cycle is completed, going from ritual to entertainment and returning to ritual use. Here is a temple dance, the *Pendet*, which because of the risk of profanation that it ran in being performed outside its ritual context, gave birth to a secular copy at the urging of the religious authorities. Henceforth appropriate for commercialization, the new version ended up being reintegrated into the temple ceremonies from which it originated: in a curious reversal that the religious authorities did not anticipate, the tourist "welcome dance" became a sacred dance for welcoming the gods.

In conclusion, then: although it is easy to show that the conversion of Balinese dance into a tourist attraction upsets relations between its ritual and theatrical aspects — which we have seen are not so easy to distinguish traditionally — we also see that this upheaval leads to results that are hardly uniform or predictable:

- the performances of Legong Dance and Ramayana Ballet are part of a general movement, initiated by the *Kebyar*, that tends to detach dance from its dramatic content as well as its ritual context — a movement that these accentuate in that they have been taken up on their own account by the Balinese;

- performances exploiting the spectacular nature of the *Barong* and *Rangda* have a more ambiguous effect in that they contribute to a dissociation of theater from ritual, and at the same time they blur the boundaries that distinguish them;

- finally, the commercialization of the *Sanghyang* and the *Pendet* resulted in the converting of a ritual dance into a tourist attraction.

3. The Seminar on Sacred and Profane Dance

Such confusion between ritual and spectacle, between what the Balinese offer to the gods and what they stage for the tourists, was alarming to the Balinese authorities. They reacted by trying to consolidate the religious foundations of Balinese art, while attempting at the same time to draw a boundary between that which belongs to religion and that which pertains to art. This meant first reminding the population of the religious value of their art, so that they would not be seduced by the aestheticizing gaze with which the tourists regard their ceremonies and ritual performances. But it was equally important to inform them of the distinctions to be applied between the art forms that must be maintained according to tradition and those they were permitted to adapt for the tourist market. Hence the necessity of setting out precise and explicit rules that would allow artists to know what they are authorized to sell to tourists and what in no case should be commercialized. It was with this objective that in March 1971 — even before the publication of the Master Plan and the convocation of the Seminar on Cultural Tourism — the cultural authorities of the province held a Seminar on Sacred and Profane Dance (*Seminar Seni Sakral dan Provan Bidang Tari*) (Proyek 1971).

The sacred and the profane

The objectives of the seminar were formulated in the following way: to separate "sacred art" (*seni sakral*) from "profane art" (*seni provan*) in regard to dance, and to distinguish among different sacred dance forms those that "could be profaned" (*boleh di"provan"kan*) and those which "must preserve their sacred character" (*harus tetap di"sakral"kan*). The task proved to be a delicate one, to judge from the difficulty experienced by the participants of the seminar, a council of academics and high Balinese officials solicited to write a paper on the subject, and who confessed to being unable to separate the sacred and the profane in regard to dance. This is hardly surprising, given that the Balinese language has no terminology that would permit its speakers to think about the conceptual opposition of these two terms. And in fact, like any public matter in Indonesia, the seminar was conducted in Indonesian, a language which no more than Balinese has terms for "sacred" and "profane". As a result, the organizers had to fall back on neologisms borrowed from the Latin languages for the very framing of the problem to be resolved (17).

This semantic borrowing resulted in some awkward attempts on the part of the participants to forge a distinction that was foreign to them. Bewildered by the given terms of reference, two of them looked for clarification in their Dutch dictionaries, which led them to commit a revealing reversal of sense. Instead of framing the problem that they were enlisted to resolve as an attempt to discriminate between domains until then undifferentiated — or more precisely, that they were not accustomed to distinguish explicitly in terms of "sacred" and "profane" — they ended up speaking of "sacred and profane dances" as one and the same category, and in so doing, they conferred upon the same dances the attributes of both sacred and profane, attributes that these Balinese intellectuals obviously confused.

Such is the "challenge" that tourism has thrown up to the Balinese. Not only are they called upon to slice into the living flesh of their culture, to perform a new, unknown incision, to draw a "boundary" (*batas*) where they knew only a continuum, but also, to make things worse, they are obliged to think in a borrowed terminology that visibly makes no sense to them. In their perplexity, they see no other recourse than to look for rescue in the language of their former colonizers. And so they are reduced to searching within a foreign mode of thought for the concepts that are supposed to help them protect the most inalienable of their cultural values from the threat wrought by the presence of foreign tourists in their territory.

Lacking the conceptual apparatus required to treat the question in terms of sacred and profane, I Gusti Agung Gede Putra, the Head of the Provincial Office of the Department of Religion (the highest official authority for religious affairs in the province), tried to transpose the problem to a more familiar terrain, that occupied by the terms *agama* ("religion") and *adat* ("custom") (18). This, in fact, only shifted the problem: although now there were terms available in which to think — even if their meanings are fairly different in Indonesian and Balinese — their semantic fields largely

---

(17) When I tried to find out the reasons for using the terms *sakral* and *provan* in the title of the seminar, I was told that this decision was imposed by the Provincial Office of the Department of Education and Culture with the idea of enlarging the debate by giving it a bearing that was at once "national" and "scientific". Moreover, some of the organizers admitted that the choice of a foreign terminology had been considered necessary in that the younger generation no longer understood the meaning of traditional Balinese terms. Whatever the reason, by deciding to treat their dances in terms of opposition between the sacred and the profane, the Balinese officials stepped into an impasse that had long trapped foreign observers.

(18) In contemporary Indonesia, the term *agama* (of Sanskrit origin) officially defines "religion", considered under its universalist and monotheistic aspects, while that of *adat* (of Arabic origin) designates "custom", understood in the sense of the ways and customs bequeathed by the ancestors and consequently specific to a particular ethnic group.

overlap. Unlike transcendental religions of a universal scope, the Balinese religion is in many respects localized. Its rituals are directed toward affirming relations between social groups, with their ancestors and with their territory. Participation in these rituals is part of the customary obligations incumbent upon an individual as a member of his surrounding community and as part of a particular descent group. That is to say that in Bali, custom is a religious reality, custom is the expression of an immutable cosmic order that has been codified in a social order bequeathed by the deified ancestors, at once defining the ideal order and prescribing the behavior required to achieve that order.

I Gusti Agung Gede Putra, recognizing the difficulty of clearly distinguishing that which pertains to custom from that which belongs to religion, tried to extricate himself from the difficulty by separating from *adat* all that should, according to him, belong to the sphere of *agama*. This latter part of *adat* he qualifies as "religious custom" (*adat keagamaan*) in order to distinguish it from what he considers as pertaining to "ordinary customary practices" (*adat kebiasaan*). By doing this, he embarks on a semantic re-casting, where *agama*, now augmented by *adat keagamaan*, is differentiated from *adat*, a category that becomes residual because now what remains is only that which relates to *adat kebiasaan* (Putra 1971). In this way, a Balinese conception of the "sacred" was created by dividing up the semantic field previously covered by the category *adat*, and removing those practices considered non-religious. These would then be grouped with modern activities to compose the sphere of the "profane".

Now, why was it so important to the Balinese authorities to separate the "sacred" from the "profane"? Since they perceived tourism as the unleashing of a tidal wave battering their coasts, the Balinese tried to build protective dikes against this foreign assault, to keep their most "sacred" values from being "profaned" by the tourists. The firm base to which they cling in confronting this assailant is their religion, conceived as the "foundation" (*sendi*), the "origin" (*induk*), the "essence" (*intisari*) of their cultural identity. And having circumscribed the hard kernel of what constitutes their "religion" (*agama*) — which henceforth defines the sphere of the "sacred" — that which does not pertain to the religion but to the sphere of "custom" (*adat*) becomes available for "profane" use.

The result of this conceptual re-casting is that the meaning of *adat* as the expression of a world order that is at once cosmic and social has become secularized, relativized and, by being deprived of its religious foundations, is rendered negotiable. This desacralization of *adat* — besides raising inextricable epistemological problems — is causing widespread incomprehension and resentment among the Balinese population. Be that as it may, once *adat* is secularized, its practices can be either discarded like a worn out old "skin" (*kulit*) — if they happen to displease the authorities or the tourists — or they might be converted into tourist attractions, thus regaining in aesthetic quality what they had lost in religious prerogatives, and thereby becoming "art" (*seni*) (19).

But one should be aware that in this case it is not only tourism that is the issue. The delimitation of a "sacred" sphere, dissociated from the rest of the social practices to become the exclusive property of *agama*, is part of a strategy long employed by the

Balinese authorities to circumscribe a reserved domain and have it recognized by the Indonesian government (20). In this sense, the Balinese response to the challenge of tourism is part of a movement of religious rationalization which strives to reform the religious practices and beliefs of the population toward a monotheism of Hinduist inspiration, with the aim of having them admitted to the ranks of *agama* — in the same standing as Islam or Christianity — by the Department of Religion (21, overleaf).

It remains now to see how this religious rationalization is expressed in Bali. Difficult as it is to obtain precise formulations on this point, one can perhaps discern among the Balinese a tendency to reduce the ambivalence traditionally attached to expressions of the supernatural. This tendency manifests itself in an attempt to conceptually dissociate that which pertains to religion from that associated with magic, the divine from the demonic, or perhaps more precisely, that which is vested with a supernatural power (*sakti*) from that which is ritually consecrated and purified (*suci*). One of the most common signs these days of this trend is the growing propensity of Balinese intellectuals — particularly marked among those eager to explain their culture to tourists — to interpret the conflicts played out in Balinese theater in terms of "good" (*kebaikan*) and "evil" (*keburukan*). This is especially the case with the theatrical confrontation between the *Barong* and *Rangda*, where the morally ambivalent notion of *sakti* is more and more frequently substituted with an unequivocal moral view. The epistemological dangers of this were pointed out already long ago by de Zoete & Spies:

> *To express the fight between the Barong and Rangda in terms of good and evil is to miss the point.* (de Zoete & Spies 1938: 97) (22, overleaf)

Sacred, ceremonial and secular dances

The inability of the Balinese authorities to separate the sacred from the profane, as they had intended, led the participants of the seminar to create a new set of problems:

---

(19) Marked as it is by the touristification of Balinese culture, this evolution of the meaning of *adat* is not particular to Bali, as is shown by the studies of Susan Rodgers and Rita Kipp on the Batak of Sumatra and by Greg Acciaioli and Toby Volkman on the Toraja of the Celebes (Acciaioli 1985; Kipp 1993; Rodgers Siregar 1979; Volkman 1984). There is an interesting selection of articles on the relations between *adat* and *agama* in various Indonesian societies in Kipp & Rodgers (1987).

(20) A characteristic example of this strategy is furnished by the response of the Balinese authorities to the prohibition of cockfights (*tajen*) by the Indonesian government in 1981 in the framework of a national campaign to put an end to gambling. Refusing to renounce *tajen* altogether, the Balinese were constrained to discriminate between that which must be conserved as a sacrifice to chthonic forces (*tabuh rah*) — in this respect constituting a ritual necessity — and that which should be suppressed as a simple pretext for gambling (*judi*). To this end, they formulated the problem in terms of a distinction between that which pertains to *agama* and that which pertains to *adat*, defined as an opposition between "that which arises from reason" and "that which relates to customary practice". On this subject, see Picard (1983).

a nomenclature distinguishing three categories of dance and accompanied, moreover, by a gloss in English, which its authors somehow thought would make things clearer.

1 - *Seni tari wali* ("sacred, religious dances") - performed in the inner courtyard (*jeroan*) of a temple or wherever a ceremony is taking place, indissociable from the carrying out of the ceremony (*pelaksana upacara*). These dances are generally devoid of narrative elements (*Pendet, Rejang, Baris Gede, Sanghyang*) (23).

2 - *Seni tari bebali* ("ceremonial dances") - performed in the central courtyard (*jaba tengah*) of a temple or elsewhere, accompanying a ceremony (*pengiring upacara*). These dances are narrative in character (*Wayang, Topeng, Gambuh*, and the principal theatrical genres derived from them) (24).

3 - *Seni tari balih-balihan* ("secular dances") - performed in the outer courtyard (*jaba*) of a temple or elsewhere, as pure entertainment (*hiburan*), with no relation to a ceremony, and not belonging to the category of *wali* or *bebali.*

One will notice that the term *balih-balihan* has no intrinsic content, in that it is defined in a residual manner — that is, it is whatever does not qualify as *wali* or *bebali.* That said, its sense is quite clear, in that being constructed from the base *balih* (literally, "that which is watched"), it can be rendered as "spectacle" or "performance". The distinction between the respective semantic fields of *wali* and *bebali*, on the other hand, is more difficult to discern. These two words have a common etymology in the Sanskrit base *bali* — and although it need hardly be pointed out that this is the very name of the island, it is interesting to note that it signifies "offering". The official Balinese-Indonesian dictionary distinguishes the two terms, however, translating *bebali* as "offering" (*sesajen*) and *wali* as "ceremony" (*upacara*) (Warna et al., 1990: 55, 789).

If one turns now to the Balinese literati and to the dancers themselves, one finds that the distinction between *wali* and *bebali*, drawn by the authorities responsible for

---

(21) Although in fact this dates from the colonial period, the movement for religious reform in Bali was precipitated by independence. While the Indonesian Constitution guaranteed religious liberty to its citizens, the Department of Religion, controlled by the Muslims, required that they espouse a religion professing a strictly monotheistic conception of the divine and not limited to a particular ethnic group — which initially restricted the choice to Islam or Christianity. The Balinese found themselves relegated to the residual category of peoples "not yet having a religion" (*belum beragama*) in the sense that their rituals were considered to pertain to "custom" (*adat*) and not to "religion" (*agama*). Consequently, if they wanted to avoid having to convert to one of the recognized religions, they had no other recourse than to reform their rituals in order to make them eligible for the status of *agama.* To do this, the Balinese reformers reaffirmed their Indic heritage in such a way as to benefit from the internationally recognized stature of Hinduism, citing as their supreme deity *Sang Hyang Widi Wasa*, with a view to presenting their beliefs in a monotheistic light. This initiative was fruitful, for the Balinese religion was officially recognized by the Department of Religion in 1958 — first as *Agama Hindu Bali*, then abandoning all reference to Bali in 1964, as *Agama Hindu*. The following year, the Council of Hinduism (*Parisada Hindu Dharma*, which became *Parisada Hindu Dharma Indonesia* in 1986) was founded in Bali, which set itself the mission of regenerating the religious life of the Balinese community in conformity to the teachings of Hinduism. On these matters, one may refer to the study by F.L. Bakker (1993).

regulating dance performances for tourists, is not current in the villages. The literati and dancers I questioned about this agreed on the whole that the *wali* dances could be characterized as offerings dedicated to the gods, presented in the context of religious ceremonies. As to *bebali* dances, however, my informants showed real perplexity, and many of them admitted that they did not understand the meaning of this term, which was apparently hardly ever used before the seminar.

This conceptual difficulty was further aggravated by the fact that the categories comprising the nomenclature of 1971 were conceived in terms of contents, that is, certain dances were described as belonging intrinsically to certain categories — whereas in fact the choice of dances required for a particular ceremony varies with local custom. It is not surprising in these circumstances that opinions diverge when it comes to deciding whether such and such a dance should be considered *wali* or *bebali*. In an attempt to resolve this difficulty, I Gusti Agung Gede Putra, the Head of the Provincial Office of the Department of Religion who had had a crucial part in the seminar, proposed in 1978 to revise its conclusions. Emphasizing this time the function of each category rather than the contents, he suggested that *bebali* dances be considered *wali* when they "contribute to the execution of a ceremony" (*menunjang pelaksanaan upacara*) and as *balih-balihan* when they are presented as an "ordinary performance" (*tontonan biasa*) (Putra 1978: 1).

This revision led to the disappearance of the *bebali* category, with the result that "ceremonial" dances, which associate a ritual purpose with a dramatic content, now tend to be thought of either as ritual (*wali*) or as entertainment (*balih-balihan*) depending only on the context — religious or secular — of their performance.

What happened between the sudden appearance of this *bebali* category — or at least its revival — in 1971 and its discreet disappearance in 1978? For the participants in the seminar, most "traditional dances" (*tari tradisional*) — in this case, those

---

(22) Thus by an ironic reversal, the Balinese intellectuals fell (and continue to so) into the error for which foreign observers had long been reproached, tending to project an ethical interpretation inspired by the Judeo-Christian vision of personal choice and individual responsibility, whereas the forces looming on the Balinese stage express the reverberation of cosmic principles in the human world. Literati refer to these principles by the term *dharma* — and its opposite *a-dharma* — which should be understood as the harmonizing of behavior to the social order and its cosmic foundation.

(23) The *Pendet* and the *Rejang* are dances generally executed by women as members of a religious congregation. In the first, the dancers ceremonially consecrate offerings to the divinities who have descended into their shrines during the course of a temple festival; whereas in the second, it is the dance itself that constitutes an offering. The *Baris Gede* is a kind of male counterpart of these, in which ranks of men dance, carrying various implements.

(24) *Wayang* is a generic term, designating both shadow theater (*Wayang Kulit*) and the theatrical genres presenting episodes drawn from the *Ramayana* (*Wayang Wong*) or the *Mahabharata* (*Parwa*). *Topeng* is a masked theater that dramatizes the ancient chronicles of the Balinese princely houses. *Gambuh* is the oldest known form of court theater, which tells of the exploits of the prince *Panji*, known in Bali under the title of *Malat*.

pre-dating the advent of *Kebyar* and the coming of the tourists — were executed in the context of a religious ceremony and thus all qualified as *wali* (25). The risk of profanation by tourist commercialization constrained the Balinese authorities to make a conceptual discrimination where there had been none before, deciding which dances could be detached from their ceremonial context in order to be presented to tourists. This necessitated the creation of an intermediate category, that of *bebali*. But the fact that these dances had a "double function" (*dwi fungsi*) — a ritual function (*fungsi rituil*) and an entertainment function (*fungsi hiburan*) — required additional distinction, which finally led to the splitting of the *bebali* category.

The difficulties of discrimination

In 1973, a decree by the Governor of Bali officially ratified the conclusions of the seminar by prohibiting the commercial exploitation of "sacred dances", those considered to belong to the category *wali*. This decree forbade organizing performances of *wali* dances for tourists, although visitors were still permitted to watch these dances when they were performed in the ceremonial context in which their execution was required (26). But this did not yet solve the problem. Not only were the provincial authorities unable to enforce the new regulation, the character of dances classified as *bebali* remained ambiguous: while not explicitly forbidding their commercialization, in principle it reserved their presentation to the context of religious ceremonies.

The indecisiveness of the authorities was in fact a reflection of the perplexity of the performers themselves. When, in the same year, Udayana University launched its first survey on the sociocultural impact of tourism, most of the dancers interviewed — while unanimously deploring the growing commercialization of dance in Bali — believed that Cultural Tourism should promote the most authentic of the Balinese arts. Consequently, far from wanting to restrict the tourists to "floor shows" presented in the hotels — programs of Legong Dance composed of *balih-balihan* dances — these dancers were in favor of organizing authentic "art performances", that is, performances of *bebali* dances expressly for tourists (UNUD 1973a: 166).

A few years later, researchers from Udayana University asked the leaders of the most famous troupes of Badung and Gianyar — many of whom performed profitably for the tourist market — whether the *bebali* dances ought to be "touristified" (*ditoriskan*) or not. The responses this time contrasted starkly: while most dancers disapproved of commercializing the *bebali* dances, arguing that a dance was condemned to lose its value if it were adapted for tourists, there were some who saw in the presentation of *bebali* dances for tourists a welcome opportunity for their necessary "restoration" (*pemugaran*) (UNUD 1976: 48).

---

(25) As I Made Bandem remarked to Ed Herbst:
there are really only phenomena which are "very wali, wali, and less wali". (Herbst 1981: 50)

(26) In 1991, a circular from the Governor confirmed the dispositions of the decree of 1973, furnishing a list of the "sacred dances" (*tarian sakral*) expressly subject to this prohibition.

This disagreement expresses the unresolved tension between two divergent views of dance among the Balinese. For some, the image is one of a living tradition which runs the risk of becoming degraded by being offered for tourist consumption. Others believe that the Balinese cultural heritage should be not merely "protected" (*dipertahankan*), but also "excavated" (*digali*), "cultivated" (*dibina*) and "developed" (*dikembangkan*) (Listibiya 1973: 5-6), with the aim of stimulating tourism and at the same time reinforcing Balinese cultural identity. In other words, the issue here is a strategy — that of Cultural Tourism — in which tourism, rather than being a threat to the Balinese cultural heritage as some insist, is seen and employed as a promotional tool for Balinese culture.

Leaving aside for the moment an elucidation of this conflict, one may ask how the decree prohibiting the presentation of sacred dances expressly for tourists applies to the different genres of tourist performances described above. In the case of the Legong Dance and the Ramayana Ballet, it is clear that they belong to the category *balih-balihan* and that their presentation for tourists is therefore authorized. On the other hand, the *Pendet* and *Sanghyang* are defined as *wali* and thus may not be organized for tourists. But what of the Barong and Kris Dance, which does not figure in the nomenclature? And what of those performances derived from the *Sanghyang*, whose commercialization is in principle prohibited?

Although the *Kecak* was originally part of a ritual, it is generally considered by the Balinese today to be an entertainment for tourists. This is not the case of the so-called "Angel Dance" and "Fire Dance", imitations of the *Sanghyang Dedari* and the *Sanghyang Jaran*. As such, they are strictly prohibited — but this evidently does not prevent the Tourism Office from advertising them to tourists. As for the performances of the Barong and Kris Dance, they seem to have an ambiguous status among the Balinese authorities, at least to judge from the array of opinions that I was able to gather in this regard (27).

In an attempt to resolve this ambiguity, I Gusti Agung Gede Putra returned again to the question in 1982, this time proposing as a criterion of distinction for *wali* dances the prior "purification" (*penyucian*) which the dancers and their accessories must undergo before a performance. Consequently, the tourist performances derived from *wali* dances would be authorized as long as they did not use consecrated accessories (Putra 1982: 3) (28, overleaf).

Once it was agreed that the use of consecrated accessories should be restricted to *wali* dances, it is hardly surprising that the Balinese officials consulted on this point

(27) Thus wrote one cultural authority of the island:

There is the central question of the people to separate the ritual Barong from the secular Barong performance for the tourists. (Moerdowo 1977: 88)

Unable to resolve this problem, the Balinese tend to seek subterfuge of a semantic order, slightly modifying the name of a litigious dance in such a way as to tone down its "sacred" implications. And thus one speaks commonly today of *bebarongan* in regard to the Barong and Kris Dance.

quickly affirm that they are sure that the headdresses, masks, and kriss used in tourist performances indeed have not been consecrated. It is rather more surprising to find the same conviction among certain foreign observers who write without apparent hesitation that the masks of *Rangda* and of the *Barong* used in the Barong and Kris Dance are not consecrated (Bandem & deBoer 1981: 148; Eiseman 1985: 118; Emigh 1984: 38; Ramstedt 1992: 74; Rickner 1972: 27; Sanger 1987: 153).

Observation of the Barong and Kris Dance at Batubulan and performances of the Monkey Dance, Angel Dance and Fire Dance at Bona is enough to call this assurance into question. Indeed, it shows how difficult it is for the Balinese to distinguish between the ritual and theatrical dimensions of a performance, however commercial its intentions. Specifically, these performances, created expressly for tourists, tend to use similar ritual procedures as the ceremonies that inspired them, be they the presentation of offerings or the use of consecrated accessories (29).

Why do the Balinese dancers seem to be so reluctant to do without consecrated accessories, even when they perform for tourists? Because, they explain, they count on the "inspiration" (*taksu*) that emanates from them (30). According to the dancers of Batubulan interviewed, without the proper consecration rituals a *Rangda* or *Barong* mask is just a "dead" (*mati*) piece of wood. On the other hand, the use of consecrated masks allows a performance to be "living" (*idup*), and thus assures its success for the audience — and this is so even if the audience is non-Balinese and obviously incapable of knowing whether a mask is consecrated or not. But the consecration of a *Barong* or *Rangda* mask makes it the vehicle of a supernatural power that may manifest its presence by taking "possession" (*karauhan*) of the dancer wearing it. Thus the use of consecrated masks in the performance of the Barong and Kris Dance may make the performance magically active and consequently dangerous — hence the necessity of taking the normal ritual precautions (31).

In these conditions, we understand that the dancers, while admitting that the "trance" episodes are generally simulated, recognize that occurrences of genuine

---

(28) Every performance, whether it is given in the inner courtyard of a temple or beside a hotel swimming pool, is preceded by offerings, some to the "powers on high" (*ring luhur*), others to the "powers below" (*ring sor*). Moreover, the dancers undergo a succinct purification and invoke "inspiration" (*taksu*) of supernatural forces before going on stage. More specifically in regard to *wali* dances, the dancers are required to have undergone a ritual purification called *mawinten*. The theatrical accessories, such as headdresses (*gelungan*), masks (*tapel*) and kriss (*keris*), are consecrated after their fabrication. As for the masks of *Rangda* and the *Barong*, they are charged with a "magical power" (*sakti*) rendering their manipulation "dangerous" (*tenget*), by means of complex procedures, after which they become receptacles for the unearthly forces they represent.

(29) This observation is confirmed by Suryani & Jensen who write in regard to the tourist performances at Bona:

It is significant that the religious aspect of Sang Hyang Dedari is retained, even though the performance is for tourists: the dancers always pray beforehand and the priest is conspicuous. It can be assumed that if the religious context is not present, the little girls will not experience trance-possession. (Suryani & Jensen 1993: 111) possession are not unusual (32), and even that accidents sometimes happen during the "kris dance" that concludes the performance. Moreover, in both Batubulan and Bona, the villagers readily attest to supernatural benefits for their community resulting from the tourist performances, as if they made no distinction between a commercial enterprise and a rite of exorcism. This is all the more astonishing in the case of Bona where — at least according to my informants, unanimous on this point — the *Sanghyang* ceremonies died out in the 1930s with the medical eradication of the periodic epidemics they were supposed to combat (33, overleaf).

In this sense, contrary to the intellectuals and religious officials, the Balinese literati and dancers in no way wish to dissociate the sacred from the profane, and the ambiguity seems not to trouble them. In short, while the authorities strive to "disenchant" the world, the dancers in search of inspiration continue to evolve in an "enchanted" world.

But is this not perhaps still the case of the intellectuals themselves, despite their denials and their evident will to rationalize? During the course of my fieldwork, I happened to show to Balinese of different backgrounds a particular promotional image, a montage showing *Rangda* embraced on either side by a tourist couple in a high party mood. As far as I could tell, their first reaction was always identical: shocked by what they said was the impropriety of the scene and manifestly disturbed by its incongruity. Then came the moment of discrimination, depending on the intellectual sophistication of my interlocutor and his equanimity in the face of the conflicting values and different systems of reference that modernity imposes. That is, depending on whether or not he was able to conceptualize the difference between the authentic and its imitation, my interlocutor either declared that

(30) This assertion is subject to qualification, to say the least. While, like the cultural officials, the dancers who perform for tourists readily cite the invocation of the *taksu* that animates them, many Balinese observers say that *taksu* deserted tourist performances long ago, chased away by the race for dollars.

(31) Three troupes perform regularly for tourists in Batubulan (Denjalan, Tegaltamu, and Sahadewa), and one in Singapadu (Sengguan). The Denjalan troupe has two *Barong*, one of which is consecrated, and five *Rangda* masks, of which three are consecrated. Recourse to non-consecrated masks is considered necessary when the actors who wear them find themselves in a situation of ritual impurity, as for example following the death of a relative. This is also the case, with some variations, for the troupes of Tegaltamu and Sengguan. Only the Sahadewa troupe uses masks especially made for tourist performances and which are not consecrated.

(32) For Suryani & Jensen, there seems to be no doubt that the dancers performing the Angel Dance in Bona are genuinely in trance:

When the authors first observed this dance at the village of Bona in South Bali, they questioned if the little girls, who danced in nearly perfect synchrony with eyes closed, were truly in trance, but subsequent observations and interviews convinced them that the trance was real. (Suryani & Jensen 1993: 110; see also Thong, Carpenter & Krippner 1993: chapter 8) such a manipulation of cultural symbols for promotional ends was of absolutely no importance because it was obvious that the mask in the picture could only be a non-consecrated one — or, to the contrary, he remained locked in his first impression and could only continue to express the discomfort into which this vision had cast him.

From discrimination to confusion

This analysis obliges us to question the implications of the measures adopted by the Balinese authorities to confront the undesirable consequences of the commercialization of the performing arts.

To recapitulate that process: as long as performances intended for tourists made do with dances which were already disengaged from their dramatic contents and their ritual context, nobody had any objections (except perhaps for a few old-fashioned literati, egged on by a handful of foreign connoisseurs distressed by the impoverishment and standardization of dance in Bali). After all, the Balinese were only adapting performances initially created as mere entertainment to suit foreign audiences. But when the tourist industry began to interfere a bit too overtly with dances that until then had been restricted to ritual use, the island's cultural and religious authorities stirred themselves and decided that it was time to intervene. In the first instance, the tourist performances were part of a general movement among the Balinese to dissociate entertainment from ritual — but in the second, it was a matter of ritual being turned into an entertainment for tourists. The response of the authorities was thus to try to distinguish those dances which must remain "tied" (*terikat*) to their ceremonial context and

---

(33) The inhabitants of Bona do not seem to be the only ones to confound the *Sanghyang* ritual and its touristic version, judging from the photographs of "*Sanghyang Dedari*" illustrating Bandem & deBoer's book, which were all taken in Bona (Bandem & deBoer 1981). If the *Sanghyang* ceremonies have in fact disappeared from this village, these photographs of "*Sanghyang* in trance" can only be a tourist performance. Given that it would have been difficult and intrusive to photograph a ritual *Sanghyang*, the same reflection goes for the photographs of "*Calonarang*" illustrating this book and many others, which were taken during a performance of the *Barong and Kris Dance* of Denjalan, which treats the theme not of *Calonarang* but of *Kunti Sraya*. Moreover, most of the photographs of the *Barong* and *Rangda* published in books and magazines, in Bali and elsewhere, are drawn from the same show, for the simple reason that it was created in such a way as to be conveniently photographed. Thus, just as the interest of foreigners conferred an emblematic status on the *Barong* and *Rangda*, a performance created for tourists has become emblematic of the *Barong* and *Rangda* in Bali.

(34) The fate of the category *bebali* somewhat evokes that of the category *adat* under the rationalization of the religion. One could illustrate this double parallel process by means of the following diagram:

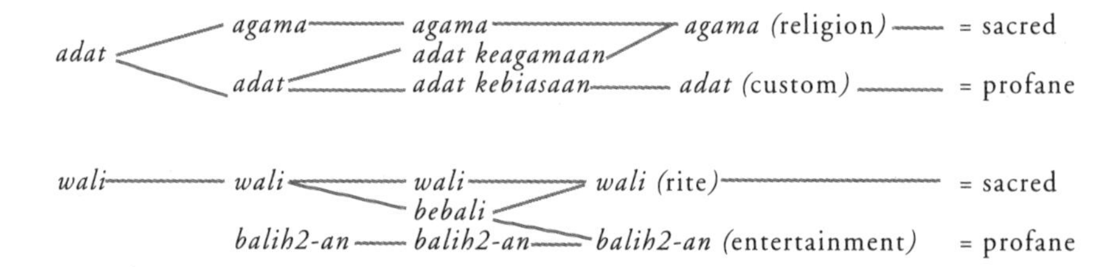

those which may be "detached" (*terlepas*) from it without excessive remorse.

This response led first to widening the gap between the ritual and theatrical aspects of dance. Thus the postulated distinction between dances classified as *wali* and *balih-balihan* had the effect of rendering residual the intermediary category *bebali*, whose ritual and theatrical components had until then composed an indissociable whole (34). But we also note that the performances of *bebali* dances tend to become standardized: the same dances are presented in the same way whether it be in the context of a religious ceremony or a spectacle for tourists. More precisely, the recent evolution of certain theatrical forms classed as *bebali* — such as *Gambuh*, for example — reveals that the *balih-balihan* version initially created for tourists — simplified, shortened and standardized on the *Sendratari* model — is now being taken up by the Balinese for their own purposes and executed in exactly the same way when it is performed in a ceremonial context, that is, as *wali*. Thus there is a risk of confusion between performances where there is nothing to distinguish them except the circumstances of their presentation.

In the endeavor to keep ritual separate from spectacle and avoid the "profanation" of "sacred" dances by their indiscriminate exploitation for commercial ends, the resolutions adopted by the Balinese authorities may well have added to the confusion they were trying to dispel between performances reserved for the Balinese and attractions intended for tourists.

Chapter Seven

Touristic Culture

Once Cultural Tourism became the official tourism doctrine of Indonesia, the Balinese infatuation with this formula seems to have become more tempered. Since the 1970s, studies of the sociocultural impact of tourism and seminars on the relationship between tourism and culture are rarer. Not that interest in tourism has dropped — to the contrary — but it has become an integral part of the Balinese cultural landscape (1). And while Cultural Tourism remains the inescapable point of reference — that which characterizes Bali as a tourist destination — the term itself has become somewhat reduced: it has become abridged, and it has lost the capital letters that previously exalted it. The formula has served its purpose and become banal, and now it is one product among many in the gamut of Balinese tourism. For tourism in Bali is seeking to diversify its production, and these days one hears not only of "cultural tourism" (*wisata budaya*), but also "nature tourism" (*wisata alam*), "marine tourism" (*wisata bahari*), "forest tourism" (*wisata rimba*), "village tourism" (*wisata desa*), "agricultural tourism" (*wisata pertanian*), "sports tourism" (*wisata olahraga*), "convention tourism" (*wisata konvensi*), "spiritual tourism" (*wisata spiritual*) and — but only to deplore it — "sex tourism" (*wisata seks*). In short, Cultural Tourism has become just one item among many.

Parallel with this change in the import of Cultural Tourism, one may observe a shift in the order of concerns. The question that occupies the Balinese these days seems to be, rather than assessing the impact of tourism on their culture, how to exploit their culture in the most profitable way. This is what is suggested by the one seminar of any importance on tourism held during the 1980s: whereas the earlier seminars were aimed at "fostering culture and developing tourism", the 1987 seminar organized by the provincial government addressed only "the fostering and development of tourism" (Pemda Bali, 1987). And the only paper dealing with the culture, presented by the Head of the Regional Office of Culture, was devoted mainly to defining what Balinese culture should be to contribute efficiently to the development of tourism.

In the face of such a statement, it is very tempting to conclude that, between the

(1) As shown by the incorporation in scenes of Balinese life of tourists occupied in their favorite pastimes — photographing a temple festival or abandoning themselves to the joys of surfing near fishermen — in the canvases of successful painters like I Wayan Bendi and I Made Budi. It was, by the way, a painting of the latter that Garuda chose to illustrate its publicity campaign for the Visit Indonesia Year. The most troubling, perhaps, is that the tourists have Balinese features, as if they were no longer really foreign to Bali.

"Seminar on Cultural Tourism" of 1971 and the "Commission of Cooperation for Fostering and Developing Cultural Tourism" in 1979, the Balinese authorities had capitulated and sacrificed their concern for the fostering of culture to the demands of developing tourism; that it is no longer a matter of protecting the Balinese from the corrupting contact with tourists, but of enrolling them in the tourist promotion of their island; that the problem is no longer to circumscribe the domain conceded to tourism, but to capitalize on every possible asset to enhance the Balinese tourist product. Nonetheless, I do not believe that things are as simple as that, and I am inclined to think that the radical change in the attitude of the Balinese authorities in regard to tourism is but the outcome of a logic set in motion from the time of the very conception of Cultural Tourism.

By the beginning of the 1980s, tourism clearly no longer frightened the Balinese. The best proof of this lies in the shift of meaning attributed to the notion of "touristic culture", which underwent an evolution symmetrical with that of "cultural tourism" — not only becoming trivial in its abridgment (from *kebudayaan pariwisata* to *budaya wisata*), but in fact becoming the object of a tacit rehabilitation. Instead of being held up as a threat, describing the peril from which Balinese culture must at all costs save itself, it is presently used in the media to designate a state of mind appropriate to tourism, and defines a culture that has been able to adapt itself to tourists and their demands. In short, in becoming banal it has become respectable — to the point even that the syntagms "cultural tourism" (*wisata budaya*) and "touristic culture" (*budaya wisata*) are employed today in conjunction rather than opposition.

Moreover, the fears initially aroused by the advent of tourists have given way to expressions of undisguised satisfaction. There has been a spectacular reversal in regard to the imputed effects of tourism. Accused not long ago of being a vehicle of "cultural pollution", tourism is now considered by the Balinese authorities to be a factor of "cultural renaissance" (*renaissance kultural*). As to the justification for this buoyant reappraisal, it is exactly the same argument already advanced by McKean: the tourist money stimulated the interest of the Balinese for their cultural traditions, and the admiration of visitors for their culture reinforced their sense of identity and their pride in being Balinese. This is also a point made by a growing number of foreign observers, manifestly reassured to find that their initial fears have proven unfounded:

> *If anything, tourism has pumped more life into the Balinese cultural Renaissance that began earlier this century. Although the vast majority of wood carvings, paintings and "antiques" passed off on visitors is strictly mass-produced souvenir stuff, there are probably more superb artists and craftsmen in Bali today than at any time in its history. With the infusion of dollars from tourist performances, village dance companies have been able to afford new costumes that inspire continued pride in their art.* (Zach 1986: 9) (2, overleaf)

This argument became the official word in Bali when it was upheld by Ida Bagus Mantra, appointed the new Governor of the province in 1978 by President Suharto, replacing the Javanese colonel imposed on the Balinese 11 years earlier to bring the island back under control after the bloodshed that marked the fall of the Sukarno regime. The new Governor was wreathed with all the credentials one could wish for to establish his authority — among the Balinese as well as vis-à-vis Jakarta. First and foremost, he was Balinese, and a *Brahmana* besides, who held a doctoral degree from a prestigious university in India, and was known as an expert in matters of religion and culture. After having been one of the founders of the *Parisada Hindu Dharma*, he was named Rector of the University of Bali and then Director General of Culture in Jakarta; and he was said to be a protégé of President Suharto. His accession, moreover, was consecrated by the celebration in 1979 of the solemn ritual purification *Eka Dasa Rudra* at the temple of Besakih — in the presence of the President of the Republic, foreign television crews and thousands of tourists — which, unlike its tragic precedent in 1963, was carried out successfully, attesting to the legitimacy acquired by the Balinese religion in the Indonesian nation (Stuart-Fox 1982). For the Balinese, anxious about the expanding Javanese influence on their territory, the appointment of a Balinese governor was perceived as a sign of both national reconciliation and the legitimization of Balinese identity on the part of the central government. The hitherto perceptible anxiety gave way to serenity, and the defensive attitude of the Balinese authorities became jubilant.

Thus, to judge by the declarations of the Balinese authorities, one could surmise that Cultural Tourism — after going through an initial period of adjustment when the onslaught of foreigners on the island raised legitimate fears — had successfully accomplished its mission. However, before congratulating the Balinese, we should look carefully at the arguments presented to us as proof of the "renaissance" of their culture — for upon examination, it turns out that under the guise of a cultural renaissance, what we are seeing is the joint process of the touristification and the Indonesianization of Balinese culture. I will show first what happens to the Balinese culture when it is called on to contribute both to the development of international tourism in Indonesia and to the fostering of the national Indonesian culture. And then we shall see how, under the constraint of this double imperative, the Balinese

---

(2) This enthusiasm is not limited only to travel writers; it appears to be generally shared by academics, as in this already old assertion of Stephen Lansing:

The performing arts on Bali are experiencing a renaissance of sorts, with tourists as the new patrons. (Lansing 1974: 46)

The same opinion has been affirmed, time and again, especially by Elizabeth Young (1980: 297, 305) and Annette Sanger (1988: 99–100). In this chorus of praises, certain discordant voices nonetheless manage to make themselves heard, such as that of Robert Brown:

The constantly increasing bubbling of activity in the arts during the past twenty years is phenomenal. Is it a healthy sign of energy, the fermentation of a wine of character, or is it the effluvism of decay, of something rotten in the state of Ubud? (Brown 1979: 50) have come to search for their cultural identity in the image that the tourists and the Indonesians hold of them.

1. The development of international tourism and the fostering of the national culture

From the denunciation of "cultural pollution" to the proclamation of a "cultural renaissance", what is signified by the term "Balinese culture" has undergone a revealing change (3). What had been above all a matter of "cultural values" (*nilai budaya*) is today primarily a matter of what the Indonesian language designates as *seni budaya*, which may be translated as "cultural arts" (4).

When tourism was accused of corrupting Balinese culture, the issues were the desacralization of the temples and the profanation of religious ceremonies, the monetarization of social relations and the weakening of community ties, or the relaxing of moral standards and the rise of mercantile attitudes. These days, whether they are worrying about the commoditization of their culture or rejoicing in the creativity of their artists, the Balinese authorities seem to be concerned above all about what is likely to be shown and sold to tourists. The "culture" in question is not to be thought of in the anthropological sense of a "complex whole which includes knowledge, belief, art, morals, law, custom, and any other capabilities and habits acquired by man as a member of society", to cite the canonical definition proposed by E.B. Tylor. Its sense here is restricted to only those aspects that may be made the object of a representation and give rise to an aesthetic appreciation — that is, to artistic expressions. And it is to this that the Balinese refer when they speak of a "cultural renaissance", as in the slogan concocted by the Directorate General of Tourism: "Tourism Ensures the Conservation of the Cultural Arts of the Nation" (*Kepariwisataan Melestarikan Seni Budaya Bangsa*).

Culture as art

This conception of "culture as art" (Acciaioli 1985) is clearly illustrated by the "Bali Arts Festival" (*Pesta Kesenian Bali*), one of the first initiatives taken by the new

(3) One may find an index of this change in the vocabulary used by the Balinese authorities. Although the discourse of Cultural Tourism is formulated in the national language, when they evoke the threat of "cultural pollution" the Balinese frequently use a vernacular term (*leteh*), while the announcement of the "cultural renaissance" goes easily by a foreign terminology (*cultural renaissance*). This double change of language, first from Balinese to Indonesian — with Balinese terms to express key concepts — and then from Indonesian to English — is an index of a displacement characteristic of the position from which the Balinese speak of themselves, as a result of their increasing integration into the Indonesian state and the international tourism industry.

(4) We should remember that the Balinese language — and this goes as well for other vernacular languages of the archipelago — does not have terms corresponding to what we call "art" and "culture", but refers always to a specific activity, inseparable from its context. This is no longer the case once one passes to the Indonesian language, which has appropriated the abstract notions of "art" (*seni*) and "culture" (*budaya*), in replacement of the Dutch terms *kunst* and *cultuur*.

Governor. Launched in 1979 at the Art Center (*Werdi Budaya*) in Denpasar — another creation of the Governor, when he was still the Director General of Culture — this annual event is the official proof of Bali's cultural renaissance. According to the booklet published by the Bali Government Tourism Office presenting both the Art Center and the Arts Festival:

> *A popular misconception is that Balinese Dance and Drama has lost much of its lustre: that gamelans are rusting in their pavilions and dancers leaving the stage for a life on the juice blender. The truth is that Bali is undergoing a cultural renaissance with bigger and brighter temple festivals, revived art forms and more orchestras than ever before.* (Wijaya, Pemayun & Raka 1981: 1)

The Arts Festival provides a perfect example of what Cultural Tourism is meant to be, in that it was created by the Governor as a means of fostering Balinese culture while contributing to the development of tourism on the island. Among the slogans calling on the Balinese to participate in the Festival, one notes in particular: "With the Bali Arts Festival We Develop Cultural Tourism" (*Melalui Pesta Kesenian Bali Kita Tingkatkan Pariwisata Budaya*). It would be a mistake, however, to see this event as an attraction intended for tourists, if only because its public is mainly Balinese (5). Widely covered by the regional and national media, the Arts Festival is a gigantic cultural event on an island-wide scale which presents, in a manner at once magnified and sublimated, "Balinese culture" in its official version. The Bali Arts Festival was in effect ratified in 1986 by the issuing of a regional regulation; and the following year it even received the stamp of approval of the President of the Republic, who personally came to inaugurate the Festival. Since then, several other provinces have begun holding their own Arts Festivals, modeled on the precedent created by the Balinese.

What comprises the Bali Arts Festival? Mainly parades, exhibitions, performances, contests, and literary soirées (Pangdjaja 1991a). The best-attended events are the performances, among which one may find theatrical genres that have become rare and which the Festival sets itself the mission of preserving and revitalizing; local specialties unknown outside their region of origin, with the idea of presenting them to the public of Denpasar; and finally, grand productions of *Sendratari*, generally based on the *Ramayana* or the *Mahabharata*, performed in the open air theater of the Art Center, said to be able to accommodate 7,000 spectators. These super-productions are indisputably the highlight of the Festival. From the very beginning they have been the events that benefit from the biggest budget, that have the most intense rehearsals and the most sophisticated staging, and above all that draw by far the greatest crowds, Balinese and visitors together. And it is always a *Sendratari* that celebrates the opening of the Festival and its closing.

---

(5) This is the result of a deliberate decision, for the date of the Festival — which takes place every year during five weeks in June and July — was chosen to coincide with the school and university vacations in Indonesia.

It is striking that the Bali Arts Festival gives the place of honor to a performance imported in the 1960s from Java, where it was intended to be a tourist entertainment. As we have seen, for *Sendratari* to be understood and appreciated by foreign audiences, this new theatrical form departed considerably from the principles of composition traditionally found in Balinese theater (6). Nonetheless, the Festival consecrated one of the most famous tourist performances, the *Sendratari Ramayana* (better known as the Ramayana Ballet) as an "authentic Balinese tradition" (*tradisi Bali yang asli*). And its success, renewed year after year, is supposed to testify to the island's artistic vitality, to the point that the president of the organizing committee could declare, in the second year of the Festival, that:

> ... *its priority objective is in the development of traditional Balinese art under the form of a presentation of the Sendratari Ramayana.* (7)

The up-grading of the *Sendratari* to an authentic Balinese tradition seems to be well-established today, judging from the paper presented by the Head of the

---

(6) Fredrik deBoer rightly notes that

> ... *what was, in the beginning, a product imported from Java has been subject to a process of localization. Features of the imported medium found interesting and workable by the artists and audiences of Bali have been retained, while aspects judged lacking have tended to fall away.* (deBoer 1989: 184)

In fact, once *Sendratari* was no longer aimed at a foreign audience, the choreographers of the Arts Festival have progressively brought it back to the taste of the Balinese. Instead of being reduced to an hour, a performance now lasts an entire evening and its rhythm is somewhat more flexible. And most important, its verbal components have regained some of their lost importance by the addition of narrators and chorus. The fact remains nonetheless that the constraints of intercultural communication that presided over the creation of *Sendratari* — a linear narrative plot mimed by dancers — has, by suppressing opportunities for improvisation, rendered the role of the *penasar* superfluous, overturning the conception of theater as it had been until then in Bali. As a result, there is a tendency to emphasize the textual version of a dramatic theme, generally of Indian or Javanese origin, to the detriment of Balinese variations that have come about from theatrical experience. This is not to mention the "colossal" (*kolosal*) character of the performances at the Art Center — with hundreds of participants — that completely denatures traditional Balinese choreography. One notes, too, the concomitant rise of a new function, that of the choreographer, charged with staging such and such an episode drawn from the body of literature in use in Bali.

(7) Radio-televised statement, 11 June 1980; personal communication of the author.

Academy of Indonesian Dance in the course of a "Seminar on the Contribution of Balinese Cultural Values to the Development of the National Culture" (*Seminar Sumbangan Nilai Budaya Bali dalam Pembangunan Kebudayaan Nasional*), held in 1984 in Denpasar. The author in effect recommends popularizing *Sendratari* more widely in the villages, as the theatrical genre "most apt to assure the conservation of Balinese cultural values" (Bandem 1986: 55).

One may marvel that after less than 20 years of existence, the *Sendratari*, originally created for a non-Balinese audience, has been officially recognized as the vehicle par excellence of Balinese cultural values. Having become so, however, it is not surprising to read, in an Indonesian study on the pernicious effects of the commercialization of Balinese culture by tourism, that:

> *... the integrity of the Sendratari Ramayana is endangered by its presentation to tourists.* (Yoeti 1985: 14) (8)

The truth is that, rather than a tourist performance, the *Sendratari* is a composite genre whose vocation is pan-Indonesian, in the sense that it was created in such a way as to permit a communication among the various ethnic groups of the archipelago. Indeed, besides *Sendratari* "in the style of Bali" (*gaya Bali*), there flourish *Sendratari* in the style of Sunda, of Surakarta, of Yogyakarta and still others. But while the *Sendratari* performances composed for the Bali Arts Festival must be "typical" (*khas*) of the Balinese style, they must remain accessible to all Indonesians, and so they include a mix of styles originating from different regions. The result is that what distinguishes the Balinese *Sendratari* from other forms of *Sendratari* is the dosage among the elements borrowed from various regional traditions. The different styles of *Sendratari* are therefore regional variations on a national theme. This is essentially what is proclaimed in a slogan which is frequently seen posted in bill stickers during the Arts Festival: "The Development of Regional Arts Assures the Conservation of the National Culture" (*Pengembangan Kesenian Daerah Merupakan Pelestarian Kebudayaan Nasional*).

As a general rule, the *Sendratari* performances presented at the Festival are composed by the teachers and students of the High School of Traditional Indonesian Music and the College of Indonesian Arts. To a large extent, these institutions, which are under the jurisdiction of the Department of Education and Culture, have taken on the role of patronage previously held by the princely courts: the creation of styles and the establishment of standards of execution; the training of dancers and musicians; and the organization and financing of performances. There is a difference,

---

(8) Edward Bruner provides an example of similar confusion in Java, when he reports the remarks of a guide deploring that so many tourists come to performances of the Ramayana Ballet at Prambanan that the Javanese can no longer watch them. This guide, too, seems to have forgotten that this performance had originally been created not for the Javanese but for tourists, Indonesian and foreign (Bruner 1991b: 22).

however, and it is an important one. Unlike the princes, who were ever anxious to maintain their own particular styles to distinguish themselves from their neighbors, the Indonesian state through its provincial agencies deliberately strives for decontextualization, centralization and the regulated standardization of the Balinese arts (Hough 1992). Such institutionalization of the arts goes hand-in-hand with their professionalization, as witnessed by the following statement by I Made Bandem, the Head of the College of Indonesian Arts:

> *The motivations for the performing arts, so far, have been religious ones. But now, we cannot isolate ourselves from globalization any more... We have to live with overseas and domestic tourists. Therefore, now is the time for our artists to conduct themselves like professionals.* (Bandem 1991: 24)

This goes for the plastic arts as well as the performing arts, and more generally for all forms of artistic expression cultivated by the Festival; and since they are under the aegis of the Department of Education and Culture, it would be no exaggeration to say that the "Balinese culture" celebrated by the Bali Arts Festival is what the ministry concerned decides it should be.

In this regard, it is significant that in Indonesia, culture is administered in tandem with education (Lindsay 1995: 659). The Indonesian term that is habitually translated as "culture", *kebudayaan*, is an abstract derivative formed from the root *budaya*, which primarily designates a "cultivated individual" in the sense of someone who has received a good education. As to *kebudayaan*, its contemporary meaning is at once normative and evolutionist, in that it refers to the process by which the ethnic groups of the archipelago are expected to acquire the qualities judged necessary to instate order and civilization according to the ideals of the developing Indonesian nation. It is in vain that one searches therein for the idea of a cultural specificity proper to each ethnic group and, a fortiori, of a cultural relativism (Pelras 1977: 64–66).

Balinese culture as a regional culture

In these conditions, if the culture presented at the Arts Festival can be called Balinese, it is in the sense that "Balinese culture" (*kebudayaan Bali*) is seen as one of the "regional cultures" (*kebudayaan daerah*) that compose Indonesia. Unlike Sukarno, who wanted to forge a new man and an Indonesian identity by eliminating the "feudalism" and "ethnocentricity" left by the colonial period, the New Order founded by Suharto, while launching a policy of economic development and modernization, undertook to create a national culture based on regional cultural traditions — foremost among them, the Javanese culture.

As in most previously colonized countries, the Indonesian state faced problems of national integration. For Indonesia, these problems were particularly acute given the centrifugal forces at work: it is an archipelago, fragmented in a chain of islands spanning an immense territory, and populated by some three hundred ethnic groups whose language, religion and customs differ markedly. Long held in check by regional interests, the authority of the state was finally able to impose itself, and national unity became an indisputable reality with the establishment of the New Order (Drake 1989).

During the 1970s, as the financial resources of the state increased, the central government's control over the regions tightened considerably, making them more and more dependent on subsidies from Jakarta. But at the same time, the realization of development plans made it necessary to delegate partial authority to the regions and to call on the participation of local communities. Acknowledging these requirements, the 1974 Regional Government Law granted the provinces limited autonomy in the framework of a heavier control by the state. This reform was completed by the 1979 Village Government Law, which ended the diversity of local situations by imposing uniform local administrative structures across Indonesia, with the objective of transforming village administration into an arm of the central bureaucracy (Warren 1990).

Thus from the 1980s the peripheral regions found themselves incorporated into the web of the state apparatus. This includes the civil and military authorities, trade and communications networks, urbanization programs, the education system, the national language and the national ideology (*Pancasila*) — not to mention the imposition of the officially recognized monotheistic religions in order to eradicate "animist" attitudes deemed harmful to national development. Once the unity of the nation was considered established, the accent could be put on the country's diversity, as in the national motto "Unity in Diversity" (*Bhinneka Tunggal Ika*) engraved on the Indonesian coat of arms — a slogan that appears as well on the pamphlets of the Directorate General of Tourism, vaunting Indonesia as "A Destination of Endless Diversity".

As a matter of fact, ethnicity has become the fashion in Jakarta, to the extent that the media now talk of an "ethnic revival". There have been numerous exhibitions on the arts and crafts of the outer islands, accompanied by the publication of glossy coffee-table books. Traditional textiles provide a constantly renewed source of inspiration in Indonesian haute couture and interior design, while the new international airport proudly exhibits a variety of decorative patterns borrowed from the country's diverse ethnic groups. Ethnic handicrafts are sold as souvenirs to tourists — both domestic and foreign — in addition to being exported abroad. Dance troupes from the provinces are invited to perform in the capital city, and the national television offers regular regional cultural shows. In short, Indonesia appears to be going ethnic.

Some authors have lent academic validity to this "ethnic revival", by asserting that cultural mobilization based on ethnic identity might be used by the state to prevent mobilization based on class interests (Magenda 1988). And indeed, as economic development propelled Indonesian society into the modern world, it also threatened the social and moral stability of populations whose environments had been disturbed. In this context, the focus on ethnic identity can be interpreted as an attempt to re-establish a sense of continuity with an idealized past in response to urbanization, social differentiation, and the Westernization of life styles. If there is undoubtebly some truth in this statement, it is far from telling the whole story. The point is that, rather than denying the appeal of ethnicity as a focus of allegiance and identity by suppressing its manifestations, the New Order has resorted to the more cunning strategy of disempowerment and incorporation. In short, not only have ethnic identities been domesticated by the state, but they are being enlisted to contribute to the process of nation-building.

Now, while the expression of ethnic identity appears to have found official sanction, it is only as long as it remains at the level of cultural display — and even then, the kinds of cultural differences which can be displayed are strictly defined by the state. Thus, the visual and decorative aspects of Indonesian ethnic cultures have benefited from an unprecedented degree of official promotion. Needless to say, this showcase vision does not acknowledge that which forms the core of a culture — such as language, religion, legal system, economic practices, social organization, and so on — and contributes to sustaining the sense of identity of the participants in that culture. On the contrary, the destruction of traditional economic patterns, plundering of the environment and depreciation of local knowledge that ensue from the policy of national development are conducive to the deculturation of religion and the erosion of the ritual function of the arts (Dove 1988; Foulcher 1990). In Indonesia, there is no room whatsoever for diversity which asserts competing economic and political interests of different ethnic groups. In this respect, the New Order state is proceeding just as the colonial state before it had proceeded in order to prevent ethnic differences from taking on political force: that is, by "culturalizing" the expression of ethnic identity as far as possible.

But even this is only one side of the story. In truth, we are not really dealing with what appears as a strictly controlled and sanitized version of Indonesia's "ethnic cultures", but rather with what is called by Indonesian officials "regional cultures" (*kebudayaan daerah*). These regional cultures are expected to make a "contribution" (*sumbangan*) to the building of the "national culture" (*kebudayaan nasional*). As such, they are considered depositories of potential "resources" (*sumber*) that can provide "cultural elements" (*unsur-unsur kebudayaan*) to the Indonesian culture (Soebadio 1985; Yampolsky 1995).

This conception of Indonesian culture is actively promoted by the state, whether in the schools, where children learn to identify the explicitly acknowledged ethnic groups according to certain markers officially enlisted to characterize them (such as houses, costumes, dances, etc.), or in the cultural programs transmitted by television, where these same groups exhibit the duly approved traits of their ethnic identity. And this conception is staged most eloquently in the "Beautiful Indonesia-in-Miniature Park" (*Taman Mini Indonesia Indah*), a sort of Art Center on the scale of Indonesia — inspired by Mrs. Suharto after a trip to Disneyland — opened in the outskirts of Jakarta in 1975 (Pemberton 1994). Although the reason invoked at the time to justify this extravagant project was the importance of presenting a valorizing image of Indonesia's cultural diversity to foreign tourists, observation shows that the visitors to *Taman Mini* are by an immense majority Indonesians. They are invited to recognize

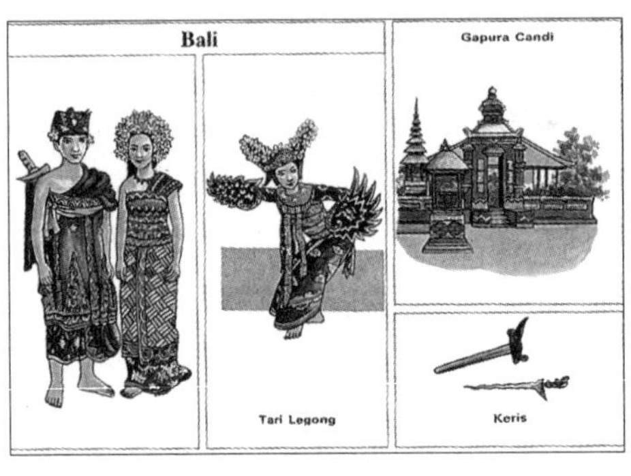

themselves in a conception of "Indonesianity" (*Keindonesiaan*) iconically signified by the juxtaposition of markers of the ethnic groups comprising the Indonesian nation. But only certain groups are represented there, and those that are, under the aegis of the province to which they belong. Each of the 27 provinces of Indonesia is represented by a "traditional house" (*rumah adat*) in which there are exhibits of "traditional costumes" (*pakaian adat*) as well as demonstrations of "traditional dances" (*tarian adat*) (9). And so it is that with the creation of a provincial *adat*, the sphere of "tradition" becomes an administrative category. The focus of identity is displaced from the ethnic group to the province, which could be seen as an attempt to substitute ethnic cultural identities with a provincial cultural identity.

Bearing this in mind, it becomes clear that "Balinese culture" should not be identified with what an ethnographic investigation would define as being the culture of the Balinese in that they constitute an "ethnic group" (*suku bangsa Bali*) — such as the Dayak or the Atoni, for example — but with the authorized culture of Bali as a "province" (*Daerah Tingkat I Propinsi Bali*) of Indonesia, such as Kalimantan Tengah or Nusa Tenggara Timur. But whereas the Dayak are dispersed across several provinces and the Atoni live among other ethnic groups in one province, Bali's situation is unique in Indonesia in that its name designates an entity that is at once geographic, ethnic and administrative — and that also happens to be the principal tourist destination of the country. This leads to shifts and overlappings in what is meant by "Bali" — and in fact, when the Balinese speak in the name of Bali, it is most often the province or the tourist destination to which they refer, rather than the ethnic group.

Thus, it is as a province, considered to be a homogeneous and distinctive entity, that Bali is encouraged to promote its "cultural arts" on the national scene — its music and dance, plastic and decorative arts, literature (but not language), costume, cuisine, handicrafts, architecture, and certain picturesque and inoffensive customs, as long as they do not run counter to good morals or economic development. I will give

(9) One finds examples of the same process in a number of books intended for school children, that show the provinces of Indonesia based on their representation at *Taman Mini*. One title among others: Nugroho (1984).

two examples of such promotion of the Balinese cultural arts.

Not long ago, the extraordinary wealth of Balinese textile traditions was disappearing fast, and its vestiges were avidly sought after by a handful of shrewd collectors (Hauser-Schäublin et al. 1991). The Balinese relegated their ancient hand-woven cloths to certain ritual contexts and adopted printed textiles for everyday wear, reserving the batiks imported from Java for their ceremonial clothing and formal dress. Then, with the rise of tourism in the 1970s, dozens of weaving studios began to sell yardage of mechanically reproduced weft ikat (*endek*) cloth to visitors as well as to Balinese. Soon, what had recently been one Balinese textile tradition among many others became representative of Bali, much as batik is of Java. The Governor set the example by exchanging his batik shirt for one of *endek*, and was soon imitated by the Balinese elite. And today, *endek* competes seriously with batik, for clothes as well as for furnishings, in temples as well as offices. But as its use becomes more widespread, *endek* tends to lose its Balinese specificity, and cheap imitations are produced in Java and Lombok. One finds it now decorating the interiors of Jakarta, where most people are unaware of its origins. In short, Balinese *endek* has become Indonesian, like batik, which has progressively lost its Javanese connotation.

Architecture provides another illustration of a similar process. From the beginning of the colonial period, administrative and commercial buildings were strongly influenced by European architecture, as can be seen in both the Bali Hotel of 1928 and the Bali Beach Hotel of 1966, to cite only two examples. At the same time, domestic architecture gave way to prefabricated elements, more and more widely available. In 1974, in reaction to what was perceived as a loss of identity, the Governor declared that henceforth administrative and commercial buildings must bear the marks of their "Balinese character" (*ciri khas Bali*). This was expressed in a profusion of decorative motifs, derived mainly from the elaborately ornate style of Gianyar — in the form of bas-relief friezes and sculptures of scenes inspired by Balinese mythology — veneered onto a functional structure. The result, as may be seen in the architecture of the Art Center of Denpasar and the international hotels of Nusa Dua, is marked by the double seal of gigantism and mannerism, in a concoction of styles that astonishes admirers of traditional Balinese architecture (Wijaya 1986). Under the name of "Bali Style" (*Stil Bali*), this monumental ornamentalism now represents "traditional Balinese architecture" in Jakarta, where the Indonesia Museum at *Taman Mini* was designed by the architect responsible for the Art Center in Denpasar. As such, *Stil Bali* has also become representative of "traditional Indonesian architecture", and in this capacity it served as a source of inspiration for the French architects of the airport in Jakarta. Once consecrated as a recognized example of Indonesian architecture, *Stil Bali* was reinterpreted by the Javanese for their own use to be finally taken up again by the Balinese in a now standardized form (10).

(10) *Stil Bali* is not the same thing as that which is celebrated in "Bali Style" (Helmi & Walker 1995), a visual contemplation of traditional Balinese architecture and its reinterpretation in building styles in Bali's expatriate community.

In the light of these examples, and of many others as well, it is clear that what we are seeing is a conscious neo-traditionalism that can be called a "folklorization" of the culture (11). The folklorized cultural elements are extracted from their original context and combined in an imagery with ethnic connotations to be consumed by the urbanized and Indonesianized Balinese middle classes (those who make up the greater part of the Arts Festival's public). In effect, only the most mobile members of Balinese society — those already cut off from their rural roots — can recognize themselves in an idealized image intended to represent the Balinese cultural identity on the national scene. One could even say that, as a regional culture, "Balinese culture" refers more to a social group than to an ethnic group. But since this authorized version of Balinese identity, elaborated in Denpasar, is transmitted to the villages via the cultural programs of Indonesian television, the island's rural population, too, ends up recognizing it as its own.

National integration and provincial differentiation

Now, through the pervasive reference to "regional cultures", what we actually are witnessing, in conjunction with the process of national integration, is a policy emphasizing homogenization within each province and differentiation between the provinces. The Indonesian state is aiming to induce in each of its provinces a distinctive homogeneous provincial identity, grounded on a single set of unique cultural features, at the expense of the diverse ethnic cultures enclosed within their boundaries (12). Such provincial identities are promoted by the regional governments and supported by synthetic images based on a notion of culture stripped down to the "cultural arts". These images are proposed to the nation for consumption and to the local populations they allegedly represent for authentication. And they are displayed in the regional museums that are being opened in the provincial capitals (Taylor 1994).

Just as "culture" (read "cultural arts") is being used as a means to defuse potential political problems, the risks inherent in ethnic mobilization are defused by means of a focus on the "region" (read "province"), that is, by shifting the locus of identification from a primordial to an administrative entity. In addition to the rather conspicuous "folklorization" of culture, there is a more discrete, yet no less crucial "provincialization" of ethnicity. In this perspective, the promotion of provincial cultural identities can be interpreted as a safe way for the state to bridge a gap between ethnic identities — regarded as being either irrelevant or else detrimental to the process of nation-building — and the still remote national identity.

While the relative cultural homogeneity of a province like Bali can be reconstituted without too much difficulty into a "typically" Balinese style, the process is rather more delicate with provinces comprising several ethnic groups. The solution, then, is

---

(11) Hélène Bouvier describes an analogous process of the "folklorization" of the performing arts in Madura (Bouvier 1994).

(12) Bernard Sellato explains clearly how this movement is proceeding in Kalimantan (Sellato 1990).

either the selection of certain cultural traits belonging to one prominent ethnic group which are promoted to the provincial level, or the combination of traits borrowed from several different ethnic groups to compose an image considered to be representative of the province.

Be that as it may, not all ethnic groups of a province are called upon to contribute to the regional culture, and not all the constituent elements of a regional culture are called upon to contribute to the national culture — only those judged worthy to be selected as the "cultural summits" (*puncak-puncak kebudayaan*) of each regional culture. Thus the issue is one of a double-barreled process of selection: on the one hand, only certain ethnic groups are considered representative of the Indonesian nation, and as such their culture is destined to become a regional culture; on the other hand, only certain elements of that culture are considered significative of the regional culture, and as such they are called upon to become part of the Indonesian national culture. Two examples will suffice to give an idea of the selection procedure in force in different contexts.

In 1983, the year when the fall of oil revenues prompted the government to give international tourism a greater role, the Indonesian Foreign Minister launched the catch-phrase "Cultural Diplomacy" (*Diplomasi Kebudayaan*). The declared objective of the operation was to promote the image of Indonesia as "a highly civilized nation" *(bangsa yang berkebudayaan tinggi*). The province of Bali, famous for its wealth of cultural traditions, was particularly solicited to contribute, and the troupes of musicians and dancers sent abroad on tour — now called "artistic missions" (*misi kesenian*) — were charged with both promoting Indonesian culture and developing tourism in Indonesia. From this point of view, Cultural Tourism and Cultural Diplomacy seem to be two sides of the same cultural policy. Indeed, the Balinese dance performances shown in foreign capitals are generally the same as those that have already been successfully staged for tourists in Bali — a practice that goes back, as we have seen, to the Colonial Exposition of 1931. These tourist performances — backed by the "Certificate of Artistic Excellence" granted to troupes authorized to perform for a foreign audience — are considered "summits" of Balinese culture and thus to "reflect" (*mencerminkan*) simultaneously the identity of Bali (*identitas kedaerahan*) and the identity of Indonesia (*identitas Keindonesiaan*). Thus Cultural Diplomacy is intended not only for foreign nations, invited to admire the cultural summits attained by Indonesia, but also for Indonesians — and thus the Balinese —, encouraged to identify themselves with the approved manifestations of the regional cultures composing the national Indonesian culture (Geriya 1988).

The zenith of Cultural Diplomacy to date is unquestionably the gigantic "Festival of Indonesia" in the United States, composed of several hundred cultural events in some 50 cities and which lasted 18 months (1990–92). The Festival was decided in 1987 with the signing of an agreement between the Indonesian Minister of Foreign Affairs and American Secretary of State. According to its coordinator, its objective was nothing less than to sell to Americans the image of Indonesia as a highly civilized nation where the artistic spirit is constantly awake (Tanen 1991) (13, overleaf). Not surprisingly, the approved components of the Indonesian culture are nearly identical to the attractions promoted by the tourism industry, as one may see by the theme of the main exhibitions. There was classical sculpture from the Indo-Javanese period, the court arts (which obviously favor Java and Bali), and the most aesthetically evolved examples of the material culture of the most picturesque ethnic groups of the archipelago — but virtually nothing illustrating Islamic culture as such, in a country where almost nine-tenths of the population is Muslim. One finds more or less the same attractions in the program of cultural events composing the Visit Indonesia Year, which was a sort of local counterpart to the Festival of Indonesia.

Another illustration of the contribution of the regional cultures to the national culture is provided by the "Project for the Research and Study of the Nusantarian Culture" (*Proyek Penelitian dan Pengkajian Kebudayaan Nusantara*) (14). The aim of this project, elaborated in 1984 by the Department of Education and Culture, was to record and register the "summits" of the regional cultures of Indonesia in order to reinforce the national culture as the foundation of Indonesian identity. The Balinese culture was one of the five regional cultures selected, along with the Sundanese, Javanese, Malay and Bugis. At the official opening of the "Baliology Project" (*Proyek Baliologi*) held at the Art Center in Denpasar, the Minister of Education and Culture declared that the Balinese cultural traditions must be "conserved" (*dilestarikan*) and "fostered" (*dibinakan*) with the aim of "supporting" (*menunjang*) the national culture, while at the same time exhorting the Balinese to beware of the seductions of "ethnocentricity" (*sukuisme*). He also launched an appeal to the academics and other experts on Balinese culture — primarily the Balinese themselves, but also their foreign colleagues — to select elements of the Balinese culture that are most deserving of being "elevated" (*ditingkatkan*) to become fully part of Indonesian cultural traditions (Bagus 1986) (15).

What is important in this regard is to understand that the conception of Balinese culture as a regional culture implies its decomposition into discrete cultural elements, abstracted from their context to be passed through the sieve of the national ideology and subjected to classification: those judged worthy of contributing to the development of the national culture are safeguarded and promoted, while those considered too primitive or too stamped with ethnicity — those that "smell of ethnocentricity" (*yang berbau sukuisme*) — are to be eradicated. Among the elements of Balinese culture that merit being enlisted into the Indonesian culture, the Minister of

---

(13) One can imagine that the expected revenues from such an event were sufficiently tangible for large Indonesian and American firms to have invested more than $6 million — of which $1.3 million from Mobil Oil alone, who was due to renegotiate drilling rights in Indonesia in 1995.

(14) The term *nusantara* designates the Indonesian archipelago, in the sense of the space encompassing lands and seas (*tanah air*).

(15) Unlike Cultural Diplomacy, the Project for the Research and Study of the Nusantarian Culture lasted only long enough to publish a few pamphlets before its budget was sharply reduced.

Education and Culture mentioned the irrigation cooperatives (*subak*); on the other hand, he rejected cockfights (*tajen*). The Head of the Regional Office of Culture, for his part, retained the following among the "eminent values of the Balinese culture" (*nilai-nilai luhur kebudayaan Bali*) worthy of inclusion in the Indonesian culture: community mutual help (*gotong royong*); the harmony between human beings, their environment and their Creator (*Tri Hita Karana*); the subjection of beings to the fruits of their actions (*karma phala*); understanding and tolerance (*kerukunan dan toleransi*); and, of course, artistic excellence (Rata 1988). But if the list of Balinese cultural elements destined to join the Indonesian national culture is subject to negotiation and argument, the very principle of a selection of elements with a view to their promotion is never questioned.

This enterprise of selection between the Balinese cultural elements to be conscripted into the Indonesian culture and those which are not judged worthy recalls the attempt of the Balinese authorities to discriminate between that which belongs to religion and that which pertains to custom when it was a matter of deciding which elements of their culture the Balinese should reserve for themselves — those which they hold "sacred" — and which elements may be abandoned to "profane" uses. Once this selection had been made, the task still remained of distinguishing among the elements available for extra-Balinese use those which may be promoted as tourist attractions from those which, to the contrary — because they do not appeal to the tourists or because they may present an unseemly image of Bali — must be eliminated.

It certainly would be wrong to see the regional cultures as the simple result of the cultural policy of the Indonesian state, if only because, on the one hand, state intervention is often locally contested, and, on the other hand, national integration is at the crux of the internationalization of capital and the globalization of culture. Nonetheless, the "Balinese culture" does indeed appear to be in the same position in regard to both tourism and to Indonesia — that is, it is considered a "resource" and as such it is expected to put its "summits" at the disposition of the development of international tourism in Indonesia and of the fostering of the national Indonesian culture. But for this to be possible, Balinese culture must first be divested of its anthropological singularity, in order to be commensurable with other regional cultures of Indonesia and with the other tourist destinations with which it competes. The touristification of Bali and its Indonesianization combine their implications to place Balinese culture in a series where it is nothing more than one item among others. At this point, the diversity of regional cultures, like that of tourist destinations, appears to be little more than a decorative motif.

2. The discourse of Cultural Tourism

This interaction between touristification and Indonesianization is legible in the discourse of Cultural Tourism. As we have seen, perhaps because it could not really be implemented, the slogan of Cultural Tourism gave way to a remarkable profusion of discourses and incited genuine fervor in Balinese public opinion. But it would be wrong to see this discursive frenzy as mere verbal gesticulation, as a confession of impotence on the part of the Balinese authorities. For, to the extent that they comprise a doctrine, these discourses express the attempt of the Balinese to appropriate tourism after it had been imposed upon them by the Indonesian government.

Culture as heritage and culture as capital

In less than a decade, the doctrine of Cultural Tourism has come to blend the "fostering of culture" with the "development of tourism", to the extent of entrusting the fate of Balinese culture to the care of the tourism industry. To come to such a point, the conflict of interests between culture and tourism had to be defused beforehand, since it is this conflict that had governed the elaboration of the doctrine of Cultural Tourism in the first place.

A structural analysis of what I have chosen to call the "discourse of Cultural Tourism" — that is, the discourses emitted by the Balinese authorities which engage a representation of the relation between the signifiers "tourism" and "culture" — allows us to understand how this conflict is resolved in the discourse itself. The initial antagonism between culture and tourism is expressed by a system of opposites contrasting the respective attributes of each of these terms along two principal axes: "inside"–"outside" and "cultural values"–"economic values". The solution of Cultural Tourism will be to deny the reality of this fundamental opposition, and it will do so in such a way that culture and tourism will exchange their respective attributes. This will make it possible to move between the two terms.

This movement takes place by reconciling simultaneously tourism to culture and culture to tourism. On the one hand, the very fact of qualifying tourism as "cultural" bestows it with the attributes of culture, thereby exorcizing the threat of destruction that it carries and legitimizing its penetration of Bali. But this is not enough: while it is stressed that tourism must become "cultural" in order to be acceptable to the Balinese, it is just as necessary that their culture be marketable as a tourist product. This implies that culture must bear the attributes of tourism.

In other words, it is not enough that tourism becomes "cultural"; Balinese culture must become to some extent "touristic". This is expressed in the discourse of the Balinese by a splitting of their conception of their culture, according to whether or not it is conceived in relation to tourism: whereas before the coming of the tourists their culture was, for the Balinese, a "heritage" (*warisan*) that must be safeguarded, it has since then also become a "capital" (*modal*) that they should profit from.

In the discourse of Cultural Tourism, "Balinese culture" (*kebudayaan Bali*) is invariably defined in reference to three concomitant elements, which are like superimposed strata: its source is in the Hindu religion (*bersumber pada agama Hindu*); it inspires the customs (*mengilhami adat istiadat*) of the Balinese community and animates its customary institutions (*menjiwai lembaga adat*); it incarnates artistic forms of high value (*menjelma didalam bentuk seni yang bernilai tinggi*).

And when it comes to specifying how these components of Balinese culture are inter-connected, it is the metaphor of a tree that seems to present itself most naturally — a tree whose roots are the religious foundation, the trunk the customary order, and the fruits artistic expressions. Thus defined by the network of relations woven between "religion" (*agama*), "custom" (*adat*) and "art" (*seni*), culture is presented as the "distinctive marker" (*ciri khas*) of "Balinese identity" (*identitas Bali*), expected to protect Bali against the risks of penetration and pollution propagated by foreign influences (*kebudayaan yang dengan kuat mengaitkan agama, adat, dan seni sehingga sukar sekali dapat ditembus atau dicemarkan oleh pengaruh budaya dari luar*). In this sense, their culture constitutes for the Balinese a heritage bequeathed by their ancestors (*warisan yang kita mendapat dari leluhur kita*) and that therefore must be considered a value to defend, nurture and promote (*nilai yang harus ditahankan, dipelihara, dibina*). Moreover, because of the intrinsically religious character of their "cultural heritage" (*warisan kebudayaan*), it is difficult for the Balinese to distinguish within it that which belongs to religion and that which pertains to custom, and therefore to trace a boundary between the sacred and the profane (*sulit untuk memberi batasan yang tepat tentang mana yang sakral dan mana yang provan*).

Since the introduction of tourism, Balinese culture is no longer the exclusive property of the Balinese alone — for it is precisely this characteristic fusion between religious celebrations, customary practices and artistic creativity that forms Bali's "image" (*citra*) as a "Tourist Destination" (*Daerah Tujuan Wisata Bali*) and that gives it a decisive pre-eminence over other destinations with which it competes. The result is that thanks to the appreciation that Balinese culture has managed to inspire in the tourists, it has become for the Balinese a "capital" (*modal*) — indeed their one and only capital — and as such, it must be considered as a value to exploit, commercialize and promote on the international tourist market (*nilai yang harus dimanfaatkan, dipasarkan, dipromosikan di pasaran pariwisata internasional*). That being the case, the Balinese authorities miss no opportunity to remind the population that if they want to be able to sell the artistic fruits of the Balinese culture, they must not cut down the trunk but, to the contrary, make sure that it is always well irrigated and deeply rooted. But they recognize that the task is very delicate, in that from the moment it becomes a "touristic capital" (*modal pariwisata*), Balinese culture is so intimately mixed with tourism that it is difficult to separate the cultural from the touristic (*demikian eratnya kedua unsur pariwisata dan kebudayaan sehingga sangat sukar untuk dipisahkan*).

Genealogy or itemization

At the outcome of this double process in which tourism and culture exchanged their respective attributes — the inside opening onto the outside as cultural values acquire economic value — the initial opposition between tourism and culture is defused, authorizing at the same time their fusion in the formula of Cultural Tourism. But this is done at the risk of confusing that which belongs to culture and that which pertains to tourism, a confusion in which the Balinese authorities saw, not long ago, the symptoms of a "touristic culture".

In effect, from the moment that what the Balinese consider the "identity marker" (*ciri khas*) of their culture — that is, the integration between religion, custom and art

— becomes the "brand image" (*citra*) of Bali's tourist product, it becomes very difficult to keep tourism separate from culture. And that is what the observation of the touristic exploitation of Balinese dance has shown, for we have seen that the Balinese proved unable to maintain a boundary between the performances reserved for their own use and those intended for tourists.

It is precisely this play permitted by the evolution from a heritage value to a capital value that authorizes the discourse of Cultural Tourism to justify the priority given to the development of tourism — for it is tourism now that is supposed to ensure the vitality of the culture on which its development depends. The fact remains that despite repeated declarations that cultural values will in no case be sacrificed to the interests of the tourism industry, it turns out that the reason why the Balinese authorities call on the population to safeguard their culture is that the economic value of Bali's touristic capital depends on the cultural value of its cultural heritage — or in more trivial terms, to attract ever more tourists. The culture in question here is already no longer a cultural heritage but has become a touristic capital. What was a cultural value to be preserved has become an economic value to be exploited.

But one must push the reflection further to ask whether the vision that the Balinese hold of their culture as heritage — presented as being its original state, anterior to the arrival of tourists — does not in reality presuppose its conversion into a tourist attraction. To the extent that it is possible to assess, one could say that it is only after they came to consider their culture as capital, as a source of fruitful financial transactions, that the Balinese began to regard it as a heritage to safeguard with care. In this sense, it is the conception of culture as capital that induces that of culture as heritage, as if the culture is justified in making money if this safeguards the culture. If this interpretation is correct, one may suspect that the indivisible and harmonious unity between *agama*, *adat* and *seni* by which the Balinese define their culture — rather than expressing the primeval essence of their identity, as they claim — is the product of the semantic borrowings and conceptual recasting that the Balinese intellectuals were forced to carry out in response to the colonization, Indonesianization and touristification of their island. Rather than being a heritage bequeathed by the ancestors, tradition is invented for the needs of the present situation (Handler & Linnekin 1984).

Nonetheless, it would be wrong to see in this splitting of Balinese culture between a heritage and a capital only a rhetorical device. Such a distinction between the origin of a patrimony and its exploitation expresses in reality the literally untenable situation in which international tourism puts the cultures of the world. At the very moment that the Balinese are called upon to exhibit their cultural identity — their uniqueness as it was shaped by their singular history — the manifestations of their culture that are promoted as tourist attractions become cut off from their origin to be turned into a product. Once written into a tourist brochure, once itemized, they become commensurable — that is, at once comparable and different — to the products that other tourist destinations put on the market to attract tourists (16). In these conditions, the declared intention of the Balinese to safeguard their cultural heritage should not be dismissed as merely a desire to draw profit from their touristic capital, which one could explain away as a fear of killing the goose that lays the golden eggs. Rather, it should be understood as an attempt to strengthen the filiation that ties them to their ancestors — in short, as an aspiration to rescue their culture from being turned into an item in a tourist brochure, one element in a series — and to restore it to its rightful place within a genealogy (Lanfant 1991; Bazin 1995).

This irreducible tension between the two values of the Balinese culture — between that which anchors it in its origin and that which dissipates it in its exploitation — is resolved only in the order of discourse. This same tension breaks out over and over again in the social order, as one finds in the occasional eruption of discordant voices, generally those of the literati and the religious authorities, who from time to time let their reprobation show, frustrated by their avowed inability to alter the course of events. As an example, the Secretary General of *Parisada Hindu Dharma* at the first seminar on "The Fostering of Culture and the Development of Tourism" in 1978 stated:

> *As for converting the manifestations of the Balinese religion into tourist attractions, we must declare in our soul and conscience that we hardly appreciate our temples becoming places for the entertainment of tourists. Nonetheless, in the name of the* devotion *that we owe the government and by virtue of the tolerance of the Balinese community, we admit the necessity of it, and we support the action of the government with a view to developing tourism in Bali.* (Proyek Sasana Budaya Jakarta, 1978: 159 [emphasized in the text])

However, the obvious impotence of the guardians of the heritage goes much further than being unable to influence decision-making: apparently never doubting for an instant the cogency of the official tourism doctrine, they seem not to realize that what they deplore as "excesses" (*ekses*) or "infractions" (*pelanggaran*) is in reality written into the very logic of Cultural Tourism. For it is precisely in the consensus that it inspires that the power of persuasion of this formula resides. By defining Balinese cultural identity in reference to the "challenge" of tourism, the discourse of Cultural Tourism tightens the social cohesion that unites the Balinese under the banner of their culture, while its authors can claim to speak in the name of the superior interests of Bali. Moreover, by putting the accent on the preservation of the Balinese cultural heritage, the discourse of Cultural Tourism is able to rally the support of the literati and other traditionalists, less susceptible to the seductions of tourism. As Adrian Vickers writes, in *Bali: A Paradise Created*, no Balinese worthy of the name could refuse to

---

(16) The photograph of *Rangda* and the tourist couple already mentioned at the end of Chapter Six is a patent example of this. It is taken from a publicity campaign launched toward the end of the 1970s by an international hotel chain. Each hotel of this company in Southeast Asia is represented by an emblematic image of the tourist destination where it is implanted. While the "festivities" the tourists will find in Bali are magical and mysterious, in Singapore and Hong Kong the connotation is rather commercial, while in Bangkok and Manila it is frankly sexual.

adhere to the ideal of "Balinese culture":

> *Nobody on Bali would seriously think to challenge the idea of Balinese culture. Even those people who oppose tourism and see themselves as defenders of tradition are supporters of the idea.* (Vickers 1989: 195)

A magic formula

From where does the discourse of Cultural Tourism emanate? While its spokesmen are indeed Balinese, their authority to speak is determined by their position in the ideological apparatus of the Indonesian state, as one may see in the use of the Indonesian language, which situates its speakers in a supra-Balinese context. In fact, the place from which this discourse is spoken is mobile, and that is what makes it so effective.

On the one hand, the discourse held by the Balinese authorities purports to emanate from Bali and to speak on behalf of its inhabitants. As such, this discourse testifies to Bali's position as dominated, whether it be in presenting tourism as a challenge coming from outside, in claiming for the province the judicial responsibility to conduct its own tourism policy, or further, in trying to make use of tourism to gain recognition of Balinese cultural identity on the national scene. And its spokesmen insist, consequently, on the need to encourage the initiatives of the local population and give them a voice. In this sense, the discourse of Cultural Tourism claims for the Balinese the status of *subject.*

On the other hand, if this discourse is, in fact, a discourse of authority, it is precisely because its spokesmen are part of the apparatus of the Indonesian state, for which they diffuse the ideology of economic development and nation-building. In this regard, the appeal made to the Balinese to participate in tourism and develop their culture signals a penetration of the villages' social space by the state. In this sense, the Balinese are the *object* of the discourse of Cultural Tourism — those of whom one speaks, but who speak not (17).

The position of those addressed by the discourse of Cultural Tourism is hardly more fixed than that of its spokesmen — for in speaking in the name of the Balinese, this discourse is intended for the Indonesians and thus for Jakarta, while in speaking on behalf of the state and the general interest, it addresses the Balinese, in that they are part of the Indonesian nation — although one might ask whether the discourse of Cultural Tourism really addresses anyone at all, in that it does not seem to concern anyone in particular. It is almost as if it were speaking to itself, or rather, as if it were

---

(17) This is further accentuated by the reification entailed by the vocabulary used in Indonesia to designate sites and other tourist attractions. As Kathleen Adams points out in regard to tourism in Tana Toraja, the fact of designating a village as a "tourist object" (*obyek wisata*) can only reinforce the tendency of the officials of the Directorate General of Tourism to consider its inhabitants as passive objects, as merchandise to promote on the tourist market (Adams 1990: 33).

only a discourse for internal use, intended for its own spokesmen, whose personal identity tends to fade behind the anonymity of their function and their being part of a social group. This might explain why this discourse seems to hold its authority not from the truth of what it says or even from the eminence of those who propound it, but from the simple fact of its very enunciation.

The fact remains that it is precisely the ambivalence of the location of both the spokesmen and the receptors of the discourse of Cultural Tourism — it is this play allowed by the movement of its spokesmen and receptors between a Balinese position and an Indonesian one — that makes its enunciation effective. The movement from one position of discourse to another may be charted in particular in the way its speakers manipulate the categories of "we" — the inclusive (*kita*) and exclusive (*kami*). And, to follow the alternate play of their respective referents, one finds that the moment in the discourse when culture as the exclusive heritage of the Balinese becomes capital because of the tourists' interest in it is also the moment when the "we" of the Balinese community must integrate itself in the "we" of the Indonesian nation. And so it is that in ratifying the conversion of the Balinese culture from heritage into capital, the doctrine of Cultural Tourism works not only to touristify Balinese culture but also to Indonesianize it.

In this regard, the discourse of Cultural Tourism shows a propensity for syncretism characteristic of the Indonesian "mentality", which tends to avoid conflict by seeking consensus. It is in this capacity that Cultural Tourism is presented by the Balinese authorities as a *kebijaksanaan*, a term commonly translated as "policy" but which must be understood as a position that is wise, well-informed, judicious and prudent, aiming to satisfy all the parties involved (Raillon 1984: 195). And it is precisely in its aptitude to reconcile contradictions that the formula of Cultural Tourism proves its "power" (*kesaktian*) and its quasi-sacred character. Thus one must consider the contradictions harbored by the discourse of Cultural Tourism not as an incoherence of logic, but as the proof of its capacity to conciliate contradictory positions, which allows it to offer to those who proclaim it the possibility of alternative interpretations that, while they may be logically incompatible, still profess the same doctrine.

In these conditions, the ambivalence may be deciphered as an attempt to overcome in discourse the conflicts arising in society — not only among the Balinese but also between the Balinese and other Indonesians. This accounts for the imperative character of the discourse of Cultural Tourism, whose incantatory pronouncements multiply and which functions as a truly magical formula, a holy mantra, promising that social reality will be determined by its inscription into the discourse and will thus coincide with what one says about it. Indeed, as long as the problem that Cultural Tourism is expected to resolve is formulated in terms of a dilemma, it cannot be resolved: strictly speaking, there is no resolution to a dilemma, since each of its terms leads to the same result which appears to be at once undesirable and inevitable. Choice being impossible, the perception of the problem as a dilemma leads to a search for a subterfuge — such as, for example, naming the situation in the hope of controlling it symbolically. If this interpretation is correct, the discourse of Cultural Tourism puts a Balinese label on a tourism policy imposed from outside the island. In proclaiming it, the Balinese authorities try to make their own that which they cannot dispel, after having magically exorcised its subversive implications.

3. Brand image and identity marker

With the acceleration of the touristification of Bali in recent years, the consensus assured until now by the formula of Cultural Tourism is disintegrating. While the rise of tourism and its related activities is undeniable, so also, unfortunately, are the problems engendered by its wild growth. Escaping all control, tourism today appears to the Balinese in the sly and fatal guise of AIDS, whose victims are starting to multiply on the island, and which is denounced as a poisoned apple brought by the visitors. And whereas formerly the Balinese perceived tourism as a bounded phenomenon, associated with the outside, now they see it as all-pervasive. For anyone observing the evolution of the situation over the years, it is hard to banish the impression that the barriers meant to contain the surge of tourism and to control its development are about to crash. Regularly predicted by the prophets of doom since the 1920s, and always held at bay, the fall of the Balinese from the Garden of Eden looks more imminent than ever.

Bali: what they are saying

Faced with these dangers, the Balinese authorities seem to be increasingly divided in their appraisal of the situation and the measures to be taken. And above all, since the appointment of a new Governor, Ida Bagus Oka, in 1988, one now sees the crystallizing of a public opinion that dares to confront the government. The criticism expressed concerns mainly the ruin of the environment and the impotence of the provincial administration to control the runaway growth of tourism and to take action against the flagrant violation of regulations governing its development.

Although the Balinese hardly speak of "cultural pollution" anymore, they are more and more openly anxious about the havoc wrought on the landscape and apprehensive about outsiders usurping their island — perhaps not so much foreign and domestic tourists as Javanese migrant workers and Jakarta-based conglomerates. Mercantilism is rampant; land speculation has reached dizzying proportions; and crime is growing — organized rackets and recurring waves of temple thefts are plaguing the island. The environment is becoming inexorably degraded as the rice fields and beaches are covered with concrete and the anarchic proliferation of hotels and souvenir shops ravages the beauty of the landscape for which Bali was once famous (18).

(18) About 1,000 hectares of irrigated rice fields disappear every year; the total surface of irrigated rice fields in Bali is around 90,000.

Ecologists do their best to render the Balinese "conscious of the environment" (*sadar lingkungan*, abridged as *darling*), while they alert the authorities to the erosion of the coasts and warn them that soon there will be a shortage of drinking water. Meanwhile the rivers and beaches and the air itself are becoming more polluted every week, and the trash collection services no longer

know what to do with the garbage piling up in dumps that were already saturated long ago. And this is not to mention the deterioration of infrastructures, groaning under the weight of a demand that seems to grow heavier by the hour. Even the tourism industry is beginning to admit that if something is not done soon, the degradation of the environment could condemn the future of tourism in Bali. In short, due to the lack of control and planning, it seems that the development of tourism can only end in the destruction of Bali. The "Garden Island" (*Pulau Taman*) is becoming the "Island of Concrete" (*Pulau Beton*) (19).

At the same time that these ills are being regularly denounced, tourism is becoming the issue of openly displayed political struggles. The splits follow a double line of fracture: a muffled opposition to the government and a divergence of views between Bali and Jakarta. Prominent Balinese periodically call for legal authority, for lack of which the provincial government is ever unable to control tourism and develop it in the interests of the population. They denounce the directives from Jakarta which too often override provincial regulations, while recognizing that it is very difficult for local officials to stand up to this type of pressure. Their concerns are echoed by the regional press which — along with the Jakarta papers — do not hesitate to publish articles accusing Indonesian and foreign capital of having made a clean sweep of Bali's real estate at the expense of the Balinese, who find themselves progressively becoming foreigners in their own land (some say that nine-tenths of the coast is owned by non-

---

(19) The opposition between these two images is unfortunately not as marked as it would seem, as may be seen in the recent vogue of *tamanisasi*, instituted to restore to Bali its intrinsic qualities of "B.A.L.I." (*Bersih*: "clean"; *Aman*: "secure"; *Lestari*: "preserved"; *Indah*: "beautiful"). Thus in 1993, with the aim of winning a prize for cleanliness awarded by the central government and at the same pleasing the tourists, the new *Bupati* of Gianyar issued the startling decree to cut down all the trees along the roadsides — including some trees that were hundreds of years old — and to plant artificial gardens (*taman*) which make copious use of painted concrete (*beton*) to the most hideous effect. The program of *tamanisasi* vaunted by the government turned into a "cementing over" (*betonisasi*) of the environment, to the great consternation of tourists and Balinese ecologists alike.

Balinese) (20, overleaf). Aware of the gravity of the situation, the Governor has alerted the population against the risk of dispossession, recommending that they lease their land rather than sell it to investors from Jakarta.

But the new fact is that the Governor himself — although he was appointed with the benediction of his predecessor and enjoys the same impeccable credentials — is no longer immune to criticism. Caught between injunctions from Jakarta and the discontent of a growing portion of the Balinese intelligentsia, he is openly accused of weakness. This might explain the publication by the Public Relations Bureau of the Provincial Secretariat of Bali of a book called: "Bali: What They Are Saying" (*Bali, Apa Kata Mereka*) (Pangdjaja 1991b). It is a compilation of articles on tourism in Bali published in 1990–91 in the Indonesian press, articles that are for the most part very critical. One may read in the preface that the interests of the province are in conflict with the aims of Jakarta: while the Balinese try to limit the growth of tourism on their island in order to control it better, the Indonesians want to develop it ever more. Under the circumstances, it would seem that the provincial government, by deliberately stressing the harmful consequences of uncontrolled tourism in Bali, was trying to lay responsibility for the situation on the central government. And the Governor personally affirms the determination of the Balinese, declaring:

---

(20) One finds more and more frequently in the Indonesian press accusations of this sort:

Bali is like a damp towel that one wrings until it's dry. And when the towel is in tatters and won't hold any more water, there's nothing left to do but throw it away. (Suara Pembaruan 30/7/90)

Believe me, Bali will not change. Bali will always be Bali. In the past, a hundred years ago, today, and even a hundred years from now. Bali has never sold itself to tourism. The Balinese people are determined that it is tourism that must submit to Bali. Tourism is for Bali, not Bali for tourism. (Pangdjaja 1991b: 11)

Although one should not be taken in by the inevitable rhetoric of such declarations when it is known that many highly placed individuals are filling their pockets as quickly as possible, it remains that the Balinese — even those with the bulging pockets — are truly worried about the future of tourism on the island. The fact is that there is a growing gap between what the tourists are supposedly seeking in Bali — unspoiled landscapes and an authentic culture — and that which they actually find. Hence the insistent rumor that Bali is becoming too touristic. In an attempt to restore an already tattered authenticity, influential spokesmen for Balinese tourism have come to propose that certain villages considered to be especially picturesque should be conserved in their traditional state for the tourists.

This idea received a resounding confirmation at the International Conference on Cultural Tourism held in 1992 in Yogyakarta (Java), under the joint auspices of the Department of Tourism, Post and Telecommunications and the Department of Education and Culture, with the support of UNESCO, the WTO, the UNDP and PATA (Nuryanti 1993). In the paper that he presented at this conference — whose theme was "Universal Tourism: Enriching or Degrading Culture?" — the Governor of Bali advanced the concept of "village tourism" (*pariwisata pedesaan*), publicly announcing the decision to make the three villages of Panglipuran (Bangli), Sebatu (Gianyar) and Jatiluwih (Tabanan) "tourist villages" (*desa wisata*) (Oka 1993). It seems for the moment that the implications of this concept remain rather vague and that its implementation raises unforeseen difficulties.

But whatever the future has in store for this formula, the fact remains that tourism is now presented as the last hope — the only hope, in fact — for safeguarding the cultural traditions sorely tried by the present evolution of Balinese society, assailed as it is by a multitude of interconnecting influences — cultural and economic globalization, national development, the media, technology, etc. (21). Thus one sees yet another reversal in the relationship between tourism and culture. Formerly, the Balinese culture was perceived as a living tradition that ran the risk of being corrupted by tourist commercialization. Now, however, tourism is not only absolved of the sins it was so recently accused of, but it is actually called on to "revitalize" a traditional culture threatened by the homogenizing perils of modernity. The Balinese

(21) This regenerative role of tourism was strongly affirmed at the conference of Yogyakarta where the first theme, entitled "Revitalizing the Cultural Heritage" was presented as follows:

Tourism should be viewed as an asset or tool for the preservation of heritage... However, the concept of preservation should not be a "protectionist" one but rather it should be seen as an integrated concept for the revitalization and development of culture. (Nuryanti 1993: 2) authorities' change of attitude toward sacred dances is significant in this regard: where not long ago, the concern was preventing their profanation by restricting their performance to ritual use only, now it is a matter of saving them from obsolescence by tapping them to inspire new dances that can in turn regenerate tourist performances that have grown dull from years of routine (22).

GWK and BNR

Until recently, Bali's image had been based on the attractions that originally made the island's reputation well before they were elevated to the rank of "tourist objects". But since the 1980s, there has been a shift of focus from culture to landscape and into the resort, with its tourist amenities. And now, to revive Bali's power of attraction, fading with excessive exploitation, the idea has dawned of making new "tourist objects" to broaden the market appeal of Bali's tourist product (23). It was with this in view that in 1993, the project of "Garuda Wisnu Kencana" was presented, better known in Bali as "GWK".

This project consists of a monumental statue of Wisnu, the Hindu deity who protects and conserves the universe, astride his mount, the royal eagle Garuda, and plated in gold (*kencana*). Proudly presented as the biggest statue in the world by its promoter — I Nyoman Nuarta, a Balinese living in Java, who compares the project to Borobudur, the pyramids of Egypt, and the Eiffel Tower, and who readily points out that it will be taller than the Statue of Liberty — the monument will be 125 meters high: the statue itself, measuring 65 meters, will be placed on an 11-story building equipped with elevators allowing visitors access to a panoramic terrace at the top of the building. It is to be built on the Bukit peninsula near the village of Ungasan on a site covering 180 hectares. The monument — which is expected to cost $200 million and to be able to receive some 20,000 visitors a day — will be "the most prominent tourist attraction for those who visit Bali" (GWK 1994: 1). It will have theaters and exhibition halls, amusement parks and museums, restaurants and souvenirs shops, and many other facilities as well, all carved out of the limestone highlands of the peninsula. Among the most eminently promoted attractions, according to a brochure produced as work-on-site begins in 1994-95, are the three dimensional projections reconstituting Balinese life of yesteryear. Foremost among

(22) Thus one of the principal figures of the Seminar on Sacred and Profane Dance of 1971, I Gusti Bagus Nyoman Pandji, declared in 1985 that now it was not only *bebali* dances that were threatened by imminent disappearance but *wali* dances as well, since many of these were no longer executed in the context of the religious ceremonies for which they were created. Consequently, while admitting that *wali* dances should not be performed out of context, he proposed that they should be "exploited" (*diolah*) in such a way as to provide inspiration for the composition of new dances — which, he said, would facilitate a "mutation of sacred values into artistic values" (*peralihan nilai sakral ke nilai artistik*) (Pandji 1985: 480–481).

(23) Thus 20 new 18-hole golf courses have been approved for development, comprising a total investment of around $1.3 billion. These are in addition to the 3 existing golf courses on the island.

these is the "Gunung Agung Memorial" which is perhaps best described in the following transcription from the brochure:

> *The eruption of Gunung Agung in 1963 has resulted in thousand [sic] of victims. This calamity is recorded in the history of Bali island and becomes a legend eversince [sic]. Natural phenomenon initiated the eruption. The earth shaking the flowing of the lava and the panicking people have shown how severe the eruption is. History cannot certainly be repeated. However the picture which can vividly depict the incident is now able to be visualized by the aids of sophisticated technology. It will be performed in a very impressive and tense attraction as if the visitors are really experiencing when nature shows its anger.* (GWK 1994: 2)

Other attractions include: "From the Historic Time to the Present", presenting scenes from Balinese history in diorama in the pedestal building; "Puri Bali", a recreation of a Balinese palace, where "art performances" will be staged in a manner reminiscent of olden times, and spectators will be required to get dressed up as Balinese aristocrats; and the "Calonarang Theater", described as presenting this "Balinese folk tale in a mixed media setting" and which will give visitors a chance to see *leyak* — the fiendish minions of *Rangda*, able to assume fantastic forms in order to carry out their evil deeds, and still feared by all but the most world-weary Balinese. As if this were not magical enough, the "Gapura Seribu Amphitheatre" — which proposes "a comfortable ambiance for over 4000 viewers watching the collosal [sic] show executed by 1000 (*seribu*) performers" — will be equipped with "the most sophisticated technology", which perhaps explains how, as the text immediately promises, "the time starts at dawn when the sun sets" (op.cit.: 4).

The initiative for this grandiose project, which dates from 1990, seems to arise jointly from the then Director General of Tourism and the Governor of Bali, who agreed on the idea of building a landmark visible from the airport to greet visitors upon their arrival in Bali. Taking into account Bali's being the "gateway" (*pintu gerbang*) to Indonesia, this landmark should become, in the words of the Minister of Tourism, "the image of Indonesian tourism" (*citra kepariwisataan Indonesia*) (Suara Pembaruan 4/9/1993). In this regard, it is significant that the same newspaper article reporting the Minister's words, also quotes the Balinese artist responsible for the project, who declares that the statue will represent "the image of Balinese culture" (*citra budaya Bali*).

Almost the moment that it was made public, this project unleashed a heated debate which the *Bali Post* — the island's main daily newspaper — echoed quite thoroughly by, among other things, soliciting the opinions of its readers and organizing a public debate. The GWK, supported as it is by the government and the tourism industry, is favored by a considerable part of the intelligentsia and public opinion. Its partisans cite the glory of Indonesia and the pride of the Balinese in being able to construct a colossal monument comprising the very leading edge of technology, worthy of the prestigious heritage of their ancestors and of comparison with the most celebrated monuments of the world, and which will surely be admired by the tourists who will come *en masse* to experience it. The opponents of the project are mostly artists and intellectuals, students, and the activists of various NGOs. Accusing their adversaries of "megalomania", they assert that the monuments of the past were not "objects" empty of sense like the GWK but had a religious function. They do not fail to point out as well that tourists do not come to Bali to see a statue taller than the Statue of Liberty but, to the contrary, to discover the traditional Balinese way of life in all its authenticity. In a particularly striking formulation, a group of intellectuals declared about the project:

> *Considerations of profit again take precedence over spiritual affairs as Bali becomes a Hindu Theme Park where everything is made quaint and neatly packaged for sale for the sake of foreign eyes.* (IRIP News Service 1993: 25) (24)

It is on this point that the divergence of opinion is most significant (Warren 1995). The opponents of the GWK seem convinced that the traditional Balinese life, rural and harmonious, which so seduced the visitors of the era of the Netherlands Indies, is still viable and visible, if one will only take the trouble to ensure its preservation and accessibility with the appropriate measures. It is, by the way, on this same idealization of tradition that the Governor's idea of "tourist villages" is based. Conversely, the fictive reconstitution of a décor illustrating scenes from traditional Balinese life by

(24) Whatever its promoters, and detractors, might say, it is clear that the public for which the GWK is intended — like that of *Taman Mini* in Jakarta — is Indonesian, and particularly Balinese, rather than foreign.

the aid of sophisticated technology implies a rupture with the world it recreates — as if, in short, the *leyak* were nothing more to the Balinese than a belief from the past.

The passions inflamed by the GWK had only begun to cool when the *Bali Post* published an alarmist article informing its readers of the construction of a vast tourist complex, the "Bali Nirwana Resort" (BNR) (25), on the site of the famous temple of Tanah Lot, included by the Governor in the 15 "tourist zones" decreed in 1988. The project, which covers 121 hectares, includes a 292-room luxury hotel, a 152-villa residential park, a 330-unit condominium complex, and an 18-hole golf course. It is being developed by the Bakrie Group, based in Jakarta, and is calling for foreign

capital to finance 80% of the $324 million it is estimated to cost. But this is only the first stage of a new seaside resort that will eventually cover some 600 hectares, considerably bigger than Nusa Dua.

Since the announcement of this project in late 1993, Bali has been shaken by a wave of protest of unprecedented force — student demonstrations, petitions by intellectuals, parliamentary debates, seminars, delegations to the Governor, editorials and letters to the Editor of the *Bali Post*, and so forth. It is important to point out that this is the first time that the development of tourism on the island has incited such a massive and unanimous opposition of Balinese public opinion. In fact, not since the massacres of 1965-66 preceding the birth of the New Order have so many Balinese dared to so openly confront the government.

Although the opponents of the project denounce the forced conversion of fertile rice fields into a playground for the idle rich, and a handful of villagers from the surrounding area have for some time refused to sell their land, it is not land but religion that has rapidly emerged as the issue at the heart of the controversy. With remarkable unanimity, the opponents of the BNR insist that Tanah Lot is a symbol of Bali throughout the world and that the Balinese see it as the symbol of their identity.

(25) Opponents of the Bali Nirwana ["paradise"] Resort have dubbed it the Bali Neraka ["hell"] Resort.

It is under this banner that they reject the BNR, protesting that the temple will be desecrated by the resort and accusing the government of trampling their faith for the sake of tourism.

The fact is that religion has proved to be the most effective (and the most emotionally charged) means of mobilizing public opinion against the project. Student groups and Hindu intellectuals across the country showed immediate support, and the most radical have urged *Parisada Hindu Dharma Indonesia* to take up the defense of their religion, not hesitating to accuse this august institution of being no more than a rubber stamp for government decisions. In January 1994, *Parisada* finally decreed that no building could be built within a two kilometer radius of the Tanah Lot temple. This decree was approved by the President of the Republic and, had it been applied, it would have wiped the BNR off the map, since the hotel was situated less than 500 meters from the temple. But, as is often the case in Indonesia, it was more a maneuver to save face than a measure likely to be implemented. Rather than risk an outright confrontation, *Parisada* agreed to a compromise. The promoters undertook to modify their publicity campaign — which made free use of the image of Tanah Lot, famous among tourists for its picturesque silhouette against spectacular sunsets — in order to appease the critics accusing them of exploiting the Balinese religion for commercial ends. Some other concessions were made: the hotel site was moved somewhat inland and the construction of other buildings was postponed; other tourist installations very close to the temple, however, seem not to have been called into question. Meanwhile, the army put down the student demonstrations, and articles about the BNR disappeared from the front pages of the *Bali Post.* In May 1994, the government confirmed its approval of the project and work is proceeding apace.

As to its immediate effect, the BNR affair shows that the mobilization of Balinese public opinion did not weigh very heavily compared to the importance of economic interests and pressures from Jakarta. But this affair has brought to light the state of exasperation in which a growing portion of Balinese find themselves, most especially the influential faction of opinion — students and intellectuals — who no longer intend to let themselves be subjected to whatever the government dictates in the name of "development" and the "national interest". The vehemence of the reactions published by the *Bali Post* testifies to this: their authors complain of being "cheated" (*kecolongan*), and fear that they will become foreigners on their own territory, that their island will be sold to the highest bidder. After Tanah Lot it will be the temple of

Sakenan on Serangan Island to serve as the décor for frolicking tourists. And who knows, say the critics, if foreign investors will not soon be sniffing around the mother-temple of Besakih. Facing the threat of dispossession, the Balinese close ranks behind their religion, held aloft as the inalienable emblem of their identity. The situation seems to be precarious: how long can the Balinese population tolerate the proliferation of tourist facilities and the omnipresence of tourists before irritation and frustration turns openly hostile? (26).

Are the Balinese losing their Balinese-ness?

In this uncertain state of affairs, the proposition of a "cultural renaissance" of Bali through tourism, however complacently affirmed by the authorities, does not escape the wave of criticism. Thus one finds allusions in the press accusing the Balinese of holding ever more spectacular ceremonies with the intention of impressing the tourists rather than pleasing the gods, or of wearing traditional dress only when they entertain foreign visitors in their village. But there are more radical accusations, such as the debate which stirred up the Balinese intelligentsia a few years ago, following the publication in the *Bali Post* of an article entitled, "The Balinese Are Losing their Balinese-ness" (*Orang Bali Semakin Kehilangan Kebaliannya*). The author, I Nyoman Naya Sujana a Balinese sociologist, professor at the University of Surabaya in Java, took his compatriots to task and — defending his critical position by virtue of seeing things from outside the island — declared that the Balinese were intoxicated with the prestige of their touristic reputation abroad and unaware that "the authenticity of Balinese cultural identity" (*keaslian identitas budaya Bali*) was gravely compromised. More precisely, he explained how the opening of Bali to the outside world through international tourism brought a simultaneous movement of abandoning indigenous cultural elements and adopting foreign cultural elements that overturned the relationships of the Balinese with their gods, their fellow human beings, and their environment:

> *Little by little, the Balinese cultural elements are being diluted and carried off into the ocean of world culture by the wave of tourism.* (Sujana 1988)

This cry of alarm did not pass unnoticed on the island, and the next day, the *Bali Post* devoted its editorial to the question of the cultural identity of the Balinese. In the days and weeks that followed, the newspaper published the reactions of its readers — distressed or incensed — as well as interviews with various prominent Balinese, for the most part academics and high officials.

The counter-attack followed an evolution of issues that reveal much about the challenge of tourism in Bali, in that it recapitulated in an accelerated fashion the

---

(26) The exhibition of satirical drawings organized by the Galleria Bebek in Denpasar in December 1993, ironically titled *Bali Sing Ken-Ken* ("Bali No Problems") testified eloquently to the rise of this state of mind among the Balinese.

transformation of Cultural Tourism into touristic culture. The editorial began by reminding the Balinese that they must consider themselves above all Indonesians, and that from the moment the central government decided to make their island the touristic show-window of Indonesia, it was inevitable that their traditional world would suffer upheaval, some of which would be painful. It was up to them, therefore, to show themselves equal to the test and to rise to the challenge of tourism.

Then the first articles began to question the foundations of the argument of the Balinese sociologist, insisting: "It Is Not True that the Balinese-ness of the Balinese Is Weakening" (*Tidak Benar Kebalian Orang Bali Memudar*). This is because the cultural identity of the Balinese must be seen in a double dimension: a superficial structure (*luar*) and an inner structure (*dalam*). The inner structure — the religious foundations of Balinese society (*agama*) and the values of communal solidarity supporting the customary institutions (*adat*) — is not threatened. Only the superficial structure — and in fact it is proof of the cultural dynamism of the Balinese that they have been able to utilize the wealth of their culture's artistic fruits (*seni*) to develop tourism — is wedded to the exigencies of the times and adjusts itself to the transformations of the environment.

After a period of lively debate, the figures interviewed affirmed that, in fact, "The Balinese-ness of the Balinese Is Stronger Than Ever" (*Makin Bertambah Kebalian Orang Bali*) — for the Balinese culture is justly reputed for its dynamic resilience, for the propensity of the Balinese to adopt only what is appropriate from foreign influences and, above all, to transform and incorporate them according to the dictates of their own genius. In these conditions, the very interest of the tourists in their culture is a heady stimulant, in that it is a matter of both pride and profit for the Balinese. Nothing surprising about this, so far. But what seems significant to me — and this is my point — is that one of the principal arguments put forward to refute the doomsday view of Bali's imminent ruin by tourism was, remarkably, this: that the best proof of the cultural authenticity of the Balinese is the fact that there are ever more tourists coming to the island. And this, they point out with some pride, would certainly not be the case if the Balinese culture were no longer what it is reputed to be.

A survey among the newspaper's readers was taken on this occasion, showing that while 40% of the persons interviewed attributed to the influence of tourists an erosion of Balinese-ness, 60% thought that, to the contrary, the increasing number of tourist arrivals in Bali was the best proof of the force of attraction of the Balinese cultural identity (Widminarko 1989).

Thus, called upon to conform to their image, the Balinese not only are required to be Balinese, but they must be worthy representatives of "Balinese-ness"; they must become signs of themselves (27). And all their attempts at the *affirmation* of their identity are but a reaction to this *injunction* from which they are unable to extricate themselves. They appropriate the touristic vision of their culture while at the same time they try to prise themselves free of its grip. Such is the identity crisis to which the Balinese are submitted — a crisis that shows itself in a paradoxical injunction.

If this analysis is pertinent, one could say that what the Balinese authorities cel-

ebrate today — but for how much longer? — as a "cultural renaissance" is nothing other than the logical conclusion of what they not long ago denounced under the name of "touristic culture". In becoming Bali's *brand image* — that which marks the uniqueness of its tourist product, that by which the island of Bali tries to distinguish itself on a highly competitive international market — culture has become, indissociably, the *identity marker* for the Balinese, that which characterizes them as a particular society, that by which they define and recognize themselves. The "Balinese culture" in this double sense is the interface between the inside and the outside, and at the same time, it is the ground where the Balinese and outsiders may come together.

It seems to me that one can speak of a *touristic culture* at that point when the Balinese come to confuse these two uses of their culture, *when that by which the tourists identify them becomes that by which they identify themselves* — or, more precisely, when the imperatives of the touristic promotion of their culture have so far infiltrated the considerations that motivate their will to preserve it that the Balinese end up taking the brand image of their tourist product for the identity marker of their cultural productions (28). Thus it is that the Balinese, enjoined to preserve and promote their cultural identity in reference to the outside world's view of them, have come to search for confirmation of their "Balinese-ness" in the mirror held to them by the tourists.

(27) The validity of this conclusion is certainly not limited to Bali, as may be seen in a number of analyses tending to show that touristified peoples come to question their identity as tourists expect them to present an authentic image of themselves (Bruner 1991a; Errington & Gewertz 1989; MacCannell 1984; Simpson 1993; Volkman 1990).

(28) One should beware that this could have serious consequences for the future of tourism in Bali. Pico Iyer expresses the point well:

> *When we choose a place to visit, the way a country carries itself and markets itself — the way it knows itself, really — is everything. We flee certain resorts not just because they are touristed but more because they have begun to see themselves through tourists' eyes, to amend themselves to tourists' needs, to carry themselves in capital letters: because, in short, they have simplified themselves into their sense of what a foreigner wants.* (Iyer 1993: 115-116)

Conclusion

It should be clear at the conclusion of this study that tourism has neither "polluted" Balinese culture nor kindled its "renaissance", much less simply contributed to "preserving" it. What has happened is that the decision to promote "cultural" tourism made the Balinese self-conscious about their culture. It is as if tourism had convinced the Balinese that they were the inheritors of something at once precious and perishable called "culture", which they perceived as a value to be conserved and promoted. And as it was distinguished and enhanced by the tourist gaze, their culture became reified and externalized in the eyes of the Balinese, by becoming an object that could be detached from themselves in order to be displayed and marketed to others.

Once they had become convinced of its value, their culture became an issue for the Balinese — a source of pride, certainly, but also of anxiety — and they faced the question already posed by tourists and the foreign experts: "Will Balinese culture survive the impact of tourism?" And in order to address the challenge imposed upon them, the Balinese authorities endeavored to raise protective barriers against the tourist invasion by attempting to fall back on an unassailable core of identity.

This attempt failed, as may be seen in the manifest inability of the Balinese to maintain a boundary that would allow them to discriminate between that which they should reserve for themselves and that which they could sell to tourists, to keep that which belongs to the culture separate from that which pertains to tourism. Certainly, the Balinese know perfectly well if they are dancing for tourists, for their community, or for their gods. They are entirely capable of differentiating among the audiences they address. But for the Balinese, commerce and art, entertainment and ritual, are not clearly distinct categories — and, as we have seen, the content of a cultural performance overflows from one category to another.

If the effort at discrimination by the Balinese authorities failed, it was not only because their language does not have words differentiating the sacred from the profane, but because it was doomed to fail. For it was based on an illusory vision of an indigenous culture as autonomous, precisely bounded and clearly identifiable that was assaulted by an external force in the form of tourists. In short, the challenge of tourism was not where the Balinese expected it to be.

The analysis of the Balinese strategy and the reasons for its failure allows one to see that, far from being an external force striking a local society from without, as the problematic of the impact would have it, tourism — or, rather, what should be called the "touristification" of a society — proceeds from within, by changing the way its members see themselves. Or, more exactly, while stressing the dichotomy between what is inside and what comes from outside, the process of touristification operates by blurring the boundaries by which the members of a society distinguish between "us" and "them", between that which belongs to the culture and that which pertains to tourism.

Consequently, international tourism, far from being foreign to Balinese culture, is an integral part of a process of cultural invention. Moreover, this process must be seen in the context of the opening-up of the Balinese world following the island's integration into, first, the Netherlands East Indies, then into the Republic of Indonesia. In short, the touristification of the Balinese culture cannot be dissociated from Bali's colonization and its subsequent Indonesianization.

In this perspective, Balinese culture is the product of a dialogical interaction between the Balinese and their different interlocutors: tourists and the tourism industry, certainly, but also the artists, orientalists and anthropologists who contributed to the composition of Bali's tourist image, as well as the Dutch officials who worked relentlessly to fashion Balinese society according to what they believed it to be — now emulated in this process by their Indonesian and Balinese successors. As this confrontation with significant "Others" made the Balinese conscious of their cultural identity, it also obliged them to elucidate what it meant to be Balinese in terms that were accessible to non-Balinese. And in this way, the same process that forced the Balinese to examine the foundations of their identity dispossessed them of their own voice by forcing them to think in foreign categories — and above all in a language that was not their own: Malay and Dutch first, and now Indonesian and English.

So it is that the Balinese — or at least the spokesmen of the native intelligentsia — have come to define themselves in terms which they call "Balinese culture", which they like to represent as a tree in which the roots are religion, the trunk is the traditional customary order, and the fruits are works of art. If the roots remain firmly implanted, they assure us, the trunk will remain strong and the tree will bear beautiful fruits.

If I may extend this naturalistic metaphor, it seems to me that one may suggest, to the contrary, that since the colonial armies subjugated the island at the turn of the century, the tree of the Balinese culture has seen its trunk atrophy while its roots have grown stronger and its fruits have multiplied. This is due to an ever greater trespassing by a foreign power on the traditional customary order — which is both an immutable divine order and the social order bequeathed accordingly by the ancestors — that regulated Balinese existence until then. More precisely, the emergence of the modern world in their traditional universe ushered in a new socio-cosmic order and forced the Balinese intelligentsia to make a series of conceptual discriminations, distinguishing what was "customary" from what was, respectively, "politics", "religion", and "art". It was, in fact, as though "custom" was progressively stripped of its "political" and "religious" prerogatives as it began to be seen in terms of its "artistic" qualities. And it is precisely these artistic qualities — for which the Balinese culture is justly famous — that have been conscripted to promote the development of international tourism in Indonesia and to help build the national Indonesian culture.

In this sense, it would hardly be paradoxical to suggest that the international tourism industry and the Indonesian state have taken on the project of "Balinizing Bali" started by the colonial administration. Today it is the Balinese authorities who, to the applause of the tourists and the Indonesians, are engaged in the "Balinization" of Bali.

Glossary

[Balinese terms are in **bold** type and Indonesian ones are in *italics*].

adat – custom; local customary law, institutions, and ritual.

Adipura – national program of village development incentives.

agama – religion; in contemporary Indonesia, the term is officially restricted to those religions claiming to be monotheistic and universalist.

amok – to go beserk, run amuck.

Asprananta – *Asosiasi Penyelenggara Tontonan Wisata*: Association of Organizers of Tourist Performances, founded in Bali in 1986.

ASTI – *Akademi Seni Tari Indonesia*: Academy of Indonesian Dance, founded in Denpasar in 1967.

ayah – service; to do unpaid service to a temple or to a lord.

bale banjar – a public pavilion where members of a *banjar* meet regularly in council.

BALI – *Bersih*, clean; *Aman*, secure; *Lestari*, preserved; *Indah*, beautiful.

balih-balihan – "secular dances", performed in the outer courtyard of a temple or elsewhere, as pure entertainment, without any relation to a ceremony.

Baliseering – "Balinization"; the Dutch cultural policy aiming to make Balinese youth conscious of the richness of their cultural heritage.

banjar – hamlet; customary (*banjar adat*) or government (*banjar dinas*) unit.

Bapparda – *Badan Pengembangan Kepariwisataan Daerah*: Regional Board for Tourist Development, founded in Denpasar in 1970.

Bapparnas – *Badan Pengembangan Kepariwisataan Nasional*: National Board for Tourist Development.

Bappeda – *Badan Perencanaan Pembangunan Daerah:* Regional Development Planning Board.

Bappenas – *Badan Perencanaan Pembangunan Nasional*: National Development Planning Board.

Baris – group of male warrior dances performed during a ceremony (*Baris Gede*); dramatic genre with Baris dancers in the leading roles (*Baris Malampahan*); modern solo dance (*Baris Panglembar).*

Barong – a mask featuring an animal or a supernatural being; the most common and most powerful is the *Barong Ket* which resembles a dragon and which controls the *buta kala.*

bebali – "ceremonial dances", performed in the central courtyard of a temple or elsewhere, accompanying a ceremony.

Bhinneka Tunggal Ika – "Unity in Diversity"; the Indonesian national motto.

Bina Wisata – Ubud Tourist Information, founded in 1982.

BKPMD – Badan Koordinasi Penanaman Modal Daerah: Regional Capital Investment Board.

BNR – Bali Nirwana Resort: project to build a vast tourist complex on the site of the famous temple of Tanah Lot.

Brahmana – the first "caste", from which high priests are drawn.

BTDB – Bali Tourism Development Board; instituted in 1972 to coordinate the implementation of the Master Plan.

BTDC – Bali Tourism Development Corporation; incorporated in 1973 to supervise the Nusa Dua project.

bupati – head of a district (*kabupaten*).

buta kala – demons who transmit illness and are responsible for all sorts of calamities.

Calonarang – exorcistic dance-drama based on an Old Javanese text telling the story of a widow-witch defeated by a powerful sage.

ciri khas – distinctive feature, identity marker.

citra – image, brand image.

Daerah Tujuan Wisata – Tourist Destination.

dagang acung – peddler.

darling – sadar lingkungan: "conscious of the environment".

Departemen Pariwisata, Pos dan Telekomunikasi – Department of Tourism, Post and Telecommunications.

Depparnas – Dewan Pertimbangan Kepariwisataan Nasional: National Advisory Council for Tourism.

desa – village; customary (*desa adat*) or government (*desa dinas*) unit.

desa wisata – tourist village; that is, a village kept "authentic" and "traditional" in order to appeal to the tourists.

dharma – religious duty according to one's "caste"; the harmonizing of behavior to the social order and its cosmic foundation.

Diparda – Dinas Pariwisata Daerah: Bali Government Tourism Office, opened in 1970.

Diplomasi Kebudayaan – "Cultural Diplomacy"; launched in 1983 by the Indonesian Foreign Minister.

Direktorat Jenderal Pariwisata – Directorate General of Tourism.

Drama Gong – popular theatrical genre, created in 1966, giving up choreography for the sake of verbal comedy and melodrama.

endek – Balinese weft ikat cloth.

Galungan – main Balinese holiday held every 210 days and lasting for ten days.

Gambuh – the oldest known form of court theater, which tells of the exploits of the prince *Panji*, known in Bali under the title of *Malat*.

Garuda – the Indonesian national airline.

gelungan – headdress used by Balinese dancers.

gotong royong – community mutual help.

GWK – Garuda Wisnu Kencana: project to build a monumental gold-plated statue of Wisnu, the Hindu deity who protects and conserves the universe, astride his mount, the royal eagle Garuda.

jaba – "outside" or "outsider"; commoner, as opposed to members of the nobility (*triwangsa*); outer courtyard of a temple.
jaba tengah – central courtyard of a temple.
jalur hijau – green belt; road alongside which no construction is permitted.
jeroan – inner courtyard of a temple.
kabupaten – district; subdivision of a province.
kaja – "the world on high"; the direction of the mountains, considered to be the source of fertility and life, the seat of the gods and deified ancestors.
kalangan – traditional Balinese arena stage.
Kanwil Depparpostel – *Kantor Wilayah Departemen Pariwisata, Pos dan Telekomunikasi*: Provincial Office of the Department of Tourism, Post and Telecommunications, opened in Denpasar in 1978.
karauhan – possessed, trance possession.
Karma Phala – the subjection of human beings to the fruits of their actions.
kawasan wisata – tourist area; refers to the 21 areas slated for tourism development by the Governor of Bali.
kawi – poetic language; archaic and literary language spoken by the leading characters in Balinese theater.
kawitan – origin point; a sanctuary where the deified ancestors of a clan are venerated.
Kayangan Tiga – the three main village temples: the *pura puseh*, the *pura desa* and the *pura dalem*.
Kebalian – "Balinese-ness"; the Balinese cultural, ethnic and religious identity.
kebijaksanaan – policy; understood as a position that is wise, judicious and prudent, aiming to satisfy all the parties involved.
kebudayaan – culture; an abstract derivative formed from the Sanskrit root *budaya*, which designates a "cultivated individual" in the sense of someone who has received a good education.
kebudayaan daerah – regional culture; the acknowledged cultural manifestations deemed representative of a province and expected to contribute to the building of the national Indonesian culture.
(ke)budaya(an) (pari)wisata – touristic culture, defined by the Balinese authorities as a state of confusion between the values of the culture and those of tourism.
Kebyar – the modern style of Balinese music and dance, born around 1915.
Kecak – a popular tourist performance, known as "Monkey Dance", making use of a large male chorus (*cak*) derived from the one providing accompaniment for some of the *Sanghyang* trance dances.
kecamatan – subdistrict.
kelod – "the world below"; the direction of the sea, considered to be a lair of demons, associated with sickness and death.
keris – dagger.
Kirtya Liefrinck-Van der Tuuk – named after two great tutelary figures of Balinese studies, the foundation opened in 1928 by the Dutch Resident in Singaraja, for the collection and study of Balinese manuscripts.

Klub Diskusi Pembangunan Daerah Bali – Discussion Club on the Development of Bali, founded in 1970.

KOKAR – Konservatori Karawitan: Conservatory of Traditional Music, founded in Denpasar in 1960.

Komisi Kerjasama Pembinaan dan Pengembangan Wisata Budaya – Commission of Cooperation for Fostering and Developing Cultural Tourism, founded in 1979 by the Directorate General of Culture and the Directorate General of Tourism.

KPM – Koninklijke Paketwaart Maatschappij; the Royal Packet Navigation Company, founded in 1888, which had a monopoly on shipping in the Dutch East Indies.

Legong – court dance, performed by two or three young girls.

leyak – sorcerers who have acquired the ability to transform themselves and propagate illness.

Listibiya – Majelis Pertimbangan dan Pembinaan Kebudayaan Daerah Propinsi Bali: Consultative and Promotional Council for Balinese Culture, founded in 1966.

Lomba Desa – competition organized by the Indonesian government to promote the development and modernization of rural villages.

losmen – guesthouse, cheap hotel.

Majapahit – 14th century Hindu-Javanese kingdom, regarded by most Balinese as the source of their culture.

mawinten – initiation ceremony undergone by various specialists, such as dancers, to increase their ritual purity.

misi kesenian – artistic mission; refers to troupes of musicians and dancers sent abroad on tour, with a view to both promoting Indonesian culture and developing tourism in Indonesia.

modal pariwisata – touristic capital.

negara – kindgom, state.

ngurek – the self-stabbing of the followers of the *Barong* possessed by *buta kala*, usually called "kris dance" by tourists and Balinese alike.

niskala – the invisible world, unmanifested.

nusantara – the Indonesian archipelago, in the sense of the space encompassing lands and seas (*tanah air*).

obyek (pari)wisata – tourist object; any officially acknowledged tourist attraction.

odalan – periodic celebration of a temple festival, during which the gods descend from the heavens to receive homage from the temple congregation.

Orde Baru – New Order; the regime established by President Suharto after the aborted "coup" of 1965.

Pancasila – the Five Principles of the official Indonesian state ideology: belief in God, humanism, nationalism, democracy, and social equity.

Panyembrama – contemporary dance composition, based on temple dances, performed to welcome distinguished guests and to open tourist performances.

Parisada Hindu Dharma Indonesia – Council of Hinduism, founded in Denpasar in 1959.

(Pari)wisata Budaya – Cultural Tourism; the official tourist doctrine of Bali, meant to take advantage of the Balinese culture to attract tourists, while utilizing the revenues generated by tourism to preserve and promote the culture.

pasanggrahan – government resthouses, used by colonial officials on their tours of inspection around Bali.

pasar seni – art market.

Pekan Pariwisata – Tourism Week.

Pembinaan Kebudayaan dan Pengembangan Kepariwisataan – The Fostering of Culture and the Development of Tourism, seen as two sides of the same coin by the doctrine of Cultural Tourism.

penasar – "those who provide a foundation"; buffoon characters serving as attendants to the princes in Balinese theater and interpreting the *kawi* spoken by their masters in colloquial Balinese.

Pendet – ritual dance, performed by members of a temple congregation carrying flowers, rice and incense in homage to the gods.

Pesta Kesenian Bali – Bali Arts Festival; an annual event launched by the Governor in 1979.

Pita Maha – association founded in 1936 dedicated to the promotion of the Balinese fine arts.

Pramana Patram Budaya – Certificate of Artistic Excellence, granted to troupes of Balinese musicians and dancers authorized to perform for a foreign audience.

Proyek Baliologi – Baliology Project; the Balinese culture was one of the five regional cultures selected in the Project for the Research and Study of the Nusantarian Culture.

Proyek Penelitian dan Pengkajian Kebudayaan Nusantara – Project for the Research and Study of the Nusantarian Culture, launched in 1984 to record the "summits" of the regional cultures of Indonesia in order to reinforce the national culture as the foundation of Indonesian identity.

puputan – fight to the finish.

pura – temple; rather than a building, it is a walled enclosure of holy ground where human beings make contact with their gods.

pura dalem – the "Temple of the Interior", where the disruptive influences of the not-yet-purified dead are placated and the deity of death is honored.

pura desa – the "Village Temple", where the village council meets, and which is associated with fertility rites.

pura puseh – the "Navel Temple", where the village's guardian deities and founding ancestors are venerated.

puri – palace; the residence of a lord.

Puri Lukisan – Ubud Museum of Modern Arts, opened in 1956.

raja – king, lord.

Rangda – a mask of demonic aspect, charged with magical power and believed to protect the community against epidemics; this mask is believed to have the power to control *leyak*.

Rejang – ritual processional dance performed by women.
Repelita – *Rencana Pembangunan Lima Tahun*: Five-Year Development Plan.
rupiah – the Indonesian currency.
Sadar Wisata – Tourism Awareness.
sakti – magically powerful.
Sanghyang – exorcistic rites which are characterized by spirit possession, executed during epidemics.
Sanghyang Dedari – ritual dance performed by two pre-pubescent girls possessed by the spirits of celestial nymphs.
Sanghyang Jaran – ritual dance performed by a man possessed by a horse spirit, who rides a bamboo hobby-horse barefoot through the coals of burning coconut husks.
Sang Hyang Widi Wasa – the official title given by the Balinese to their supreme deity, equivalent to the Christian God and the Islamic Allah.
Sapta Pesona – the Seven Charms of Tourism (peacefulness, orderliness, cleanliness, verdancy, beauty, hospitality, and happy memories).
Satria – the second "caste", from which most of the lords are drawn.
SCETO – Société Centrale pour l'Equipement Touristique Outre-Mer; the French firm which designed the Bali Tourism Development Master Plan in 1971.
seka – voluntary association; collectives of mutual aid or cooperation organized around specific functions.
sekala – the visible world, perceived by the senses.
Sendratari – *seni*, art; *drama*, theater; *tari*, dance. Pantomimic dance—drama, created in Java in 1961 and eagerly adopted by the Balinese.
seni – art.
seni budaya – "cultural arts"; culture as art.
SMKI – *Sekolah Menengah Karawitan Indonesia*: High School of Traditional Indonesian Music, founded in 1979 in replacement of *KOKAR*.
Stil Bali – Bali Style; the official style of Balinese public architecture adopted by the Governor in 1974.
STSI – *Sekolah Tinggi Seni Indonesia*: College of Indonesian Arts, founded in 1988 in replacement of *ASTI*.
subak – irrigation association, responsible for the regulation of the rice cycle.
suci – holy; ritually consecrated and purified.
taksu – inspiration of a divine or magical origin.
Taman Mini Indonesia Indah – Beautiful Indonesia-in-Miniature Park, built in the outskirts of Jakarta in 1975.
tamanisasi – refers to the decision taken in 1993 by the Bupati of Gianyar to cut down all the trees along the roadsides and to plant artificial gardens (*taman*) making copious use of painted concrete.
tapel – mask used by dancers.
tari lepas – "free dances"; dances detached from all ritual or dramatic ties in order to be presented as mere entertainment.
tawan karang – the right to salvage any wreck stranded off the coast of Bali.

tenget – magically dangerous.
Topeng – masked theater that dramatizes the ancient chronicles of the Balinese princely houses.
Tri Hita Karana – the harmony between human beings, their environment and their Creator.
triwangsa – "the Three Peoples"; the Balinese nobility, made up of the three upper "castes" (*Brahmana, Satria, Wesia*), as opposed to the commoners (*jaba*).
UNUD – *Universitas Udayana*: the University of Bali, in Denpasar.
VOC – Vereenigde Oost-Indische Compagnie; the United East India Company, founded in 1602, which held the Dutch trade monopoly with Asia until 1800.
wali – "sacred, religious dances", performed in the inner courtyard of a temple or wherever a ceremony is taking place, indissociable from the carrying out of the ceremony.
warisan kebudayaan – cultural heritage.
Wayang – generic term, designating both shadow theater (*Wayang Kulit*) and the theatrical genres presenting episodes drawn from the *Ramayana* (*Wayang Wong*) or the *Mahabharata* (*Parwa*).
Werdi Budaya – the Art Center, founded in Denpasar in 1976.
Wesia – the third "caste", from which some of the lords are drawn.
wibawa – spiritual power, charisma.
wisman – *wisatawan mancanegara*: foreign tourists.
wisnu – *wisatawan nusantara*: domestic tourists.
yadnya – religious ceremony, ritual sacrifice.

References

Acciaioli, G. 1985. Culture as Art. From Practice to Spectacle in Indonesia, *Canberra Anthropology*, 8/1&2: 148–174.

Adams, K.M. 1990. Cultural Commoditization in Tana Toraja, Indonesia, *Cultural Survival Quarterly*, 14/1: 31–34.

Agung, I.A.A.G. 1991. *Bali in the 19th Century*. Jakarta: Yayasan Obor Indonesia.

Allcock, J.B. 1989. Sociology of Tourism, in *Tourism Marketing and Management Handbook*, eds. S.F.Witt & L.Moutinho, pp. 407–414. New York: Prentice Hall.

[Anonymous]. 1927. Bali sebagai Museum barang koeno [Bali from the Perspective of a Museum of Antiques], *Surya Kanta*, 3/3–4: 29–30.

Artaud, A. 1931. Le Théâtre Balinais, à l'Exposition coloniale, *La Nouvelle Revue Française*, 217: 655–658.

Bagus, G.N., ed. 1986. *Sumbangan Nilai Budaya Bali dalam Pembangunan Kebudayaan Nasional* [*The Contribution of Balinese Cultural Values in the Development of National Culture*]. Denpasar: Direktorat Jenderal Kebudayaan.

Bakker, F.L. 1993. *The Struggle of the Hindu Balinese Intellectuals. Developments in Modern Hindu Thinking in Independent Indonesia*. Amsterdam: VU University Press.

Bandem, M. 1983. The Evolution of *Legong* from Sacred to Secular Dance of Bali, *Dance Research Annual*, 14: 113–119.

- 1986. Transformasi kesenian dalam melestarikan nilai budaya Bali [The Transformation of the Arts in the Preservation of Balinese Cultural Values], in *Sumbangan Nilai Budaya Bali dalam Pembangunan Kebudayaan Nasional* [*The Contribution of Balinese Cultural Values in the Development of National Culture*], ed. G.N.Bagus, pp. 48–56. Denpasar: Direktorat Jenderal Kebudayaan.

- 1991. Bali's Art Czar (Interview with Dr. Made Bandem), *Nusa Tenggara* (November 23): 24.

Bandem, M. & F.E. deBoer. 1981. *Kaja and Kelod. Balinese Dance in Transition*. Kuala Lumpur: Oxford University Press (revised edition, 1995, Kuala Lumpur: Oxford University Press).

Bappeda Bali, 1985. *Peranan Nilai Tambah Sektor Pariwisata Dalam Pembentukan PDRB Daerah Bali* [*The Role of the Development of the Tourist Sector in the Formation of the Bali's GRDP*]. Denpasar: Team Pengembangan, Pengolahan dan Penyajian Data Statistik Pembangunan Daerah Bali.

Baretje, R. 1987. La contribution nette du tourisme international à la balance des paiements, *Problems of Tourism*, 4/38: 51–78.

Barnier, V. 1983. Bilan et perspectives sur l'étude des rapports entre tourisme et société d'accueil, *Cahiers de Recherche en Tourisme*, 2/3: 24–27.

Barth, F., ed. 1969. *Ethnic Groups and Boundaries. The Social Organization of Culture Difference.* London: Allen & Unwin.
Basset, C. 1990. *Bali Abianbase. Côté cour, Côté jardin.* Jakarta: TOTAL Indonésie.
Bateson, G. 1970 [1949]. Bali: The Value System of a Steady State, in *Traditional Balinese Culture,* ed. J.Belo, pp. 384–401. New York: Columbia University Press.
Bateson, G. & M. Mead. 1942. *Balinese Character. A Photographic Analysis.* New York: New York Academy of Sciences (reprinted in 1962).
Baum, V. 1937. *A Tale from Bali.* Garden City: Doubleday (reprinted in 1973, Singapore: Oxford University Press).
Bazin, C.M. 1995. Industrial Heritage in the Tourism Process in France, in *International Tourism: Identity and Change,* eds. M.F.Lanfant, J.B.Allcock & E.M.Bruner, pp. 113–126. London: Sage Publications.
Belo, J. 1949. *Bali: Rangda and Barong.* Seattle: University of Washington Press.
- 1953. *Bali: Temple Festival.* Seattle: University of Washington Press.
- 1960. *Trance in Bali.* New York: Columbia University Press.
Belo, J., ed. 1970. *Traditional Balinese Culture.* New York: Columbia University Press.
Bendesa, K.G. & M. Sukarsa. 1980. An Economic Survey of Bali, *Bulletin of Indonesian Economic Studies,* 16/2: 31–53.
Benson, S. 1935. Tourists in Bali, *London Mercury,* 31: 261–268.
Bernet Kempers, A.J. 1977. *Monumental Bali.* Den Haag: Van Goor (revised edition, 1991, Berkeley: Periplus Editions).
Bhadra, W. 1956. A Balinese Looks at Bali. Changing Patterns in the Island's Society, in *Perspective of Indonesia, Atlantic Monthly Supplement:* 70–71.
Boon, J.A. 1977. *The Anthropological Romance of Bali 1597–1972. Dynamic Perspectives in Marriage & Caste, Politics & Religion.* Cambridge: Cambridge University Press.
- 1986. Between-The-Wars Bali. Rereading the Relics, in *History of Anthropology, volume 4. Malinowski, Rivers, Benedict and Others. Essays on Culture and Personality,* ed. G.W.Stocking Jr., pp. 218–247. Madison: The University of Wisconsin Press.
Booth, A. 1990. The Tourism Boom in Indonesia, *Bulletin of Indonesian Economic Studies,* 26/3: 45–73.
Bouvier, H. 1994. *La matière des émotions. Les arts du temps et du spectacle dans la société madouraise (Indonésie).* Paris: Ecole Française d'Extrême-Orient.
Brown, R.E. 1979. The Performing Arts: Modernity and Tradition, in *What is Modern Indonesian Culture?,* ed. G.Davis, pp. 48–52. Athens: Ohio University.
Bruner, E.M. 1989. Tourism, in *International Encyclopedia of Communications,* ed. E.Barnouw, pp. 249–253. New York: Oxford University Press.
- 1991a. Transformation of Self in Tourism, *Annals of Tourism Research,* 18/2 : 238–250.
- 1991b. *Between Tourism and Ethnography: A Postmodern Tour Guide in Bali.* Manuscript.
BSDP. 1992. *Sustainable Development Strategy for Bali.* Sanur: Bali Sustainable Development Project.

Carpenter, B. & M. Hofker-Rueter. 1993. *Willem Hofker, Schilder van / Painter of Bali.* Wijk en Aalburg: Pictures Publishers.

Cazes, G. 1982. Réflexions sur la notion d'intégration appliquée à l'aménagement touristique, *Travaux de l'Institut de Géographie de Reims,* 51–52: 23–30.

Chantepleure, G. 1938. *Mes souvenirs de Bali.* Paris: Calmann-Lévy.

Clement, H.G. 1961. *The Future of Tourism in the Pacific and Far East.* Washington: Department of Commerce.

Clifton, V. 1927. *Islands of Indonesia.* London: Constable (reprinted in 1991, Singapore: Oxford University Press).

Coast, J. 1951. The Clash of Cultures in Bali, *Pacific Affairs,* 24/4: 398–406.

- 1953. *Dancers of Bali.* New York: Putnam.

Cohen, E. 1979. Rethinking the Sociology of Tourism, *Annals of Tourism Research,* 6/1: 18–35.

- 1988. Authenticity and Commoditization in Tourism, *Annals of Tourism Research,* 15/3: 371–386.

Connor, L. 1979. Corpse Abuse and Trance in Bali: The Cultural Mediation of Aggression, *Mankind,* 12: 104–118.

Covarrubias, M. 1937. *Island of Bali.* New York: Knopf (reprinted in 1972, Kuala Lumpur: Oxford University Press).

Crandall, L. 1987. The Social Impact of Tourism on Developing Regions and its Measurement, in *Travel, Tourism and Hospitality Research. A Handbook for Managers and Researchers,* eds. J.R.B.Ritchie & C.R.Goeldner, pp. 373–383. New York: John Wiley & Sons.

Cribb, R., ed. 1990. *The Indonesian Killings, 1965–1966: Studies from Java and Bali.* Clayton: Monash University, Centre of Southeast Asian Studies.

Crick, M. 1989. Representations of International Tourism in the Social Sciences: Sun, Sex, Sights, Savings and Servility, *Annual Review of Anthropology,* 18: 307–344.

Cummings, J., et al. 1990. *Indonesia. A Travel Survival Kit.* Melbourne: Lonely Planet Publications.

Dalton, B. 1990. *Bali Handbook.* Chico: Moon Publications.

Darling, D. 1992. *The Painted Alphabet.* Boston: Houghton Mifflin (reprinted in 1994, Saint Paul: Graywolf Press).

Darling, D. & R. Helmi. 1995. *Nusa Dua: Reflections of Bali.* Singapore: Archipelago Press.

Daroesman, R. 1973. An Economic Survey of Bali, *Bulletin of Indonesian Economic Studies,* 9/3: 1–34.

DeBoer, F.E. 1987. Functions of the comic attendants (*panasar*) in a Balinese shadowplay, in *Humor and Comedy in Puppetry,* eds. D.Sherzer & J.Sherzer, pp. 79–105. Bowling Green: Bowling Green State University Popular Press.

- 1989. Balinese *Sendratari*: A Modern Dramatic Dance Genre, *Asian Theatre Journal,* 6/2: 179–193.

Department of Information. 1969. *The First Five-Year Development Plan (1969/70 – 1973/74)*. Jakarta.
Ditjen Pariwisata. 1977. *Seminar Pariwisata* [*Seminar on Tourism*]. Sanur: Direktorat Jenderal Pariwisata.
- 1978. *Seminar Pariwisata* [*Seminar on Tourism*]. Sanur: Direktorat Jenderal Pariwisata.
Djelantik, A.A.M. 1986. *Balinese Paintings*. Singapore: Oxford University Press.
Dogan, H.Z. 1989. Forms of Adjustment. Sociocultural Impacts of Tourism, *Annals of Tourism Research*, 16/2: 216–236.
Doorn, J.W.M. van. 1989. A Critical Assessment of Sociocultural Impact Studies of Tourism in the Third World, in *Towards Appropriate Tourism: The Case of Developing Countries*, eds. T.V.Singh, H.L.Theuns & F.M.Go, pp. 71–91. Frankfurt: Peta Lang.
Dove, M.R., ed. 1988. *The Real and Imagined Role of Culture in Development: Case Studies from Indonesia*. Honolulu: University of Hawaii Press.
Drake, C. 1989. *National Integration in Indonesia: Patterns and Issues*. Honolulu: University of Hawaii Press.
Durtain, L. 1956. Bali, la fabuleuse et la charmante, *Les Oeuvres Libres*, 122: 21–52.
Eiseman, F.B. 1985. *Bali. Sekala and Niskala*, Volume 1. Denpasar (revised edition, 1989, Berkeley: Periplus Editions).
- 1988. *Woodcarvings of Bali*. Berkeley: Periplus Editions.
EIU. 1991. Indonesia, *International Tourism Reports*, 3: 22–40.
Elegant, R. 1987. Seeking the Spirits of Bali: Despite Fast Food and Discos, the Old Ways Live, *The New York Times*, March 8, Section Travel, p.9, 26.
Emigh, J. 1979. Playing with the Past. Visitation and Illusion in the Mask Dance of Bali, *The Drama Review*, 23/2: 11–36.
- 1984. Dealing with the Demonic. Strategies for Containment in Hindu Iconography and Performance, *Asian Theatre Journal*, 1/1: 21–39.
Erawan, N. 1994. *Pariwisata dan Pembangunan Ekonomi (Bali sebagai kasus)* [*Tourism and Economic Development (The Case of Bali)*]. Denpasar: Upada Sastra.
Errington, F. & D. Gewertz. 1989. Tourism and Anthropology in a Post-Modern World, *Oceania*, 60/1: 37–54.
Fabricius, J. 1941. *Eiland der Demonen: Een Bali-Roman*. Batavia: Unie Bibliotheek.
Flierhaar, H. te. 1941. De aanpassing van het inlandsch onderwijs op Bali aan de eigen sfeer, *Koloniale Studiën*, 25: 135–159.
Forster, J. 1964. The Sociological Consequences of Tourism, *International Journal of Comparative Sociology*, 5/2: 217–227.
Foulcher, K. 1990. The Construction of an Indonesian National Culture: Patterns of Hegemony and Resistance, in *State and Civil Society in Indonesia*, ed. A.Budiman, pp. 301–320. Clayton: Monash University, Centre of Southeast Asian Studies.
Francillon, G. 1975. *Bali. Tourism, Culture, Environment*. Paris: Unesco (revised edition, 1979).

- 1990. The Dilemma of Tourism in Bali, in *Sustainable Development and Environmental Management of Small Islands*, eds. W.Beller, P.d'Ayala & P.Hein, pp. 267–272. Paris: Unesco.
Froment, G.J. 1981. Péril à Bali, *Répertoire des Voyages*, 351: 75–84.
Gerbault, A. 1941. *Iles de Beauté*. Paris: Gallimard.
Geertz, C. 1959. Form and Variation in Balinese Village Structure, *American Anthropologist*, 61: 991–1012.
- 1963. *Agricultural Involution. The Processes of Ecological Changes in Indonesia.* Berkeley & Los Angeles: University of California Press.
- 1980. *Negara. The Theatre State in Nineteenth-Century Bali.* Princeton: Princeton University Press.
Geertz, H. 1994. *Images of Power. Balinese Paintings Made for Gregory Bateson and Margaret Mead.* Honolulu: University of Hawaii Press.
Geertz, H. & C. Geertz. 1975. *Kinship in Bali.* Chicago: The University of Chicago Press.
Geriya, W. 1988. Peranan kesenian dan kebudayaan Bali dalam Diplomasi Kebudayaan [The Role of Balinese Arts and Culture in Cultural Diplomacy], in *Puspanjali. Persembahan untuk Prof. Dr. Ida Bagus Mantra* [*Puspanjali. Contributions in Honour of Prof. Dr. Ida Bagus Mantra*], ed. M.J.Atmaja, pp. 149–159. Denpasar: Kayumas.
Gibbons, J.D. & M. Fish. 1989. Indonesia's International Tourism: A Shifting Industry in Bali, *International Journal of Hospitality Management*, 8/1: 63–70.
Goldberg, A. 1983. Identity and Experience in Haitian Woodoo Shows, *Annals of Tourism Research*, 10/4: 479–495.
Gorer, G. 1936. *Bali and Angkor. Or Looking at Life and Death.* London: Joseph (reprinted in 1986, Singapore: Oxford University Press).
Goris, R. n.d. Godsdienst en Gebruiken in Bali. Observations on the Customs and Life of the Balinese, in *Bali.* Batavia: Travellers' Official Information Bureau for Netherland India [1931].
- 1960a [1935]. The Religious Character of the Village Community, in *Bali. Studies in Life, Thought, and Ritual*, eds. W.F.Wertheim et al, pp. 79–100. The Hague: Van Hoeve (reprinted in 1984, Dordrecht: Foris).
- 1960b [1937]. The Temple System, in *Bali. Studies in Life, Thought, and Ritual*, eds. W.F.Wertheim et al, pp. 103–111. The Hague: Van Hoeve (reprinted in 1984, Dordrecht: Foris).
Graburn, N.H.H. 1984. The Evolution of Tourist Arts, *Annals of Tourism Research*, 11/3: 393–419.
Greenwood, D.J. 1982. Cultural "Authenticity", *Cultural Survival Quarterly*, 6/3: 27–28.
- 1989. Culture by the Pound: An Anthropological Perspective on Tourism as Cultural Commoditization, in *Hosts and Guests. The Anthropology of Tourism*, ed. V.L.Smith, pp. 171–185. Philadelphia: University of Pennsylvania Press (first published in 1977).

Guermonprez, J.F. 1987. *Les Pandé de Bali. La Formation d'une "Caste" et la Valeur d'un Titre.* Paris: Ecole Française d'Extrême-Orient.

- 1990. On the Elusive Balinese Village: Hierarchy and Values Versus Political Models, *Review of Indonesian and Malaysian Affairs*, 24: 55–89.

GWK. 1994. *The Blue Chip in a Tropical Tourism World.* Bandung: Yayasan Garuda Wisnu Kencana.

Handler, R. & J. Linnekin. 1984. Tradition, Genuine or Spurious, *Journal of American Folklore*, 97: 273–290.

Hanna, W.A. 1957. *Changing Bali: Romantic and Otherwise. A Letter from Willard A. Hanna.* New York: American Universities Field Staff.

- 1972. Bali in the Seventies. Part I: Cultural Tourism, *American Universities Field Staff Reports. Southeast Asia Series*, 20/2: 1–7.

- 1976. *Bali Profile. People, Events, Circumstances (1001–1976).* New York: American Universities Field Staff (reprinted in 1990, Banda Naira: Rumah Budaya).

Hassall and Associates, Scott & Furphy, PT Indulexco. 1992. *Comprehensive Tourism Development Plan for Bali: Final Report.* United Nations Development Programme & The Government of the Republic of Indonesia.

Hauser-Schäublin, B., M.L. Nabholz-Kartaschoff & U. Ramseyer, 1991. *Textiles in Bali.* Berkeley: Periplus Editions.

Helmi, R. & B. Walker. 1995. *Bali Style.* Singapore: Times Editions.

Herbst, E. 1981. Intrinsic Aesthetics in Balinese Artistic and Spiritual Practice, *Asian Music*, 13/1: 43–52.

Hiss, P.H. 1941. *Bali.* New York: Duell, Sloan and Pearce.

Hitchcock, M. & L. Norris. 1995. *Bali: The Imaginary Museum. The Photographs of Walter Spies and Beryl de Zoete.* Kuala Lumpur: Oxford University Press.

Hobart, A. 1983. Between Things: The Place of the *Pandasar* in Bali, *Archipel*, 25: 159–170.

Hooykaas, C. 1979. *Introduction à la littérature balinaise.* Paris: Association Archipel.

Hough, B. 1992. *Contemporary Balinese Dance Spectacles as National Ritual.* Clayton: Monash University, Centre of Southeast Asian Studies.

IBRD/IDA. 1974. *Appraisal of The Bali Tourism Project. Indonesia.* Washington: Tourism Projects Department.

IRIP News Service. 1993. Bali's 80 Billion Rupiah Monstrosity, *Inside Indonesia*, 37: 25–26.

Iyer, P. 1988. *Video Night in Kathmandu And Other Reports from the Not-So-Far-East.* New York: Knopf.

- 1993. *Falling Off the Map. Some Lonely Places of the World.* New York: Knopf.

Jacknis, I. 1988. Margaret Mead and Gregory Bateson in Bali: Their Use of Photography and Film, *Cultural Anthropology*, 3/2: 160–177.

Jafari, J. 1984. Unbounded Ethnicity. The Tourist Network and its Satellites, *Revue de Tourisme*, 3: 4–21.

Jayasuriya, S. & K. Nehen. 1989. Bali: Economic Growth and Tourism, in *Unity and Diversity. Regional Economic Development in Indonesia since 1970*, ed. H.Hill, pp. 331–348. Singapore: Oxford University Press.
Jensen, G.D. & L.K. Suryani. 1992. *The Balinese People. A Reinvestigation of Character*. Singapore: Oxford University Press.
Kadt, E. de, ed. 1979. *Tourism. Passport to Development? Perspectives on the Social and Cultural Effects of Tourism in Developing Countries*. New York: Oxford University Press.
Kakul, N. 1979. Jelantik Goes to Blambangan; a Topeng Play, *The Drama Review*, 23/2: 37–48.
Kam, G. 1993. *Perceptions of Paradise. Images of Bali in the Arts*. Ubud: Yayasan Dharma Seni Museum Neka.
Keyser, E. de. 1933. *L'Ile des Seins Nus*. Paris: Les Editions de France.
Kipp, R.S. 1993. *Dissociated Identities. Ethnicity, Religion, and Class in an Indonesian Society*. Ann Arbor: The University of Michigan Press.
Kipp, R.S. & S.Rodgers, eds. 1987. *Indonesian Religions in Transition*. Tucson: The University of Arizona Press.
Kleen, T. de. 1921. Bali. Its Dances and Customs, *Sluyters' Monthly*, 2: 127–132.
Koke, L.G. 1987. *Our Hotel in Bali*. Wellington: January Books.
Kop, G.G. van der. 1924. Lights and Shadows on Bali and the Balinese, *Inter-Ocean*, 5/10: 645–649, 681.
Krapf, K. 1961. Les pays en voie de développement face au tourisme. Introduction méthodologique, *Revue de Tourisme*, 16/3: 82–89.
- 1963. *Tourism as a Factor of Economic Development*. Roma: United Nations Conference on International Travel and Tourism.
Krause, G. 1920. *Bali. Volk-Land-Tänze-Feste-Tempel*. Hagen: Folkwang Verlag.
- 1930. *Bali. La population, le pays, les danses, les fêtes, les temples, l'art*. Paris: Editions Duchartre et Van Buggenhoudt.
- 1988. *Bali 1912*. Wellington: January Books.
Lanfant, M.F. 1972. *Les théories du loisir*. Paris: PUF.
- 1980a. Introduction: Tourism in the Process of Internationalization, *International Social Science Journal*, 32/1: 14–43.
- 1980b. Le tourisme international, fait et acte social: une problématique, *Loisir et Société / Society and Leisure*, 3/1: 135–160.
- 1991. *Tourisme international reconsidéré: milieu exclu, tiers exclu? Le principe de l'alternative*. Aix-en-Provence: Centre des Hautes Etudes Touristiques (partially translated in Lanfant, M.F. & N.H.H. Graburn. 1992. International Tourism Reconsidered: The Principle of the Alternative, in *Tourism Alternatives. Potentials and Problems in the Development of Tourism*, eds. V.L.Smith & W.R.Eadington, pp. 88–112. Philadelphia: University of Pennsylvania Press).
Lansing, J.S. 1974. *Evil in the Morning of the World. Phenomenological Approaches to a Balinese Community*. Ann Arbor: University of Michigan, Center for South and Southeast Asian Studies.

- 1983. *The Three Worlds of Bali.* New York: Praeger.
Last, J. 1955. *Bali in de Kentering.* Amsterdam: De Bezige Bij.
Lembaga Pariwisata Nasional. 1967a. *Pokok-Pokok Pengembangan Obyek dan Wilayah Kepariwisataan di Indonesia* [*Guidelines for the Development of Tourist Objects and Areas in Indonesia*]. Jakarta: Lembaga Pariwisata Nasional.
- 1967b. *Pokok-Pokok Rencana Perkembangan Wilayah Kepariwisataan di Bali* [*Guidelines for the Development of Tourist Areas in Bali*]. Jakarta: Lembaga Pariwisata Nasional.
Lindsay, J. 1995. Cultural Policy and the Performing Arts in Southeast Asia, *Bijdragen tot de Taal-, Land- en Volkenkunde*, 151/4: 656–671.
Listibiya. 1970. *Seminar I Drama Gong* [*First Seminar on Drama Gong*]. Denpasar: Majelis Pertimbangan dan Pembinaan Kebudayaan Daerah Propinsi Bali.
- 1973. *Pola Dasar Kebijaksanaan Pembinaan Kebudayaan Daerah Bali* [*Founding Principles of the Cultural Policy for Bali*]. Denpasar: Majelis Pertimbangan dan Pembinaan Kebudayaan Daerah Propinsi Bali.
Lombard, D. 1990. *Le carrefour javanais. Essai d'histoire globale.* Paris: Ecole des Hautes Etudes en Sciences Sociales.
Lovric, B.J.A. 1986. The Art of Healing and the Craft of Witches in a "Hot Earth" Village, *Review of Indonesian and Malaysian Affairs*, 20: 68–99.
- 1987. *Rhetoric and Reality: The Hidden Nightmare. Myth and Magic as Representations and Reverberations of Morbid Realities.* PhD Dissertation, University of Sydney.
- 1988. Balinese Theatre: A Metaphysics in Action, *Asian Studies Association of Australia Review*, 12/2: 34–45.
Mabbett, H. 1987. *In Praise of Kuta.* Wellington: January Books.
MacCannell, D. 1976. *The Tourist. A New Theory of the Leisure Class.* New York: Schocken Books (reprinted in 1989, New York: Random House).
- 1984. Reconstructed Ethnicity: Tourism and Cultural Identity in Third World Communities, *Annals of Tourism Research*, 11/3: 361–377.
Macnaught, T.J. 1982. Mass Tourism and the Dilemmas of Modernization in Pacific Island Communities, *Annals of Tourism Research*, 9/3: 359–381.
MacRae, G.S. 1992. *Tourism and Balinese Culture.* M.A. Thesis, University of Auckland.
Magenda, B.D. 1988. Ethnicity and State-Building in Indonesia: the Cultural Base of the New Order, in *Ethnicity and Nations. Processes of Interethnic Relations in Latin America, Southeast Asia, and the Pacific*, eds. R. Guidieri, F. Pellizi & S.J. Tambiah, pp. 345–361. Austin: Rothko Chapel.
Manuaba, A. 1995. Bali: Enhancing the Image Through More Effective Planning, in *Bali. Balancing Environment, Economy and Culture*, eds. S.Martopo & B.Mitchell, pp. 29–42. Waterloo: University Consortium on the Environment.
Martopo, S. & B. Mitchell, eds. 1995. *Bali: Balancing Environment, Economy and Culture.* Waterloo: University Consortium on the Environment.
Mathews, A. 1965. *The Night of Purnama.* London: Cape (reprinted in 1983, Kuala Lumpur: Oxford University Press).

Mathieson, A. & G. Wall. 1982. *Tourism: Economic, Physical and Social Impacts.* London & New York: Longman.
Maurer, J.L. 1979. *Tourism and Development in a Socio-Cultural Perspective: Indonesia as a Case Study.* Genève: Institut Universitaire d'Etudes du Développement
Maurer, J.L. & A. Zeigler. 1988. Tourism and Indonesian Cultural Minorities, in *Tourism: Manufacturing the Exotic,* ed. P.Rossel, pp. 64–92. Copenhagen: International Workgroup for Indigenous Affairs.
McKean, P.F. 1973. *Cultural Involution: Tourists, Balinese, and the Process of Modernization in an Anthropological Perspective.* PhD Dissertation, Brown University.
- 1989. Towards a Theoretical Analysis of Tourism: Economic Dualism and Cultural Involution in Bali, in *Hosts and Guests. The Anthropology of Tourism,* ed. V.L.Smith, pp. 119–138. Philadelphia: University of Pennsylvania Press (first published in 1977).
McPhee, C. 1947. *A House in Bali.* New York: Day (reprinted in 1979, Kuala Lumpur: Oxford University Press).
- 1966. *Music in Bali.* New Haven: Yale University Press (reprinted in 1976, New York: Da Capo Press).
McTaggart, W.D. 1980. Tourism and Tradition in Bali, *World Development,* 8: 457–466.
Mead, M. 1970 [1942]. Community Drama, Bali and America, in *Traditional Balinese Culture,* ed. J.Belo, pp. 341–349. New York: Columbia University Press.
- 1977. *Letters from the Field, 1925–1975,* ed. R.N.Aschen. New York: Harper & Row.
Millau, C. 1974. Pitié pour Bali, *Le nouveau guide Gault-Millau,* 68: 66–72, 101–109.
Moerdowo, R.M. 1977. *Reflections on Balinese Traditional and Modern Arts.* Denpasar: Udayana University (reprinted in 1983, Jakarta: Balai Pustaka).
Mukerda. 1968. *Hasil Musyawarah Kerja Pariwisata Daerah Bali I* [*Proceedings of the First Workshop on Tourism in Bali*]. Denpasar.
Nash, D. 1981. Tourism as an Anthropological Subject, *Current Anthropology,* 22/5: 461–481.
- 1989. Tourism as a Form of Imperialism, in *Hosts and Guests. The Anthropology of Tourism,* ed. V.L.Smith, pp. 37–52. Philadelphia: University of Pennsylvania Press (firt published in 1977).
Nehen, K. et al. 1990. *Sumbangan Sektor Pariwisata Terhadap Pembentukan Nilai Tambah Produksi Daerah Bali* [*The Contribution of the Tourist Sector to the Growth of Production in Bali*]. Denpasar: Universitas Udayana.
Nieuwenkamp, W.O.J. 1910. *Zwerftochten op Bali.* Amsterdam: Elsevier (revised edition, 1922, Amsterdam: Elsevier).
Noronha, R. 1973. *A Report on the Proposed Tourism Project. Bali.* Washington: IBRD.
- 1979. Paradise Reviewed: Tourism in Bali, in *Tourism. Passport to Development? Perspectives on the Social and Cultural Effects of Tourism in Developing Countries,* ed. E.de Kadt, pp. 177–204. New York: Oxford University Press.

Nugroho, C., ed. 1984. *Mengenal Budaya Bangsa (Tarian Adat, Pakaian Adat & Rumah Adat Daerah). Sumber Data: Taman Mini Indonesia Indah* [*Getting Acquainted with National Culture (Traditional Dances, Traditional Costumes and Traditional Houses of the Regions). Source: Beautiful Indonesia-in-Miniature Park*]. Semarang: Yayasan Telapak.

Nuñez, T.A. 1963. Tourism, Tradition, and Acculturation: Weekendismo in a Mexican Village, *Ethnology*, 2/3: 347–352.

Nuryanti, W., ed. 1993. *Universal Tourism: Enriching or Degrading Culture?* Yogyakarta: Gadjah Mada University Press.

Office for Project Services. 1992. *Management of Tourism in Bali: Final Report.* United Nations Development Programme & The Government of the Republic of Indonesia.

Official Tourist Bureau. 1914. *Illustrated Tourist Guide to East Java, Bali and Lombok.* Weltevreden: Official Tourist Bureau.

- n.d. *Short Guide to Bali.* Batavia: Official Tourist Bureau [1923].

O'Grady, R. 1981. *Third World Stopover. The Tourism Debate.* Geneva: World Council of Churches.

Oka, I.B. 1993. A Sub-System of Cultural Tourism in Bali, in *Universal Tourism. Enriching of Degrading Culture?*, ed. W.Nuryanti, pp. 123–131. Yogyakarta: Gadjah Mada University Press.

O'Neill, R.M.G.S. 1978. *Spirit Possession and Healing Rites in a Balinese Village.* M.A.Thesis, University of Melbourne.

Pacific Consultants International. 1973. *The Nusa Dua Area Development Plan.* Tokyo.

Pan American Airways. 1966. *A Quick Start Program for Tourism Development, Indonesia.* Jakarta: Lembaga Pariwisata Nasional.

Pandji, G.B.N. 1985. Seni Wali di Bali dan perkembangannya [The Wali Art in Bali and its Development], in *Laporan Pertemuan Ilmiah Kebudayaan Bali, 26–29 Desember 1985* [*Report on the Scientific Meeting on Balinese Culture, 26–29 December 1985*], pp. 469–482. Denpasar: Proyek Penelitian dan Pengkajian Kebudayaan Bali (Baliologi).

Pangdjaja, I.B., ed. 1991a. *Bali Arts Festival. Pesta Kesenian Bali.* Denpasar: Cita Budaya.

- 1991b. *Bali. Apa Kata Mereka* [*Bali. What They Are Saying*]. Denpasar: Cita Budaya.

Pelras, C. 1977. Culture, ethnie, espace social: quelques réflexions autour du cas Bugis, *Asie du Sud-Est et Monde Insulidien*, 8/2: 57–79.

Pemberton, J. 1994. Recollections from "Beautiful Indonesia" (Somewhere Beyond the Postmodern), *Public Culture*, 6/2: 241–262.

Pemda Bali. 1987. *Seminar Pembinaan dan Pengembangan Pariwisata Menuju Tahun 2000 di Propinsi Bali* [*Seminar on the Fostering and Development of Tourism Towards the Year 2000 in the Province of Bali*]. Denpasar: Pemerintah Daerah Tingkat I Bali.

Pendit, N. 1954. *Bali Berjuang* [*Bali Fights Back*]. Denpasar: Yayasan Kebaktian Pejuang (reprinted in 1979, Jakarta: Gunung Agung).

Picard, M. 1979. *Sociétés et Tourisme. Réflexions pour la Recherche et l'Action.* Paris: Unesco.
- 1980. Sur quelques rapports entre la sociologie et l'économie politique dans l'étude du loisir, *Loisir et Société / Society and Leisure*, 3/2: 325–356.
- 1983. En feuilletant le Bali Post: à propos de l'interdiction des combats de coqs à Bali, *Archipel*, 25: 171–180.
- 1986. Compte rendu de Bandem & deBoer, "Kaja and Kelod", *Archipel*, 31: 215–218.
- 1996. Dance and Drama in Bali: The Making of an Indonesian Art Form, in *Being Modern in Bali. Image and Change*, ed. A.Vickers, pp. 115-157. New Haven: Yale University Southeast Asian Studies.
Picturesque Dutch East Indies. 1925. The Official Tourist Bureau of Weltevreden (Java), *Inter-Ocean*, 6/8: 526–529.
Pizam, A. & A. Milman. 1984. The Social Impacts of Tourism, *Industry and Environment*, 7/1: 11–14.
Pollmann, T. 1990. Margaret Mead's Balinese: The Fitting Symbols of the American Dream, *Indonesia*, 49: 1–35.
Powell, H. 1930. *The Last Paradise.* London: Jonathan Cape (reprinted in 1982, Kuala Lumpur: Oxford University Press).
Prajogo, M.J. 1985. *Pengantar Pariwisata Indonesia* [*Introduction to Tourism in Indonesia*]. Jakarta: Direktorat Jenderal Pariwisata.
Proyek. 1971. *Seminar Seni Sakral dan Provan Bidang Tari* [*Seminar on Sacred and Profane Arts in Dance*]. Denpasar: Proyek Pemeliharaan dan Pengembangan Kebudayaan Daerah.
Proyek Sasana Budaya Bali. 1978. *Penanggulangan Pengaruh Negatif Kebudayaan Asing Terhadap Kebudayaan Bali* [*Tackling Negative Influences of Foreign Culture on Balinese Culture*]. Denpasar: Proyek Sasana Budaya Bali.
- 1979. *Seminar Pembinaan Wisata Budaya Bali* [*Seminar on the Fostering of Cultural Tourism in Bali*]. Denpasar: Proyek Sasana Budaya Bali.
Proyek Sasana Budaya Jakarta. 1978. *Seminar Pembinaan Kebudayaan dan Pengembangan Kepariwisataan* [*Seminar on the Fostering of Culture and the Development of Tourism*]. Sanur: Direktorat Jenderal Kebudayaan.
- 1979a. *Seminar Pembinaan Kebudayaan dan Pengembangan Kepariwisataan* [*Seminar on the Fostering of Culture and the Development of Tourism*]. Yogyakarta: Direktorat Jenderal Kebudayaan.
- 1979b. *Naskah Kerjasama Ditjen Kebudayaan dan Ditjen Pariwisata* [*Memorandum of Cooperation between the Directorate General of Culture and the Directorate General of Tourism*]. Jakarta: Direktorat Jenderal Kebudayaan.
Purbo & Mulia. 1968. *Repelita Pembangunan Kepariwisataan di Daerah Bali* [*The Five-Year Plan for the Development of Tourism in Bali*]. Jakarta: Lembaga Pariwisata Nasional.

Putra, G.A.G. 1971. Tari-tarian sakral dan provan dari segi rituil [Sacred and Profane Dances Seen from the Point of View of Ritual], in *Seminar Seni Sakral dan Provan Bidang Tari* [*Seminar on Sacred and Profane Arts in Dance*]. Denpasar: Proyek Pemeliharaan dan Pengembangan Kebudayaan Daerah.
- 1978. *Hubungan Seni Tari Bali dengan Agama Hindu* [*The Link between Balinese Dance and the Hindu Religion*]. Denpasar: Institut Hindu Dharma.
- 1982. *Cudamani. Tari Wali* [*Cudamani. The Wali Dances*]. Denpasar.
Raillon, F. 1984. *Les étudiants indonésiens et l'Ordre Nouveau. Politique et idéologie du Mahasiswa Indonesia (1966-1974).* Paris: Maison des Sciences de l'Homme.
Ramstedt, M. 1992. Indonesian Cultural Policy in Relation to the Development of Balinese Performing Arts, in *Balinese Music in Context,* ed. D.Schaareman, pp. 59–84. Winterthur: Amadeus, Forum Ethnomusicologicum 4.
- 1993. Traditional Balinese Performing Arts as *Yajnya,* in *Performance in Java and Bali. Studies of Narrative, Theatre, Music, and Dance,* ed. B.Arps, pp. 77–87. London: School of Oriental and African Studies, University of London.
Rata, I.B. 1988. Peranan kebudayaan daerah dalam menunjang pembangunan nasional [The Role of Regional Cultures in Support of National Development], in *Puspanjali. Persembahan untuk Prof. Dr. Ida Bagus Mantra* [*Puspanjali. Contributions in Honour of Prof. Dr. Ida Bagus Mantra*], ed. M.J.Atmaja, pp. 160–170. Denpasar: Kayumas.
Redfield, R. 1953. *The Primitive World and its Transformation.* Ithaca: Cornell University Press.
Rhodius, H. & J. Darling. 1980. *Walter Spies and Balinese Art.* Zutphen: Terra.
Ricklefs, M.C. 1981. *A History of Modern Indonesia.* London: Macmillan (revised edition, 1993, London: Macmillan).
Rickner, R. 1972. *Theatre as Ritual: Artaud's Theatre of Cruelty and the Balinese Barong.* PhD Dissertation, University of Hawaii.
Robinson, G.B. 1995. *The Dark Side of Paradise. Political Violence in Bali.* Ithaca: Cornell University Press.
Rodenburg, E. 1980. The Effects of Scale in Economic Development. Tourism in Bali, *Annals of Tourism Research,* 7/2: 177–196.
Rodgers Siregar, S. 1979. Advice to the Newlyweds: Sipirok Batak Wedding Speeches. Adat or Art?, in *Art, Ritual and Society in Indonesia,* eds. E.M.Bruner & J.O.Becker, pp. 30–61. Athens: Ohio University.
Rubinstein, R. 1988. *Beyond the Realm of the Senses: The Balinese Ritual of Kekawin Composition.* PhD Dissertation, University of Sydney.
Sanger, A.E. 1987. New Patrons of Old Music: The Survival and Revival of the Performing Arts in Bali, *Widya Pustaka,* 5/1&2: 151–156.
- 1988. Blessing or Blight? The Effects of Touristic Dance-Drama on Village Life in Singapadu, Bali, in *The Impact of Tourism on Traditional Music,* eds. A.L.Kaeppler & O.Lewin, pp. 89–104. Kingston: The Jamaica Memory Bank.
SCETO. 1971. *Bali Tourism Study. Report to the Government of Indonesia.* Paris: UNDP/IBRD.
Schuh, G. 1954. *Iles des Dieux.* Lausanne: Editions Clairefontaine.

Schulte Nordholt, H. 1986. *Bali: Colonial Conceptions and Political Change, 1700–1940. From Shifting Hierarchies to 'Fixed Order'.* Rotterdam: Erasmus University.

Seebass, T. 1996. Change in Balinese Musical Life: Kebiar in the 1920s and 1930s, in *Being Modern in Bali. Image and Change,* ed. A. Vickers, pp. 71–91. New Haven: Yale University Southeast Asia Studies.

Sellato, B. 1990. *Indonesia Goes Ethnic. Provincial Culture, Image, and Identity: Current Trends in Kalimantan.* Paper presented to the conference on Centres and Peripheries in Insular Southeast Asia. Paris: CNRS/DEVI.

Seminar. 1971. *Hasil Keputusan Seminar Pariwisata Budaya Daerah Bali* [*Proceedings of the Seminar on Cultural Tourism in Bali*]. Denpasar.

Sessa, A. 1970. *Tourism as a Factor of Progress in the Economy of Developing Countries.* Paris: Unesco.

Simpson, B. 1993. Tourism and Tradition. From Healing to Heritage, *Annals of Tourism Research,* 20/1: 164–191.

Singer, M. 1972. *When a Great Tradition Modernizes.* New York: Praeger.

Smith, V.L., ed. 1989. *Hosts and Guests. The Anthropology of Tourism.* Philadelphia: University of Pennsylvania Press (first published in 1977).

Soebadio, H. 1985. *Cultural Policy in Indonesia.* Paris: Unesco.

Soe Lie Piet. n.d. *Pengoendjoekan Poelo Bali Atawa Gids Bali* [*Presentation of the Island of Bali Or Guide to Bali*]. Malang: Paragon Press [193 ff.].

Soeroto, Atiek & Hendro. 1968. *Rencana Perkembangan Phisik Kepariwisataan di Pulau Bali* [*Physical Planning for the Development of Tourism on the Island of Bali*]. Jakarta: Lembaga Pariwisata Nasional.

Spies, W. & R. Goris. 1937. Overzicht van dans en tooneel in Bali, *Djawa* 17: 205–229.

Spruit, R. 1995. *Artists on Bali.* Amsterdam: The Pepin Press.

Stuart-Fox, D.J. 1982. *Once a Century. Pura Besakih and the Eka Dasa Rudra Festival.* Jakarta: Sinar Harapan.

Suci, N.L. 1977. Pariwisata dan lakon pertunjukan Barong di Desa Batubulan [Tourism and the Drama Performance of the Barong in the Village of Batubulan], *Pengkajian Budaya,* 3/1: 27–36.

Sujana, N.N. 1988. Orang Bali Semakin Kehilangan Kebaliannya [The Balinese Are Steadily Loosing their Balinese-ness], *Bali Post,* December 3, p. 7.

Suryani, L.K. & G.D. Jensen. 1993. *Trance and Possession in Bali. A Window on Western Multiple Personality, Possession Disorder, and Suicide.* Kuala Lumpur: Oxford University Press.

Tanen, T.M.G. 1991. Festivals and Diplomacy, in *Exhibiting Cultures: The Poetics and Politics of Museum Display,* eds. I.Karp & S.D.Lavine, pp. 366–371. Washington: Smithsonian Institution Press.

Tantri, K. 1960. *Revolt in Paradise.* New York: Harper (reprinted in 1981, Jakarta: Gramedia).

Taubman, H. 1968. The Isle of the Gods Faces an Earthly Dilemma, *The New York Times,* June 9, p. 55.

Taylor, P.M. 1994. The Nusantara Concept of Culture: Local Traditions and National Identity as Expressed in Indonesia's Museums, in *Fragile Traditions. Indonesian Art in Jeopardy*, ed. P.M.Taylor, pp. 71–90. Honolulu: University of Hawaii Press.

Tenzer, M. 1991. *Balinese Music*. Berkeley: Periplus Editions.

Thong, D., B. Carpenter & S. Krippner. 1993. *A Psychiatrist in Paradise. Treating Mental Illness in Bali*. Bangkok: White Lotus.

Thurot, J.M. 1981. Reformuler la problématique de l'impact socio-culturel du tourisme, *Revue de Tourisme*, 2: 2–9.

Travellers Official Information Bureau. 1935. *Bali, The Eastern Paradise*. Batavia: The Travellers Official Information Bureau of the Netherlands Indies.

Travis, A.S. 1982. Managing the Environmental and Cultural Impacts of Tourism and Leisure Development, *Tourism Management*, 3/4: 256–262.

- 1984. Social and Cultural Aspects of Tourism, *Industry and Environment*, 7/1: 22–24.

Tunnard, C. & J.C. Pollaco. 1970. *The Development of Cultural Tourism in Central Java and Bali*. Paris: Unesco.

Turnbull, C. 1982. Bali's New Gods, *Natural History*, 1: 26–32.

Turner, L. & J. Ash. 1975. *The Golden Hordes. International Tourism and the Pleasure Periphery*. London: Constable.

Ubbens, J. & C. Huizing. 1995. *Adrien Jean Le Mayeur de Merprès. Painter-Traveller / Schilder-Reiziger*. Wijk en Aalburg: Pictures Publishers.

UNCTAD. 1967. *Le tourisme culturel et la mise en valeur du patrimoine culturel aux fins du tourisme et de la croissance économique*. New York: Nations Unies.

- 1971. *Elements of Tourism Policy in Developing Countries*. New York: United Nations.

UNESCO. 1982. *The Mexico City Declaration on Cultural Policies*. Mexico City: Mondiacult.

United Nations. 1963. *Recommendations on International Travel and Tourism*. Geneva: United Nations.

UNUD. 1973a. *Laporan Hasil Penelitian Pengaruh "Mass Tourism" Terhadap Tata Kehidupan Masyarakat Bali* [*Report of the Research on the Influence of Mass Tourism on the Way of Life of the Balinese*]. Denpasar.

- 1973b. *Laporan Hasil Penelitian Pengembangan Pariwisata di Bali* [*Report of the Research on the Development of Tourism in Bali*]. Denpasar.

- 1974. *The Impact of Tourism on the Socio-Economic Development of Bali*. Denpasar.

- 1975. *The Impact of Tourism on the Village Community Development*. Denpasar.

- 1976. *Pengaruh Adanya Peraturan-Peraturan Daerah Terhadap Perkembangan Pariwisata dan Kebudayaan Bali* [*Effectiveness of Regional Regulations in the Development of Tourism and Culture in Bali*]. Denpasar.

Urbain, J.D. 1991. *L'idiot du voyage. Histoires de touristes*. Paris: Plon.

URESTI, ed. 1987. L'"impact social et culturel du tourisme international" en question: réponses interdisciplinaires, *Problems of Tourism*, 10 / 2 & 3.

Urry, J. 1990. *The Tourist Gaze*. London: Sage Publications.

Vickers, A. 1986. *The Desiring Prince: A Study of the Kidung Malat as Text.* PhD Dissertation, University of Sydney.
- 1989. *Bali: A Paradise Created.* Berkeley: Periplus Editions.
Vickers, A., ed. 1994. *Travelling to Bali. Four Hundred Years of Journeys.* Kuala Lumpur: Oxford University Press.
Volkman, T.A. 1984. Great Performances: Toraja Cultural Identity in the 1970s, *American Ethnologist*, 11/1: 152–169.
- 1990. Visions and Revisions: Toraja Culture and the Tourist Gaze, *American Ethnologist*, 17/1: 91–110.
Wallis, R.H. 1979. *The Voice as a Mode of Cultural Expression in Bali.* PhD Dissertation, University of Michigan.
Warna, W. et al. 1990. *Kamus Bali-Indonesia* [*Balinese-Indonesian Dictionary*]. Denpasar: Dinas Pendidikan Dasar Propinsi Dati I Bali.
Warren, C. 1990. *The Bureaucratisation of Local Government in Indonesia.* Clayton: Monash University, Centre of Southeast Asian Studies.
- 1993. *Adat and Dinas. Balinese Communities in the Indonesian State.* Kuala Lumpur: Oxford University Press.
- 1995. The Garuda Wisnu Kencana Monument Debate: Environment, Culture and the Discourses of Nationalism in Late New Order Bali, in *Kulturen und Raum. Theoretische Ansätze und empirische Kulturforschung in Indonesien*, eds. B.Werlen & S.Wälty, pp. 377–390. Zürich: Verlag Rüegger.
Widminarko. 1989. *Pendapat Pembaca Bali Post Tentang Kebalian Orang Bali* [*Opinions of the Bali Post Readers on the Balinese-ness of the Balinese*]. Denpasar: Forum Diskusi Bali Post.
Wiener, M.J. 1995. *Visible and Invisible Realms: Power, Magic and Colonial Conquest in Bali.* Chicago: The University of Chicago Press.
Wijaya, M. 1986. Trends in Modern Balinese Architecture. How Fares the Environment on the Fabled Isle?, *Prisma*, 39: 85–94.
Wijaya, M., C.O. Pemayun & G.P. Raka. 1981. *Bali's Art Centre, Werdi Budaya, and the Annual Festival of the Arts.* Denpasar: Diparda Bali.
Williams, A. 1994. *Covarrubias.* Austin: University of Texas Press.
Withington, W.A. 1961. Upland Resorts and Tourism in Indonesia: Some Recent Trends, *The Geographical Review*, 51/3: 418–423.
Wood, R.E. 1980. International Tourism and Cultural Change in Southeast Asia, *Economic Development and Cultural Change*, 23/3: 561–581.
WTO. 1979. *Etude sur la contribution du tourisme à l'échange des valeurs spirituelles et à une meilleure compréhension entre les peuples.* Madrid.
- 1980. *Déclaration de Manille sur le Tourisme Mondial.* Manila.
- 1981. *Etude pilote sur les effets sociaux et aspects culturels des mouvements touristiques.* Madrid.
- 1985. *Rôle de l'Etat dans la sauvegarde et la promotion de la culture comme facteur de développement touristique et dans la mise en valeur du patrimoine national de sites et de monuments à des fins touristiques.* Madrid.

Yampolsky, P. 1995. Forces for Change in the Regional Performing Arts of Indonesia, *Bijdragen tot de Taal-, Land- en Volkenkunde*, 151/4: 700–725.
Yates, H.E. n.d. *Bali. The Enchanted Isle.* Weltevreden: K.P.M. [1930].
-1933. *Bali: Enchanted Isle. A Travel Book.* London: George Allen & Unwin.
Yoeti, O.A. 1985. *Komersialisasi Seni Budaya dalam Pariwisata* [*The Commercialization of the Cultural Arts in Tourism*]. Bandung: Angkasa.
Young, E. 1980. *Topeng in Bali: Change and Continuity in a Traditional Drama Genre.* PhD Dissertation, University of California.
Zach, P. 1986. Bali: Paradise Preserved, *International Herald Tribune*, July 25, p.9.
Zoete, B. de, & W. Spies. 1938. *Dance and Drama in Bali.* London: Faber and Faber (reprinted in 1973, Kuala Lumpur: Oxford University Press).
Zurbuchen, M.S. 1987. *The Language of Balinese Shadow Theater.* Princeton: Princeton University Press.

Illustration Sources

Frontispiece: Balinese ricefields (photograph by Kunang Helmi).

Chapter 1

16–17: Indonesia map (Editions Didier Millet).

24: The Bali Hotel (coll. Leo Haks).

26: Two cartoons by O. Fabrès: "L'enthousiaste à Bali – Lovely!!", "A Bali – Tourisme". (Fabrès, O. 1933. *Aux Indes Neérlandaises.* Amsterdam: P.N. van Kampen & Zoon N.V.).

29: The Balinese beauty (Goesti Made Toewi by Willem Hofker, 1943, in B. Carpenter & M. Hofker-Rueter, *Willem Hofker, Schilder van / Painter of Bali*, Wijk en Aalburg: Pictures Publishers, 1993).

31: The Balinese dancer (photograph by Thilly Weissenborn).

33: The Balinese witch (*Bali.* Batavia: Travellers Official Information Bureau for Netherland India, undated).

36–37: "Bali Island" tourist map (P.T. Repro International, P.T. Matra).

Chapter 2

39: Administrative map of Bali (Editions Didier Millet).

60: "Is it art or business"? [*Seni* = art; *Rp* = rupiah] (*Bali Post*, 21 October 1982).

61: "Buy me, Miss"! *Dagang acung* in action (photograph by Rio Helmi).

63: Tourism in Bali: "Who benefits?" (*Bali Post*, 3 January 1991).

Chapter 3

67: Touristic map of south Bali (Editions Didier Millet).

70: The so-called "hippies" and how to make them look respectable [poster from Bali Government Tourism Office] (photograph by Jean-Claude Picard).

74: The Bali Beach Hotel rising above the tops of the coconut palms (*Bali Post*, 6 November 1982).

77: Kuta postcard (airbrush painting by Tony Tantra).

79: A Balinese view of the hippies [Well! What's happening here? Who wants to safeguard our people's morals?] (*Bali Post*, 15 February 1981).

Chapter 5

120: Balinese culture as bait [*seni budaya* = arts and culture; *wisatawan* = tourist. Judging by his outfit, the angler is a Balinese official, not an artist] (*Bali Post*, 5 September 1982).

123: "Balinese Culture. Where does it go: tradition or tourism?" [*budaya Bali* = Balinese culture; *adat* = tradition] (Jango Pramartha, 1995 calendar published by *Bali Post*).

Colour illustrations are identified in the two sections of colour plates.

Index

E

F

G

H

I

J

K

L

M

N

O

P

R

S

T

U

V

W

Y